STARS OF
THE OPERA

ENRICO STINCHELLI

STARS OF THE OPERA

THE GREAT OPERA SINGERS

ACKNOWLEDGEMENTS

We would like to thank the following people for their kind collaboration regarding the photographic material used in this book.

Eugene Rizzo and Elena Martini for the beautiful slides by Paul Ronald taken on the set of the opera film *Otello*. The Kaleidos-Roma for the slides of E. Belvedere and A. Rossetti, taken on the set of the opera film *Otello*. Franco Varini (Teatro Comunale of Bologna); Lamberto Scotti (Teatro Comunale of Florence); Giovanni Altavilla (San Carlo Theatre of Naples); Pietro Diliberto (Teatro Massimo of Palermo); Ugo Sandroni (Teatro Regio of Turin); Claudio Gherbitz (Teatro Comunale "Giuseppe Verdi" of Trieste); Carlo Felice Theatre of Genoa; Rome Opera House; La Fenice Theatre of Venice; Elena Fumagalli (La Scala Theatre of Milan); the Hon. Quintavalla (Cultural Councilman of Parma); Vincenzo Raffaele Segreto (Teatro Regio of Parma); Dr. Mariotti (Cultural Councilman of Pesaro); and Simona Barabesi (Rossini Opera Festival of Pesaro).

Dr. Hans Widrich (Salzburg Festival); Charlotte Bonello (Opéra of Nice), Sydney Opera House Trust; Tokyo Bunka-Kaikan; Louwrens Langevoort (Théâtre Royal de la Monnaie of Brussels); Metropolitan Opera House of New York; Louise Sparks (Staatsteater of Pretoria); G. Fiasconaro (Pe Operahuis of Port Elisabeth, South Africa); Valerj Glotov (Kirov Theatre of Leningrad); Anja Weigmann (Opera Theatre of Nuremberg).

A special thanks to Günther Zerbes, Ursula Glaser, Ingrid Drösler, Hartwig Bernhard, Giandonato Crico, Ermete Manzoni, Alberto dalla Tomasina, Alfredo Tabocchini, Galliano Passerini, Giovanna Deriu — and all the photographers who have kindly supplied their material.

Another thank you to Jürgen Grand (EMI); Mr. Colombo and Mrs. Marmina (Philips); Franco Guandalini, for the beautiful photos of his wife, the soprano Raina Kabaivanska; Alberto Terrani, for the photos of his consort, the mezzosoprano Lucia Valentini; to Anton Dermota; Ljuba Welitsch; Katia Ricciarelli; Peter Edelmann; Giuseppe Taddei and all the other artists who have collaborated in realising this volume.

Front Cover Photo
Luciano Pavarotti via satellite from the Terme di Caracalla in Rome, July 1990. On this historic occasion the three tenor greats — Luciano Pavarotti, Placido Domingo and José Carreras — sang on the same platform in a unique and unforgettable concert.
(Photographer: Corrado Maria Falsini)

Photos
Every possible effort has been made to give correct and detailed photo credits. Obviously not all historic data has been easily accessible or necessarily precise. The author and publisher express their regret for possible errors or omissions and shall be glad to accept any authorized revisions, to be included in future editions.

Translation of Le Stelle della Lirica
Translated by Hellé Theophilatos
Edited by P.E. Fogarty
Jacket design by Silvia Notargiacomo
Phototypeset by Graffiti, Rome
Photolithography by Studio Bondani, Rome
Printed and bound by Tipografia Ariete, Rome

ISBN 88-7301-007-5

© 1992 GREMESE INTERNATIONAL s.r.l., Rome
Casella postale 14335 - 00149 Roma

CONTENTS

PREFACE

At first I thought that I would include in *Stars of the Opera* only a restricted number of illustrious singers: fifteen at most. Choosing them was a problem — for one reason or another singers who had given much to the operatic stage continued to be left out. How can we, after all, define a "great voice"? It is not one that breaks crystal, or reaches ultrasonic high notes with ease, or one that illustrates exceptional lung power and seems never to need to take another breath; nor is it one which flaunts volume and power, hurling itself into audiences's ears. A "great voice" is a soft, malleable instrument; at the same time it is incisive, solid and equal in all the registers, built on hard study and supported by intelligence and sensitivity. It is a voice that manages to communicate, that will always be remembered for the wide range of sensations and emotions it gives the audience. *Vom Herzen möge es wieder zum Herzen gehen*, wrote Beethoven on the score of his *Missa Solemnis*: "from the heart may it reach other hearts". This is the only valid rule to be followed by any true artist.

Everybody who begins to study singing aims at this achievement. However it is easy to lose one's guidelines or to fall into imitations of previous great singers, or to adopt crowd-pleasing compromises such as enlarged notes, exaggerated acting, excessive falsetti or *poitriné* sounds. A confusion of techniques; singers who evade precise definition. Let us only mention "Pippo" Di Stefano whose voice colour was one of the most beautiful ever to have existed, who was adored by the public for his innate amiability and spontaneity; but who adopted an extremely personal singing technique and therefore was not appreciated by the critics; Victoria De Los Angeles who is a soprano of exquisite musicality and sensitivity but lacking in the high register; Mario del Monaco's exceptional talent and means were marred by a dubious taste and a sometimes inadmissible exaggeration; whilst Tito Gobbi, Mirto Picchi, Magda Olivero and Gino Bechi cannot be defined as having had beautiful voices, but they were supported by great interpretive qualities, and in the case of the divine Magda by a perfect technique.

The team of the famous fifteen therefore grew in number to include many other stars, each of whom in some way contributed to vocal history. This vast selection of names has been organised into various categories according to their voice type, (eg. dramatic tenor, *coloratura* soprano, *basso profondo*, etc.), and in chronological order. The entries are, perforce, short; but I have tried to summarise both the best and the worst aspects of each performer, without being afraid of touching sore spots or troublesome theories. We recommend the appendix to the reader's attention; there he may find extra information to complement the text; but above all we advise you to read Alfredo Kraus's master class carefully — it will be useful to all singing students and fascinating for all opera lovers.

The Author

INTRODUCTION

Acting in Song

Opera was born officially in 1567 during the Carnival at Palazzo Corsi in Florence, however this event had been preceded by many experiments which had favoured its creation. The first musical drama was Jacopo Peri's *Dafne*, with text by Ottavio Rinuccini. They were two of the most enthusiastic and gifted members of a group of people, who, animated by the new spirit of the late Renaissance, would habitually gather at the palace of the Conte de' Bardi. There the young intellectuals who were part of the *Camerata* of Via de' Benci would discuss the world in general, and especially the dream of renewing music and vocal style. They firmly proposed to return to the simplicity of the ancient Greeks: a single voice was to have supremacy over the polyphonic and contrapunctual tangles that were, by then, out of fashion and in contrast to the widespread humanistic ideals of the time. Vincenzo Galilei, one of the most militant members of the group, wrote: "Why should words be sung by four or five voices so that they become incomprehensible, when the ancients could express their most profound passions with a single voice accompanied only by a lyre? We must renounce counterpoint and return to primitive simplicity". To tell the truth the intellectuals themselves did not know to what "primitive simplicity" they were referring, for the remnants of the Greek tragedies were rather scarce. However, thanks to a few significant discoveries they were able to confirm their theories, formulate some conclusions, and set the foundation for the beginnings of opera. These were, in synthesis, that: the monodict style was the only one capable of following the thread of a natural discourse, therefore supremacy to soloist singing; melodies were to reflect and idealise the emotions; and, above all, singers were to strive for perfect enunciation so that every listener could understand the text. Really, if we think about, it, *recitar cantando* (acting in song) is probably the only real possibility of overcoming the gap that most often separates the stage from the stalls, the orchestra pit, and which distances audiences even in the presence of illustrious and acclaimed singers.

Good acting, a clearly comprehensible text, but also good singing, (without overlooking vocal ornament, the so-called *canto fiorito* which has always helped express emotion) are the basis for all singing, from opera to pop music.

The Importance of the Singer

From the days when opera was still in its infancy; from Monteverdi, Vivaldi, Handel, Mozart until the composers of the last century and those of today, the *conditio sine qua*, the ace card with which to make a world wide public love this "organised madness", is the singer — the clarity of his enunciation, his ease of emission, his agility (in a certain type of repertoire), the variety of his phrasing and the beauty of his timbre — in one word, his or her *bravura*. These are undeniable facts, despite the claims of some people, and this is why over almost three centuries of operatic history the singer has reigned supreme. Of course there have been great conductors or great directors who have been acclaimed by the public, but not one of them has ever managed to gather the ovations given to legions of singers — even ones who were not

Adelina Patti (1843-1919).

Francesco Tamagno (1850-1905) *as* Otello.

outstanding. From 1600 on (but let us not forget what happened in ancient Greece and Rome), singers have been surrounded by immense affection, and even idolisation. They have been petted, spoiled, punished fiercely for their defects, over-paid or under-paid, (and oh how many have paid, themselves, to be permitted to sing!) loved madly or hated viciously: everything is exaggerated, everything taken to extremes, just as in the plots and the music of so many operas. The singer is the centre point of an operatic performance, despite the theory that the conductor fills this role. No matter how unpleasant a bad baton might be, a conductor will never be hated or despised as will a singer when he "cracks" or suffers some other vocal mishap. Rather, as the history of belcanto teaches us, it is the good singer who manages to save productions that are lacking in conducting and direction. No matter how well the accompaniment of an aria is played, rich in colour and shading, with an impeccable performance from every member of the orchestra, applause will only be triggered in the case of an equally splendid vocal interpretation.

A Witness: the Recording

Having decided that the voice is the most important element in a performance, and mentioning only *en passant* that many awful scores were also saved by good singing, (the concept of the

singer as co-author of the work lasted well into the nineteenth century), we come to the most pressing problem, as far as we are concerned. We have taken into consideration only the "stars" of this century, leaving untouched nearly two centuries of history. Why?

First of all because from Caruso on we can listen to and judge all the most important operatic stars thanks to the recordings they have left us. Personally I am favourable to records and consider them a most important method of divulgation, which, if listened to correctly, can allow us to identify precise aspects of an artist (such as vocal technique and musicality), the customs of the time, and even a social reality, which, without these recordings, would become only dusty memories or biased writings. But the record is there: it can change a timbre, almost hiding it, making it opaque, or sometimes lightening it; a very bad record can even alter the intonation, but none can ever stop a strong stylistic and technical personality from emerging. It may be said, therefore, that Tamagno's voice was different when heard in the theatre, or that his recordings do not do him justice; but nobody can say that his *solfeggio* was correct, or affirm that he was a musician. I never had the good fortune to hear Gigli or Lauri Volpi live, and I am sure that they were great tenors; but their records reveal an abuse of bad habits, (sliding *portamenti*, posed *falsettoni*, exaggerated accents, etc.) which may have been tolerated by biased,

Mario Ancona *(1860-1931).*

Enrico Caruso *(1873-1921) in* Aida.

provincial critics who complacently forgot about authentic musician-singers such as Leo Slezak or Fritz Wunderlich, (to remain in theme with tenors). The record is not like imprecise sentences written by incompetent critics. The record restores to Alexander Kipnis all his greatness as a bass, putting him at the top of the list of his contempories. But on the other hand it re-evaluates some myths without mercy: such as Marcella Sembrich, whose high notes sound like screeching train brakes; or the baritone Kaschmann, who seems to do everything he can in his personal version of "O de' verd'anni miei" to cancel his fame as a divine stylist. Silva's aria from *Ernani* in Edouard de Reszké's rendition is one of the most eccentric pieces in the history of recordings; whilst the whining and insipid interpretation Gigli gives of "M'appari", one of his most favoured songs, cannot be excused because it is sung in his mythical *falsettone*. Many doubts are raised about the good taste of those audiences in the "good old days" when we place the *calunnie* of Shaliapin or of Navarini on the turntable or in the C.D.; or the serenades of Battistini (but his famous "Eri tu" is no joke either) from *Don Giovanni*; the arias from *I Puritani* with De Lucia or Hipólito Lázaro; Martinelli's *Otello*; or the "Ho-jo-to-ho" of Litvinne; the "Ritorna vincitor" of Giannina Russ; and the acrobatics — let us call them that — of the contralto Guerrina Fabbri battling with the melismas of Arsace. The list is long.

Leo Slezak *(1873-1946).*

Alexander Kipnis (1891-1978) *in* The Magic Flute.

Marcella Sembrich (1858-1935) *in* Il Barbiere di Siviglia.

Thanks to records, the sensitive listener and, above all the critic who has some idea of singing technique (*rara avis*) can conceive what enormous progress the singer has made towards being a musician and not just a "sound machine". Amongst the singers of the turn of the century we cannot find examples of artists such as Ged-

da, Fischer-Dieskau, Kipnis, Schipa, Hotter, Wunderlich, Taddei, Ludwig, Schwarzkopf, Olivero, Freni, Kraus, Tebaldi, Callas, Simionato, Stignani, Lemnitz, Ramey, Horne, Scotto.

These are artists who have put their voices, beautiful or ugly as may be, at the service of the composer. If by some miracle, we could have

Edouard de Reszké (1853-1917) *in* Faust.

Fernando De Lucia (1860-1925).

Hans Hotter *(1909) in* Salome.

Bidù Sayao *(1902) in* La Traviata.

recordings from the seventeen and, especially, the eighteen hundreds, it would certainly be no joke!! If it is all right to remember the "first performers" with mouldy nostalgia, without any documentation to prove their worth except the scribblings of certain "voice-ologists" who then, as now, were not always reliable, then it is also acceptable that we doubt the excellence of many famed performers, basing our judgement instead on the writings of the various Stendhal, Berlioz, Schumann, Giulio Ricordi, Boito, and other great *chroniqueurs*.

Golden Voices, Iron Nerves

How many clichés, how many lies, how many useless nasty comments we have read or heard from critics against this or that singer. One of the most shocking stances is that taken against the "fabulous fifties" of this century. Quite on the contrary, that period is the last great flowering of voices from the revolutionary advent of Caruso on. Just glancing through the theatre annals of those years we are astounded: a wide repertory to satisfy all tastes, in every theatre, even the provincial ones; excellent protagonists, even as doubles; the possibility of creating at least ten different casts for operas such as *Trovatore, Norma, Rigoletto, Traviata* or *Andrea Chénier*, for which today we cannot even find one cast; great popular enthusiasm; great rivalry; memorable performances; accounts which attest to the vitality and brilliance of opera in that period.

The *divi* transmitted emotions which justified the title, surrounded by that magic aura that lifts the singer above the level of show-business.

Now some people — surely the most singularly folkloristic in the opera world — insist that the fifties were a sort of Pandora's box, the apex of

Ebe Stignani *(1904-1974) in* Cavalleria Rusticana.

bad singing, especially when confronted with the "glorious" period that goes from the first half of the sixteen hundreds until about 1830. We believe these theories are invalid, certainly not supported by any satisfactory proof. If it is true that a good vocal organisation accompanies a singer throughout his life, protecting him from a precocious decline and vocal mishaps, then a comparison between some of the derogated stars of the fifties and their mythical colleagues of one hundred and twenty years earlier would be very interesting.

PARALLEL CAREERS

Singer	Year of Debut	Year of Withdrawal
Angelica Catalani (1780-1849). Flexible and acrobatic voice, which reached up to high E flat — but musically she was unprepared, unable to perform Mozart's accompanied recitatives correctly.	1797. (in *Lodoiska* by Mayr at Venice).	About 1830. (however already in 1824 the London and Berlin public protested against her faulted vocal condition).
Renata Scotto (1933). Her repertoire goes from *Lucia* to *Tosca* and includes the most complicated parts for *coloratura* soprano and *lirico-spinto* soprano.	She sang "Stride la vampa" in public in 1948, and in 1952 made her theatre debut as Traviata at Savona.	Still in activity after forty years of career.
Isabella Colbran (1785-1845). Stendhal praised her beauty and her acting, but thought her mostly off-key, and deplorable in her singing. Her husband, Rossini, used to arrange parts to "fit" her.	1806 (?). Madrid.	About 1824. (According to Stendhal her decline was already clear in 1816, when most of the public strongly protested against her singing).
Lelya Gencer (1929). She has sung the rare Donizetti roles and Santuzza, Charlotte and Butterfly, Violetta and Suor Angelica, Donna Anna and Gilda, — from Monteverdi to Verism.	1950. (as Santuzza in *Cavalleria* at Ankara).	1985. (Last stage performance with a little opera by Gnecco at La Fenice, Venice. She is still performing in concerts).
Giuditta Pasta (1797-1865). Right from her debut there was talk about an opaque timbre and a precarious intonation. In 1841 Mendelssohn wrote of the "catastrophic conditions of her voice" and of her "serious problems of intonation".	1815. (A small part at La Scala).	1841. (She decided to retire after a disastrous tour of Poland and Russia, however her vocal condition was already badly faulted in 1834).

Joan Sutherland (1926). Starting from *coloratura* roles she gradually included in her repertoire *Aida, Ballo in Maschera, Adriana Lecouvreur,* etc.; ranging from Handel to Tippett and Bononcini.

1952. (as the First Lady in *The Magic Flute*).

1990. (as Marguerite in *Les Huguenots* at Sydney).

How many tenors worthy of that name could have boasted a vocal longevity comparable to that of Schipa, Lauri Volpi, Gigli or Kraus? How many tenors were able to demonstrate the vocal freshness possessed by Pavarotti at fifty-three years of age? Isn't Del Monaco worth more than Donzelli, the first to perform Pollione, who had to lower the *concertato* of Donizetti's *Parisina* because he had no high notes? And we shouldn't forget that the orchestras at the beginning of last century were a much reduced unity compared with modern ones; for the ear of today's listener — deafened by record players, radio and television all at full blast — demands an increased sonority in the singer. It would be ridiculous to deny this.

From Caruso on, singers have begun to project their voices better, to abandon the constant use of falsetto and to search for a more consistent colour. They have learned to sustain sound with the help of a new method of breathing which is radically opposed to the old method used by the *castrati*, (who did not take full advantage of the diaphragm muscle since they pulled the stomach inwards during exhalation). We do not wish to generalise too much or to indulge in too many technical explanations; but if we consider the evolution in singing which has occured since the end of the eighteen hundreds until today, we realise what conquests both men and women have made in the field of operatic interpretation. However it is true that in these past few years great talents have been lacking, perhaps because of the excessive publicity given to certain exponents who are not at all exemplary. It is also true, alas, that good singing teachers are disappearing, and that there is an absurd proliferation (especially in Italy, strangely enough) of singing "gurus" or "witch doctors"; some are unashamedly active *en-plein-air* during perfection and master classes, others operate within the darkness of their home dens. A country that is incapable of guaranteeing a sound vocal study in its conservatoriums or musical academies is forced to tolerate a large amount of private initiative, which, of course, remains uncontrolled, and includes many frauds. In such conditions it is impossible to expect the birth of new opera stars.

Rome, 1.3.1992

Enrico Stinchelli

Leonard Warren *(1911-1960)*, **Jussi Björling** *(1907-1960)*, and **Zinka Milanov** *(1906-1989) in the recording studio.*

Enrico Caruso in Carmen.

16

THE TENORS

The Tenor Voice: Range and Emission

The tenor is the highest of the male voices and usually ranges from c to c″, with the most comfortable octave extending from g to g′. The type of emission used is that of chest voice for the lower and middle notes and head voice for the high notes. It is thus defined as "mixed emission". The joining of these two registers, or the *passaggio*, occurs between e′ flat and f′ sharp. Of course this *passaggio* must never be heard in a well trained voice, despite the fact that it is cultivated by many incompetent singing teachers. Worse still are the attempts to recreate it artificially, resulting in those awful "vomiting" sounds, hiccups, strangled notes, darkenings, and innumerable other unnatural voice placements.

Tenors in the *Verismo* Repertory

The dawning of the *Verismo* style occurred towards the end of the nineteenth century and coincided exactly with the decline of the Belcanto School. Verdi's compositions represent the last contribution of genius to Grand Opera but also, unwittingly, the first introduction of veristic elements into lyric drama. The mythical characters disappeared, as did their tales of idealised love. The old arias were transformed into a continuous, uninterrupted musical discourse. The naturalistic opera of the *Giovane Scuola* (Young School) in Italy (Puccini, Leoncavallo, Mascagni, Cilea and Giordano) proposed a type of drama inspired by what was "real" (*il vero*) — the harsh truth and the use of an immediate and passionate style in emotional passages. These concepts are all well demonstrated in the prologue to Leoncavallo's *Pagliacci* (1892). "L'autore ha cercato di pingervi uno squarcio di vita. Egli ha per massima sol che l'artista è un uom, e che per gli uomini scrivere ei deve, ed al Vero ispirarsi". (The author/composer has tried instead to depict a segment of life. His only belief is that the artist is a man, and that he must write for men alone, and be inspired by what is real).

Instead of trills and *roulades* which were now considered useless, screams ("A te la mala Pasqua!", *Cavalleria Rusticana*), insults ("Sgualdrina", *Tabarro*), desperate weeping ("Mario, Mario", finale of *Tosca*), laughter ("Nemico della patria", *Andrea Chénier*) and even the spoken word ("Che vuol dire...", finale *La Bohème*) were preferred. Everyday language was imitated. Little did it matter if these forms were used in a conventional way, or as tear jerkers; but they were preferably inserted into a popular context — a plebeian tragedy.

Of course the tenor vocal line was shaken up, even if the change was slow and gradual. Everything had to be adapted to the fashion and taste of the time and the changing social conditions. Two different schools arose. One consisted of the *tenori di forza*, who had strong, robust voices with intense colour and who were able to confront both Verdi's compositions and those of the *Giovane Scuola* and emerge unscathed. The other was that of the *tenori di grazia*, who were dedicated to a more virtuoso repertory and in a higher range. Unfortunately the latter group were frequently inclined to use falsetto and to resort to some highly discutable technical solutions.

Leaders of a New Line: Caruso, De Lucia and Bonci

In *verismo* opera the tenor is still the protagonist. Not any longer, however, in terms of stylised singing, with its elegiac arias culminating in stratospheric high notes. In *verismo* he has become the incarnation of the passionate male, all blood and guts, hairy-chested, just like the clichés of the typical Southern Italian male. His voice tends to be dark and widened in the central register: the so-called "Mediterranean" sound. He is not at all inclined to flowery, delicate singing or showy high notes.

We must remember that the difficult transition from the eighteen hundreds to our century was characterised by an increased voice volume due in part to the enlarged sonority of the or-

Together with **Emmy Destinn** (in the photo), and the baritone Amato, **Caruso**, under the baton of Toscanini, took part in the first historical performance of The Girl of the Golden West in New York in 1910. His rendering of the "good" outlaw, Dick Johnson, remains unequalled.

The great contralto **Gabriella Besanzoni** offers a refreshing drink to **Enrico Caruso** her friend and partner in so many Carmens.

A victorious Radames born at the foot of Vesuvius, **Enrico Caruso**. He sang in his native city during the 1901-1902 season in both Manon and Elisir d'Amore. Despite being in fine form he did not manage to equal the success made by his rival De Lucia, and had to undergo humiliating attacks from the Neapolitan critics - he who was as Neapolitan as pizza, tomato sauce and spaghetti! Naples would not see him again until shortly before his death in 1921, when, suffering from emphysema, he made his return.

chestras, a factor imposed by the new needs of the late-romantic compositions.

The head of the twentieth century tenors and the one who has remained a point of referral for all singers in this century is Enrico Caruso. In contrast to him we can examine the refined and ancient art used by Fernando De Lucia and Alessandro Bonci.

Enrico Caruso (born Naples 1873 - died Naples 1921) described his own voice as similar to a cello. In fact his sweeping use of breath, his perfect *legato* and his velvety timbre make his voice resemble this string instrument more than any other tenor voice known until then.

After having completed his studies, which remained however somewhat patchy due to his poor financial situation, Caruso debuted on November 16, 1894 in Morelli's *L'Amico Francesco* in Naples. From then until 1906-7 he was admired as a *tenore di grazia* with exceptional gifts. His Duca di Mantova, his Nadir, Nemorino, Des Grieux in Massenet's *Manon*, and his Faust were amazing for his refined phrasing, his perfect breathing technique, but above all for the exceptional natural beauty of his voice. It was rich with harmonics and brilliant in the first high notes. However from b′ flat onwards he had to use a *falsettone*, or, if necessary, lower the aria key. (This happened in Enzo's aria in *La Gioconda*, and, with Puccini's approval, in Rodolfo's aria in *La Bohème*).

The sensual bronzed colour of his voice and the passion he put into his interpretations made him synonymous with the *verismo* tenor. During his American career (from 1903/4 until 1920) his myth grew because of his memorable performances of *Carmen*, *Pagliacci*, *Bohème*, *Tosca*, *Manon Lescaut* and especially, *La Fanciulla del West* of which he was the first interpreter at the Metropolitan Opera in New York in 1920. Caruso sang more than six hundred times at the Metropolitan in a repertory of about forty different operas (amongst these the first American performances of *Armide* and *La Forza del Destino*).

After a temporary loss of voice during the 1908-9 season, his timbre became even more baritone-like, and more powerful, and his interpretations even more fascinating. In the theatre (and also on recordings) he sang "Vecchia zimarra" hidden behind the scenery whilst the indisposed bass had only to mime the words of his own aria.

Between 1902 and 1920 the great tenor made more than two hundred records, earning dizzy sums of money. His was the first really phonogenic voice and was immediately taken advantage of by the newly established recording industry.

Caruso died because of a lung abscess, which, on the 24th. of January, 1921, had forced him

De Lucia *as Turiddu. This role was really very far from the Belcanto repertory of this tenor; but he performed it often and with great success.*

to interrupt a performance of *L'Ebrea* at the Metropolitan Opera, New York.

In comparison to Caruso's rich voice and passion, **Fernando De Lucia** (born Naples 1860, died Naples 1925) exhibited a stylised art which seemed almost insipid with its exaggerated taste for *sfumature*, *diminuendi* and *filature*. It sounded as if he was simply playing with his voice in a fanciful game. He applied these same formulas to both repertories: that of the *tenore di grazia* (*Faust*, *Elisir d'Amore*, *Sonnambula*, *Rigoletto*, *The Pearl Fishers*) and that of the *verismo* school in which he specialised after 1891. He was the first to interpret *L'Amico Fritz*, *I Rantzau*, *Silvano* and *Iris*; all by Mascagni; and he often sang *Tosca*, *Cavalleria Rusticana*, *Fedora*, *Bohème*, and *Carmen*.

There is nothing to be surprised about in De Lucia's choice of repertory; it was customary in that time for tenors to sing *Barbiere* as well as *Cavalleria*; the *verismo* tenor is really only an invention of the last forty years. The first singers to perform the operas of the *Giovane Scuola* were actually a mixture, possessing the stylistic prerogatives inherited directly from belcanto and perfectly adaptable to the new works.

Certainly the *rallentandi* and *melisma* used by De Lucia surpassed any artistic licence. One example is worth another, and Lauri Volpi in his book *Voci Parallele* cites how De Lucia would presumptuously change the words at the end of the aria "Recondita armonia" from *Tosca*. (He would not say "Tosca sei tu"; but rather "Tosca sei te", thus rendering the sentence grammatically incorrect). He did this to achieve the increased resonance provided by the "e" vowel compared to that given by the "u" vowel. However the Neapolitan tenor possessed a varied and graceful manner in phrasing and a sweet timbre that became irresistible in moments of ecstatic abandon, even if hampered somewhat by an accentuated *vibrato stretto* (narrow vibration) probably due to a lack of proper sustainment.

Alessandro Bonci (Cesena 1870 - Viserba 1940) was another of Caruso's rivals as far as old school delicate singing was concerned. Bonci made his debut in January, 1896, as Fenton in Verdi's *Falstaff* and gave his farewell performance in the *Requiem* by that same composer in 1927. Bonci, like De Lucia, had as principal characteristics a pure timbre, a noticeable *vibrato stretto* and a very refined technique. He had a greater range than De Lucia, reaching up to high c″, but his repertory was more limited in *verismo*.

He preferred singing *Rigoletto, Sonnambula, Puritani, Faust, Manon* (Massenet), *Elisir d'Amore, Don Giovanni, Barbiere, Lucia di Lammermoor* and, his favourite, *Un Ballo in Maschera*. Although he did not possess an authentic Verdian incisiveness, he managed all the same to triumph in this role because of his elegant style, and his famous little laugh in the quintet "È scherzo od è follia", a variation that Verdi himself much appreciated in March, 1898.

Tenors of the Twentieth Century

Before the advent of *verismo* it was most important for all singers, and not only tenors, to be able to range smoothly over all the registers, from the low to the medium to the high. The composers would suit each opera to the vocal characteristics of each singer, just as a tailor does with the personal measurements of his clients. The best qualities of each individual were taken advantage of, and during the performance the same singers added even more ornamentation, adding complicated *cadenze*, or changing the very arias for others that they preferred. They contributed greatly to the whole outcome of the performance and the ultimate success of the work and its composer, who quite willingly accepted these liberties. Even Verdi asked the expert, Donizetti, to write some extra *cadenze* and variations for him, to add to several repeat performances of *Ernani*.

The naturalistic or *verismo* theatre ended all

this. Here it was the performer, now limited in his vocality, who chose the opera and composer best suited to himself, be it Rossini, (in declining popularity), Donizetti, Verdi or Mascagni. This is the origin of the classification of voice types used in our century, types such as lyric, dramatic, etc., catagories which are all very restricted.

We have already said that *verismo* required large voices of medium extension, but it especially needed effective actors: dynamic, passionate, and even exaggerated. And so vocal technique began to take second place to theatricality. Little by little the last masters of belcanto were disappearing, replaced by the verist performers. In the same manner the last exponents of the nineteenth century interpretations gave way to the artists who followed Caruso and who were, more often than not, unhappy imitations or bad copies of the original.

The *verismo* technique had no need for voices which were extended or extremely agile. The verist tradition required shouts, sobs, and cries, and this contributed to the advent of singers who were only interested in declaiming at full voice without any mercy for the listener. Even today some of them continue to exert a negative influence, thanks to the recording industry, which, during this century, has spread world wide.

All the same, the verist school of singing had one great value: it indicated a technique of voice production that was more or less correct, based on the homogeneity of the entire range and on the sustainment of every note. It ridded us of the ostentatious mannerisms which, at the end of the nineteenth century, had reached the absolute limits of tolerance. When listened to today, some performances given by the so-called "belcantisti", from De Lucia to Battistini, from Patti to Marcella Sembrich, become simply comical.

The change of concept regarding the singer as co-author of an opera (1600-1850) into that of the opera modelling the singers created the twentieth century separation of the tenor voice into various catagories.

The *tenore di grazia* was replaced by the light or the light lyric tenor, whose voice often lacks colour and who employs the use of falsetto frequently. The lyric tenor, who was formerly defined as of "mixed character", took on a wider repertory ranging from the later Verdi (*Traviata, Rigoletto*) to some of the verist works (*La Bohème, Butterfly*, etc.). The *tenore lirico spinto*, formerly the *tenore di forza*, was assigned the more complicated verist roles (*Andrea Chénier*, Johnson in *Fanciulla del West*, Folco in *Isabeau*, Calaf in *Turandot*) and the dramatic tenor, the classic Wagnerian *Heldentenor*, was used to interpret roles such as *Otello* or Samson in Saint-Saëns' *Samson and Dalila*.

LIGHT LYRIC AND LYRIC TENORS OF THE TWENTIETH CENTURY

Giuseppe Anselmi (Nicolosi, Catania 1876-Zoagli, Genoa 1929) came from the same mould as Bonci and De Lucia. Elegant and refined, he sang as a *tenore di grazia* from 1896 to 1916. Because of his vocal ductility and purity, and because of his noble appearance, he was a favourite in operas such as *Rigoletto, Manon, Barbiere, Lucia, Werther,* and *Tosca*. He obtained great success in London, Buenos Aires, Madrid and St. Petersburg, as well as in all the major Italian theatres.

He can be reproved only for an excessively affected pronunciation in declarations of love or, for that matter, any languid phrase, and an excessive use of embellishments in the Liberty style. These defects are easily heard in any of his recordings but Anselmi was, after all, only following the fashions of his time and he was able to do so because he possessed an extraordinary vocal organ.

Another example of vocal and physical elegance was the tenor **Edoardo Garbin** (Padua 1865 - Brescia 1943), the first Fenton in Verdi's *Falstaff*. He was gifted with a light and very con-

A group photo for Leoncavallo's Zaza. From the left: the tenor **Edoardo Garbin**, first Fenton in Falstaff at La Scala (1893), was a refined singer and actor, who, together with his wife, the soprano **Adelina Stehle**, was frequently applauded. To his right the soprano **Rosina Storchio**, Leoncavallo, and, with top hat and walking stick, the baritone **Mario Sammarco**.

trolled emission, with security in the high registers and in *mezzavoce*. Due to his talent Garbin was also an excellent verist, especially in Puccini roles, being acclaimed above all in *Adriana Lecouvreur* and in *Fedora*.

It is right to remember **Lucien Muratore** (Marseille 1876 - Paris 1954) as a historic performer of French lyric roles, from Gounod to Massenet. Formerly a prose actor, he sang very frequently in French and American opera theatres between 1902 and 1936. He was the first to interpret more than thirty new roles.

Thanks to his intelligence, which was well above average, he knew how to use his vocal and visual gifts to the utmost, wisely controlling a voice that was, by nature, deprived of any timbre charm. In 1913 he married the famous Lina Cavalieri, with whom he made several films.

Leonid Sobinov (Jaroslav 1872 - Riga 1934) triumphed in Russia. Unforgettable Lensky in

Lensky's "Farewell to Life" sung by **Leonid Sobinov** greatly moved audiences. It is rare to find a tenor who responds with such sensitivity to the plot of Tchaikovsky's opera Eugene Onegin. (Archives of the Kirov Theatre, Leningrad, 1910).

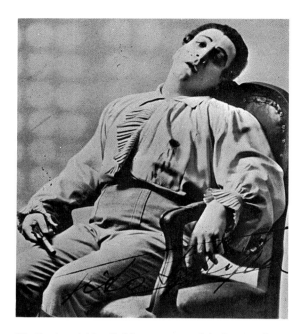

*Werther's suicide - **Schipa** was one of the best performers of the part in Massenet's opera. It allowed him to show all his poetry, elegiac abandon, and wonderful vocal nuances. However during the second half of his career he would always lower the aria ''Pourquoi me réveiller'' by a semi-tone.*

***Tito Schipa** in one of his last concerts. (Archive of La Fenice Theatre, Venice).*

Eugene Onegin he studied in Moscow and made his debut in 1894. He was most active in St. Petersburg in a very wide repertory (*Roméo and Juliette* by Gounod, *Lohengrin*, *Orfeo*, *Werther*, *Traviata*, *Fra Diavolo*, *Barbiere*, *Don Pasquale*, etc.). He also performed in Italy (La Scala: 1904, 1906, 1911) and in France, retiring in 1924.

Sobinov possessed a beautiful voice colour and a natural sweetness which made him perfect for melancholy roles, in sensitive characters who were destined to a tragic end. He was also elegant, refined, handsome and had an excellent cultural background.

John Mac Cormack (Athlone 1884 - Dublin 1945) was a rival of Bonci, De Lucia, and Anselmi for polished sound, vocal consistency, facility with high notes, moderation and varied phrasing. However he was hindered by his enormous corpulence, which rendered him hardly credible in parts such as Rodolfo, Edgardo or Pinkerton. It was because of his size that MacCormack retired early from the stage (1920) suffering from the "fatty" complex. He then dedicated himself exclusively to concert performances.

He had twenty-one roles in his repertory that ranged from lighter parts (*Don Giovanni*, *Sonnambula*, *Faust*, *Rigoletto*) to some of the verist repertory (*Cavalleria*, *Pagliacci*, *Butterfly*, *Bohème*). He made his debut in 1906 (*L'Amico Fritz*) at Savona, then at Covent Garden (*Cavalleria Rusticana*). From 1909 on he collaborated with the opera companies of Boston, Philadelphia, Chicago and New York.

He received the title of "Conte Palatino" from Pope Pious XI for his worthy activities in the sphere of sacred music in 1924. His interpretation of Gounod's "Ave Maria" recorded with the accompaniment of Fritz Kreisler on the violin has remained mythical.

The great **Tito Schipa** (Lecce 1888 - New York 1965) sang from 1910 (he made his debut in *Traviata* at Vercelli) until 1960, when he withdrew from the stage after a final triumphal series of concerts.

The secret of his vocal longevity can be found in his amazing technique and the particular formation of his facial cavities, which allowed a positioning completely in the "mask". Schipa managed to make an almost unlimited use of his voice which was, actually, neither beautiful nor extended. He passed easily from a *fortissimo* to a *filato* and vice-versa; he could attack or sing the most difficult passages in *mezzavoce*; ("Parmi veder le lagrime', for example, from *Rigoletto*); he coloured every aria poetically reaching the extreme apex of his expressive possibilities in the part of *Werther*.

The whole world appreciates his interpretations of *Bohème*, *Rigoletto*, *Manon*, *Barbiere*, *Elisir*, *Don Pasquale*, *Lucia*, *Don Giovanni*, *Sonnambula*, *Arlesiana*, and *Tosca*, all roles characterised by the use of secure technique and imagination — the two ingredients of true belcanto.

Schipa also sang a lot at Chicago (1919-1932) and at the Metropolitan Opera (1932-35, 1940-41), and at San Francisco from 1924 on.

Beniamino Gigli (Recanati 1890 - Rome 1957) enjoyed immense popularity, perhaps inferior only to that of Caruso. After his beginnings as a choir boy and his studies at the Santa Cecilia Conservatorium in Rome, he won the competition held by Maestro Cleofante Campanini at Parma for young singers, after which he debuted at Rovigo in *La Gioconda* (14th October, 1914). He had been well launched and in only a few years time he was in demand by all the major companies world wide. From 1920 until 1932 he was very active at the Metropolitan of New York, where he had taken Caruso's place. After this he returned to Europe, where he was already well-known, and continued his career until 1955 with a repertory so large that nobody has ever been able to rival it. In fact Gigli possessed a vocal apparatus that could be adapted to any operatic part. It was warm and velvety in tone, equal in all registers, reaching past c″, with a perfect *legato* and an enchanting *mezzavoce*.

He sang at Covent Garden in 1930-31, 1938-39, and in 1946, when he sang both Canio and Turiddu in the same evening.

Between 1920 and 1940, he sang Nadir, Nemorino, Canio, Turiddu, Chénier, Rodolfo,

The Irish tenor **John Mac Cormack**, in the title role of Gounod's Faust. One of the great names in the history of recordings.

Beniamino Gigli in his costume for Enzo Grimaldo in La Gioconda. The warmth of his mezzavoce and the penetrating timbre in the aria "Cielo e mar" are amongst the best things left by Gigli on record.

Riccardo: that is: from Donizetti and even Bellini (*Sonnambula*, *Pirata*, and *Norma* at Catania in 1945) to Verdi, Puccini, Giordano, Mascagni, Cilea, Wagner (*Lohengrin*), as well as the French lyric authors, all splendidly.

A huge repertory that clearly demonstrates his exceptional talent. The last costume appearance of the great tenor was in *Pagliacci* at La Fenice, Venice, on the 14th of February, 1954. It was a triumphal evening for a singer who was almost sixty-four years old.

Gigli's vocal longevity, as that of all great artists, is due to a solid technique based on correct respiration and a high resonance position in the "mask". Gigli knew how to use mixed sound (that resonates both in chest and head) with special effectiveness. With a minimum of effort he could produce high notes which were both ringing and robust. The last phase of Gigli's career was damaged by certain verist exaggerations such as sobs (the ones after "No, pazzo son" from *Manon Lescaut* are famous), inconsiderate yells (like those after the "Improvviso" of *Chénier*, or Cavaradossi's "Farewell to life"). In contrast he was given to being insipid in Neapolitan songs or popular ditties which he so often exhibited in concerts and on records. Perhaps it is the price one pays to gain world popularity and perpetuate one's own myth, particularly in America. Despite his figure, which was not a silhouette, Gigli made quite a few films.

Amongst the Great, Some Stars Shine Even Brighter

As a *tenore di grazia* **Dino Borgioli** (Florence 1891 - 1960) would not today have any rivals, whereas in his time he had many, and worthy ones at that.

He made his debut in *La Favorita* at Milan in 1917, and from then on made his presence felt

No, this is not a fattened-up Douglas Fairbanks in "The Adventures of Sinbad the Sailor"; but **Ferruccio Tagliavini** in the "Friendship" duet from The Pearl Fishers. It is a performance of 19 February, 1952, performed with the baritone Tagliabue. (Historic archives of the Rome Opera Theatre).

The 1956-1957 season of the Rome Opera was opened with Mascagni's Iris on 26 December. Gavazzeni was conducting, Wallman directing, and **Giuseppe Di Stefano** was singing with Petrella and Christoff. (Photo: Oscar Savio. Historic Archives of the Rome Opera Theatre).

world-wide, but particularly in England. He performed operas by Bellini, Donizetti, and Rossini, without mannerisms and with a well-formed and technically sound voice.

Jussi Björling (Stora Tuna 1911 - Siar Oe, Stockholm 1960): an idol at the Met and Covent Garden, he boasted one of the finest timbres ever heard in this century.

Björling had a superbly refined technique and penetrating high notes; his emission was measured and noble. He possessed a vocal flexibility which could manage the finest shadings of sound yet launch unhesitatingly into the fullest and richest dramatic passages. This tenor could produce both a tasteful Mozart Don Ottavio and an exuberant Puccini Des Grieux. And all this while carrying on a busy Lieder repertory.

Fortunately, Björling has left us a part of his musical heritage on discs, among which we would like to emphasize the complete opera recordings of *Trovatore, Bohème, Turandot, Manon Lescaut, Rigoletto,* and *Ballo in Maschera.* He also participated in many highly successful "live" recordings: one of the best being a *Roméo* and *Juliette* by Gounod, recorded at the Met, with Bidú Sayao as his partner.

To collect Gigli's heritage, there came a small and amiable Italian tenor, **Ferruccio Tagliavini** (Barco, Reggio Emilia 1913), who made his debut at Florence in *La Bohème* in 1938. There were many similarities to Gigli: the lovely colour of his voice, the sweet *falsettone*, the clear enunciation, the passionate phrasing, and, unfortunately, also some of his defects, such as the well known "hiccups" and the unnecessary *acciaccature*.

Until the mid-fifties Tagliavini was one of the best performers of the *Pearl Fishers*, *L'Amico Fritz*, *Arlesiana*, *Werther*, *Manon*, *Lucia*, and, above all, he was an unforgettable Nemorino. Later a choice of unsuitable repertory (*Tosca, Fedora, Ballo in Maschera*) hardened his voice and he lost polish and roundness in the *passaggio*.

Tagliavini sang regularly at the Metropolitan Opera between 1941 and 1954, and at Covent Garden in 1950 and 1955-56, touring with La Scala.

Amongst the great *tenori di grazia* of the 40's and 50's **Cesare Valletti** (Rome 1922) is not to be forgotten. He was the most worthy follower of Tito Schipa. His timbre was clear and limpid, extended up to b', warm and caressing in the *mezzavoce*. Valletti made a varied and imaginative use of shadings. And he gave the right colouring to every phrase, pleasureably modulating his voice. From 1947 until 1962 he was one of the best as Werther, Elvino, Edgardo, Nemorino, Des Grieux (*Manon*, Massenet), Don Ottavio, Almaviva in Rossini's *Barbiere* and Alfredo (*Traviata*). However towards the end of the fifties the first signs of decline began to appear. His high notes became forced, the emission open and the voice opaque and veiled. Perhaps his permanence at the Metropolitan between 1953 and 1960 accelerated the setting of Valletti's star.

Giuseppe "Pippo" Di Stefano (Motta, S. Anastasia, Catania 1921) has always declared with extreme honesty that he was never subjugated to singing technique but was guided by his instinct. He has always preferred generous emotional participation and a psychological characterisation of his roles to the purely vocal. This put at risk his own vocal integrity and finally sacrificed it. Such, however, was the price to be paid for the really revolutionary contribution made by Di Stefano to the diffusion of opera in our century. He was able to fully involve the general public in a performance by changing the usual technique/instinct values and giving first place to the poetic text through his clear enunciation and phrasing. He managed to enthuse audiences world-wide, involving them completely — a rare gift indeed.

The Swedish tenor **Jussi Björling**, in the title role of Gounod's *Faust*. He was admired in Verdi and Puccini as well as in French music.

We must not forget that the early Di Stefano (he made his debut at Reggio Emilia in 1946 in *Manon*) until 1952-53 was confident in the most arduous belcanto repertory: from *Puritani* to *Barbiere*, from *Favorita* to *Sonnambula*, displaying high c″'s, c″ sharps and d″'s, with perfect *filati* in the most difficult phrases (the "Dream" in *Manon* and the incredible high c″ in *diminuendo* in the New York *Faust*) as well as a velvet sound of incomparable beauty.

Usually the reason for Di Stefano's early decline is attributed to his particular technique of "open singing". We think these are comments by people who know little about singing. The truth is that the Sicilian had a great technique based on word articulation and on the purity and height of his sound, which was not ruined by horrible darkenings or "coverings". Problems occurred as soon as "Pippo" moved away from his natural repertory to explore roles that were not adapted to his precious instrument, in works such as *Iris, Forza del Destino, Turandot* and even *Aida* and *Otello*. There was a

Di Stefano sang Andrea Chénier *more than once, even if the part was not adapted to his purely lyrical voice. The best results were to be heard in the two arias: "Un dì all'azzurro spazio" and "Come un bel dì di maggio". (Photo Oscar Savio. Historic Archives of the Rome Opera Theatre).*

progressive and inexorable decay: the *mezzavoce* became *falsetto*, the high notes became harsh and nasal; he lost the ability to respect dynamic signs and sang everything in full voice, helped, it is true, by a beautiful timbre; but finally it was monotonous and forced.

However the public adored Di Stefano and even during his worst moments it rewarded the Sicilian tenor for his amiability and generosity. During the seventies he participated in performances of little known operas and specialized in operetta. Even now it is still possible to hear "good old Pippo" in the concert hall, where he sings Neapolitan songs and chamber arias.

*The young partner of the beautiful **Virginia Zeani** is **Alfredo Kraus** in a 1960* Traviata, *All the most important post-war Violetta's have enjoyed singing with this exceptional Alfredo. (Photo F. Villani. Historic Archives of the Teatro Comunale di Bologna).*

Alfredo Kraus (Las Palmas 1927) has happily wed the Italian school of Pertile and Schipa with the great Spanish tradition exemplified by Fleta. For over thirty years (starting in a *Rigoletto* at Cairo in January, 1956) he has performed in a restricted number of operas that have all been perfectly suited to his means: *Rigoletto, Traviata, Werther, Manon, Faust, Lucia, La Fille du Régiment, La Favorita, Don Pasquale* and *Elisir*. As can be seen these are all very difficult parts of which, today, Kraus can be said to be the best interpreter.

With intelligent and persistent study he has formed a voice that is incredibly smooth and flexible. He began with a modest vocal colour and an inconspicuous volume, but a breathing technique calculated to the tiniest part has allowed him to perform *smorzature* or *rinforzandi* whenever he wishes. The wonderful *messa di voce* at the end of the aria "Pour me rapprocher de Marie" from *La Fille du Régiment* is an example. He can make his breath last forever, as in the duet from *Lucia*, "Verranno a te..." or the endless "Ah! Manon" from the end of the "Dream Scene", (*Manon* by Massenet), and he has an extension that reaches e″ flat at full voice. It is all the more incredible if you consider that Kraus has now reached an age when all his predecessors have already concluded their careers.

Kraus is a true gentleman in both life and art. He is always extremely elegant, never lapses into a failure of good taste, is never given to excess, He is still offering his artistic treasures to world wide audiences. There are particularly fond ties with the Metropolitan (from 1962), Covent Garden (from 1959) and with the Chicago and San Francisco Operas. Here we must note that for over the last twenty years Alfredo Kraus has been virtually ignored by the recording industry.

Luciano Pavarotti (Modena 1935) studied with Arrigo Pola and made his debut in 1961 at Reggio Emilia, in *La Bohème*.

As we can hear in the recording of that first evening, he was destined to a Bellini or Donizetti repertory with an occasional escapade into Verdi (*Luisa Miller, Rigoletto*) or Puccini (*Butterfly, Bohème, Turandot*). His voice is light and clear, almost light in the high notes which are ringing, penetrating and extending past high d″. His diction and *legato* are impeccable. These are characteristics of the old *tenore di grazia* and it is not a coincidence that, together with Alfredo Kraus, the tenor from Modena was the best interpreter of operas like *Puritani, Favorita, Fille du Régiment, Lucia*, and *Rigoletto* from 1962 until 1975, forming, during this period, a most wonderful partnership with Joan Sutherland.

Pavarotti first sang at Covent Garden in 1963 in the role of Rodolfo, and he then went on to sing *Sonnambula, Traviata, Rigoletto*, and *Lucia*.

"Libiamo, libiamo nei lieti calici..." sings **Kraus** in an impeccable dinner suit, whilst being observed by the soprano **Adriana Maliponte** and the noble guests present at the first act party of La Traviata. *(Photographic Archives of the Pretoria Opera Theatre, 1981).*

In a role that has become identified with his name, **Alfredo Kraus** as the Duke of Mantova in Rigoletto.

In 1964 he sang Idamante in *Idomeneo* (Mozart) at Glyndebourne; with Joan Sutherland and Richard Bonynge, he made a triumphal tour of Australia. Since 1968 he has sung regularly at the Metropolitan in New York.

With the increase of his popularity in the United States Pavarotti let himself be exploited by the show-business industry. In exposing himself in any and every type of musical exhibition in town squares, parks, sporting stadiums, etc., and in television and recording studios, he passed himself off as the typical Italian tenor export. In 1990 he was the symbol of Italy in the World Cup Soccer Competitions, singing everywhere with rather dubious artistic results. In fact it was the dictates of the marketplace that forced Pavarotti to gradually abandon his natural belcanto repertory and accept more lucrative engagements such as *Tosca*, *Trovatore*, *Gioconda*, and *Aida*. In the past few he has given good performances in these roles, thanks to the beauty of his voice and his solid technique; but it is clear that he was more at ease in the parts of Nemorino, the Duke of Mantua, Rodolfo in both *La Bohème* and *Luisa Miller*, and Riccardo in *Ballo in Maschera*. His rather large size has imposed some very understandable limits to his appearance in the French *lyrique* repertory of which he would have been an ideal interpreter (Romeo, Werther, Des Grieux).

Veriano Luchetti (Tuscania, Viterbo, Italy, 1939) has built himself a sturdy reputation in the catagory of lyric tenor over the years, and is one of the most complete artists in recent times. It was a hard-won battle since Luchetti began his career towards the second half of the sixties, his first big success being in Meyerbeer's *Africana*. It was a time when the operatic circuit was still quite crowded with old glories; and at the same time Pavarotti, Domingo and Carreras were emerging and immediately becoming public favourites.

Luchetti, however, had all the qualities to equal and, occasionally, to surpass his illustrious colleagues. His voice has always been very flexible and smooth in all the three registers, with a not particularly charming tone-colour, but with an extended range, an authentic *mezzavoce*, and a perfectly placed sound. His is the voice that is exact for Pinkerton, Edgardo, Rodolfo, the Duke of Mantua, but also adaptable to more dramatic roles such as Don Alvaro, Don José, or Arrigo (*Vespri Siciliani*). Luchetti has specialised in parts not favoured by the superstars, such as Foresto in *Attila*, Macduff in *Macbeth* and Gabriele Adorno in *Simone Boccanegra*, offering wonderful perfor-

A gala at the San Carlo of Naples, 1973. **Pavarotti** *has always been characterised by the great variety of his repertoire in concerts. He covers Bononcini, Scarlatti, Gluck, Mozart, Donizetti, Verdi, Tosti, Liszt, Massenet and Puccini. One of his favourite encores is "Nessun Dorma"* (Turandot). *Another is "Una furtiva lagrima" from Donizetti's* Elisir d'Amore. *(Photo Troncone. Archives of the San Carlo Theatre, Naples).*

*The ideal Verdi part for **Pavarotti** is Riccardo in Ballo in Maschera. In this photo we see the final death scene. To the left is the soprano **Maria Chiara**. (Photo Marchiori. Archives of the Teatro Comunale of Florence).*

*Naples, 24 April, 1973: Caruso's home town commemorates him one hundred years after his birth. A galaxy of illustrious tenors participate. From the left **Mario Del Monaco**, Maestro De Fabritiis, **Alain Vanzo, Luciano Pavarotti, Vladimir Atlantov**, and **Ferruccio Tagliavini**. (Historic Archives of the San Carlo Opera Theatre, Naples. Photo: Troncone).*

mances in these roles all over the globe.

There are two important Spanish tenors who would have been able to have long and memorable careers if they had not fallen victim to a mistaken repertory and faulty technique. **José Carreras** (Barcelona 1946) was a fantastic lyric tenor until the second half of the 1970's: a very brief period of vocal glory indeed. During this time he was able to perform triumphantly in *Lucrezia Borgia* (Barcelona 1971), *Butterfly* (New York 1972), *Rigoletto* (Vienna 1975) and *Don Carlos* (Salzburg 1976) and in other operas such as *Traviata, Lombardi,* and *Bohème,* singing with an unequalled sweetness. His silken tone and his clear enunciation seemed, miraculously, to reincarnate the great Giuseppe Di Stefano. In fact Carreras has never denied his admiration for Di Stefano, and has always said he is proud of such a comparison. The same gifts, but, perhaps, also the same defects. The choice of a harsh repertory (*Tosca, Aida, Forza del Destino, Andrea Chénier, Trovatore, Turandot*) has produced an even more drastic decline than that of his predecessor. It was already noticeable in the Salzburg *Aida,* 1979, with von Karajan. Carreras' vocal organ was compromised by hard sounds, *falsetti,* a defective *legato* and throat 'pushing'. The 1986 *Don Carlos* (Salzburg) mercilessly showed the accentuation of these faults.

In July of 1987, during the shooting of Comencini's opera-film, *La Bohème,* Carreras was taken ill with a serious form of leukaemia. Both his life and his career were at risk; but thanks to efficient treatment and the affectionate moral support of opera lovers the world over, he has returned to singing, first only in concerts, then in a victorious *Carmen* in Vienna in 1990.

Jaime Aragall (Barcelona 1939), more than a victim of his voice, is a victim of his nerves. Mother Nature gave him a seductive, almost voluptuous timbre, and good high notes, especially when they were emitted with due calm and concentration. The only real enemy of this singer is his character. In Vienna a few years ago he interrupted a performance of *Tosca* announcing his withdrawal from the stage. It was an evening full of shock and distress for his numerous fans at the Staatsoper. The tenor sang "E lucean le stelle" with his voice broken by weeping. He seemed a mere shadow of himself.

Two years later he returned to the stage interpreting with renewed enthusiasm *Ballo in Maschera, Don Carlos,* and *Tosca,* finding occasional bursts of his former glory. The role of the Spanish Infante is the one that most suits Aragall, vocally and psychologically. Alas, he tends to sing it all loudly, without shadings or *mezzevoci* and this makes his interpretative style often monotonous and inelegant. During his early career years, Aragall was an excellent Donizetti tenor, often singing with Montserrat Caballé.

Among the lyric tenors that are valid today let us mention **Dano Raffanti** (Lucca 1948) who is a good Nemorino, Duke of Mantua and a noteworthy Rossini tenor. He has a rare vocal colour and penetrating high notes but is too emotional and inconsistent and often gives negative results.

The American **Neil Shicoff** (New York 1949) is also of worthy vocal means. He is in demand in the major theatres as Faust, the Duca di Mantova, and Rodolfo. Meanwhile the Puccini roles and early Verdi parts are successfully upheld in the United States by **Giuliano Ciannella** (Bologna 1940). He personally knew, and was appreciated by the old Lauri Volpi. The Argentini-

*It was the 1982-83 season, and after an absence from the stage which had lasted almost two years, **Jaime Aragall** returns to perform the part of Mario Cavaradossi at the San Carlo. He is not at his best; but the public is happy to be able to once again applaud the Spanish tenor. (Archives of the San Carlo Opera Theatre of Naples. Photo: Troncone).*

an **Luis Lima** (Cordoba 1950), after having debuted as Turiddu in 1974 at Lisbon, has changed to a repertory more suited to his means (*Traviata, Don Carlos, Faust, Bohème, Lucia,* and *Buttefly*). He has revealed good qualities such as clear enunciation and a pleasant vocal colour. **Alberto Cupido** (Portofino 1950) is very active in Italian theatres. He, also, has a lovely clear voice colour, more suited to the lyric than the "spinto" repertory.

THE LIGHT TENORS: AN ENDANGERED SPECIES

The light tenor, or *lirico-leggero,* tends often to be a parody of the former *tenore di grazia.* Their voices are under-nourished, colourless, insipid; and they make frequent use of falsetto, with squealing high notes and difficulty in any forceful *coloratura* passages (the true Rossini *coloratura*). They are the heirs (or imitators) of the little tenors that proliferated in the era of Bonci and De Lucia (but descended from the previous century), who made use of a clavicular breathing technique resulting in an inconsistent sound and false colouring.

Because of these truly bad qualities light tenors were summoned to sing the comic operas of the eighteenth century but also Handel, Rossini, Bellini, Donizetti and sometimes Verdi. We shall restrict ourselves to mentioning the best — those who, in our century, have left good memories of their peak years. **Luis Alva** (Lima 1927) has been singing for more than thirty years, even now sporadically returning to the stage; he was the protagonist of many revivals and also gave many famous performances of Nemorino and Almaviva.

Alvino Misciano (Narni, Terni 1915) was active in a very wide repertory and participated in many eighteenth century revivals. **Nicola Monti** (Milan 1920) was an undoubtedly stylish performer and was often applauded as Elvino in *La Sonnambula* and Paolino in *Il Matrimonio Segreto.* **Luigi Infantino** (Regalbuto, Enna 1921 - Rome, 1991) was, at first, considered an up-and-coming promise as a light lyric tenor for general repertory; but, after an early vocal decay, he was relegated to first performances or revivals of forgotten operas.

Worthy of a different comment is **Agostino Lazzari** (Genoa 1920 - 1981) whose voice had a greater timbre and a broader technical base. Lazzari was an excellent Almaviva, Don Ramiro (in *Cenerentola*), Hoffmann, Nemorino, and Werther, as well as being a specialist in operetta and contempory opera. The same can be said for **Pietro Bottazzo** (Padua 1934) who is a tenor with a clear and well positioned, agile voice with an extension into the *falsettone,* to whom goes the merit of bringing Rossini back into his true dimension during the sixties and seventies. He participated in many recordings for the RAI. (Italian Television and Radio).

Not really a Rossini singer but more orientated towards the French *lyrique* repertory (*Lakmé, Mireille, Mignon*) is **Alain Vanzo** (Principality of Monaco 1928). He is a very refined singer, agile and able in the use of *falsetto* in the highest parts of the score.

The Great Mozart Tenors in the Twentieth Century

Many of the best Mozart singers and those of the German lyric repertory of our century can be found amongst the lyric, dramatic and occasionally even amongst the Wagnerian tenors: Roswänge, MacCormack, Schipa, Gigli, Kraus. However we must mention a few important names, starting with **Herman Jadlowker** (Riga 1877 - Tel Aviv 1953). A tenor with a dark timbre, almost baritone like, outstanding in fast vocalising and trills, he was a great interpreter of *Idomeneo.* His execution of the bravura aria "Fuor del mar" is unsurpassable. He also sang many other dramatic works, from Verdi to Wagner. Another Mozartian great in the 20's and 30's was the Hungarian **Koloman von Patacky** (Alsö Neudra 1896 - Hollywood 1964) whose voice was sweet and seductive and emission heavenly. He was a skilled artisan of expressive nuance. To be remembered: the high B flat "in morendo" ("dying") at the end of *Celeste Aida.* He was an exceptional Florestano, Tamino, and Don Ottavio.

Richard Tauber (Linz 1891 - London 1948) was a great Mozart singer. He put a large sensual voice at the service of this repertory, a voice he was able to soften and sweeten at will, as demonstrated in his performances of Don Ottavio, Tamino, and Belmonte, between 1913, when he started his career, and 1947, when he retired

31

permanently after his last performance as Don Ottavio at Covent Garden.

Anton Dermota (Kropa, Slovenia 1910 - Vienna 1989) belongs to the last great generation of Mozart singers. From 1936, the year of his debut in *Traviata*, until his retirement in January, 1982, singing Tamino at the Vienna Staatsoper, he was Mozart's knight in shining armour. He executed a style of phrasing that belongs entirely to the Italian Belcanto tradition — the same which inspired Mozart when he wrote his operas: singing while breathing, a light emission, imagination and style.

He was accompanied by all the greatest conductors of this century. Dermota offered a perfect interpretation, without ostentation, of Don Ottavio, Belmonte, Ferrando, and, above all, Tamino. Even in his last performance of this role, at the sprightly age of seventy-two, Dermota offered a lesson to all his current colleagues.

Fritz Wunderlich (Kusel 1930 - Heidelberg 1966) sung his last opera as Tamino (*The Magic Flute*) during the first days of September, 1966 at the Festival of Edinburgh. Soon after, a tragic accident in Germany was to interrupt his brilliant career, a career which had begun as Tamino in 1954 at Fribourg, Switzerland. Thus the most beautiful tenor voice ever heard in Germany, and one of the most beautiful voices heard this century disappeared from the stage. An immaculate voice, warm and sensual in the centre, fluid in emission with radiant high notes. It was a miraculous combination of the best qualities of Björling with those of Di Stefano. Wunderlich was superb in Mozart, in contemporary German and Austrian works, in Handel oratorios, in the Masses of Bach, Haydn, and Beethoven, in the leideristic repertoire and in operetta, of which he has universally been crowned king. But he was also an unforgettable Lensky and a passionate Alfredo or Count Almaviva, the latter being finally subtracted from the unbearable falsetti of so many dandies.

Wunderlich, who had a degree as a French horn player, was above all a musician able to eliminate from his singing all the bad habits of his predecessors, such as excessive *portamenti* and *solfeggio* inaccuracies.

With **Nicolai Gedda** (Stockholm 1925) we come to the end of the era of Great Mozart Singers. He was capable of singing in all languages in an extremely wide repertory, had a long lasting career (true of all real singers) and was stylistically perfect. In Italy at the Maggio Musicale in Florence, 1980 he created a Lensky melancholic and intense, rich in different shadings and details. You must hear his Lieder concerts, which are works of art in the use of vocal fantasy and style. These qualities are evident even in recent concerts. (And we would like to remind the reader that Gedda can no longer be

April 1986. Time does not seem to pass for one of the most intelligent and refined tenors of our time: **Nicolai Gedda** *receives just applause during a concert at the San Carlo. (Historic Archives of the San Carlo Opera Theatre of Naples).*

thought of as a "spring chicken"). We can say for Gedda what we have already said for Wunderlich in regard to musical capacity and preparation — superb.

The Rossini Renaissance and the Search for the *Tenore Contraltino*

During the last decade we have been able to witness the triumphal return of Rossini to the operatic stage. This was thanks to the Rossini Opera Festival of Pesaro and to the critical studies sponsored by their Foundation (accompanied by the release of all of Rossini's operas on record in their new philological form). Among the younger generation a new interest has risen regarding the long-gone ways of performing: florid singing, variations, decorative fantasy.

It has been particularly difficult to find an authentic Rossini tenor, someone who could perform accurately in complex roles, ranging from Almaviva to Otello, from Ramiro to Giacomo V (*Donna del Lago*), from Argirio (*Tancredi*) to Arnaldo. However there is a good crop of singers willing to try and some have proved their value not only at Pesaro but in theatres all over the world which have participated in the Rossini Renaissance. Amongst these we remember **Ernesto Palacio** (Lima 1946) and **Francisco Araiza** (Mexico City 1950); both are discreet virtuosi although with precise limits. Araiza, in particular, is capable in *coloratura* passages and reaches up to high d″ flat; however he tends to be unpleasantly nasal. He is also much appreciated as a Mozart tenor (Tamino, Don Ottavio, etc.) especially in the Germanic countries. **Dalmacio González** (Olot 1946) possesses a small but very high voice. He is often asked to perform Argirio and Lindoro in *L'Italiana in Algeri*. In the more demanding Rossini roles **Rockwell Blake** (Pittsburgh 1951) and **Chris Merritt** (Oklahoma City 1950) have given excellent results, being able to sustain *messe di voce*, trills, and corpulent *falsettoni*.

Undoubtedly, Blake, of the two, is the one who has studied the most and with better results. Starting with a vocal material of not outstanding quality, he has constructed a solid technique. With a correct breath measurement he has been able to achieve incredible speed and agility in vocalised passages and easily overcome the almost unsurmountable difficulties contained in *Zelmira*, *Otello*, *Ermione*, *Armida*, *Donna del Lago*, and *Elisabetta Regina d'Inghilterra*, all by Rossini. Merritt's case is quite the opposite He had great natural gifts: a dark colour in the middle register, a high register reaching up to e″ (by the use of a reenforced *falsettone*); but for these enviable quali-

ties there was no adequate technical support. Equality of sound between the registers has always been missing. These defects can be better hidden in the Rossini vocality; but they are, alas, blatantly audible in the Romantic repertory and in Verdi roles (as is proved by the La Scala performances of *Vespri Siciliani* in 1989).

The boom of the Rossini revival and that of the proto-romantic repertory has seen **William Matteuzzi, Luca Canonici**, and **Giuseppe Morino** featured in Italy. The first has specialized in the roles of Lindoro (*Italiana in Algeri*) and Almaviva. His phrasing is refined and he distributes sounds sweetly, though sometimes even passing the limits of affectation. He rises easily to high f″ in *falsettone* and, to the joy of his audience, he generously distributes this note wherever he can. Morino is a special case: his tremulous voice extends over a wide range, his phrasing is varied (characterised by a repeated passing from loud to soft), and when he sings it sounds as if one is listening to an old 78 recording of De Lucia or, more likely, of Carlo Dani, a little turn-of-the-century tenor whose voice was identical, in every respect, to that of Morino. Lastly, Luca Canonici, a pupil of Gobbi's, was internationally launched by his participation in Comencini's film of *La Bohème* when he replaced the ailing José Carreras. This tenor has a small voice but with a pleasant tone, easy high notes, and a great spontaneity and amiability — gifts which, continually being refined by technique, promise a noteworthy career.

Rockwell Blake in L'Italiana in Algeri; *one of his favourite roles. (Photo: A.B. Williamson).*

THE DRAMATIC AND *LIRICO-SPINTO* TENOR IN THE ITALIAN REPERTORY OF THIS CENTURY

One of the immediate followers of Caruso at the beginning of the nineteen hundreds was **Giovanni Zenatello** (Verona 1876 - New York 1949) another ex-baritone who changed quickly into a tenor. His first studies gave his voice a rich colour, resonant in the middle and lower registers but hindering a smooth emission or ease in the high register. During the first twenty years of this century he was much in demand as Otello, Don José, Canio, Des Grieux in Puccini's *Manon Lescaut*, Riccardo in *Ballo in Maschera*, and above all, as Radames. It was he that sang this part in the *Aida* which opened the summer festival at the Verona Arena (August, 1913). Zenatello became the mentor of this project and for various reasons would personally organise the performances.

*The great **Miguel Fleta** in the fourth act of Bizet's Carmen. Few have been able to equal his rendering of "The Flower Song". (EMI Archives. Photo from 1929).*

A great verist performer was to be found in **Piero Schiavazzi** (Cagliari 1875 - Rome 1949) who was mostly active, between 1899 and 1924, in operas such as *Cavalleria, Iris, Conchita* by Zandonai, and *Fedora*, but was also a good interpreter of the *tenore di grazia* repertory (*Lucia, Rigoletto*). Alas, his voice became strained from 1911 on, due to excessive work and a rather unconventional singing technique.

Bernardo De Muro (Tempio di Pausania, Sassari 1881 - Rome 1955) was amazing for his length of breath, his sonority and volume as well as his polished and forceful high notes. These skills derived from a very solid breathing technique — his diaphragm muscles were made of iron — and from Mother Nature, who had given such a voice to this stocky little tenor from Sardinia. He was known to abuse his abilities, conceding himself artistic licences left, right and centre. His interminable high note on the phrase "Sacerdote, io resto a te" from the third act finale of *Aida* has remained famous to this day. He would hold the note whilst walking all the way from the back of the stage to the very front edge where he would consign his sword to a spectator in one of the front boxes. It was a gesture of defiance and spite towards Ramfis, but above all a demonstration of superhuman lung power.

The risky *tessiture*, the exaggerated *corone* and the vocal athletics performed in *Cavalleria, Pagliacci, Andrea Chénier, Iris, Fanciulla del West, Trovatore* and *Isabeau* (which was De Muro's favourite opera) helped accentuate the decline of his voice about half way through the twenties. However his withdrawal from the stage took place in 1938 at Rome with a last amazing interpretation of Falco in *Isabeau*.

Fleta, Cortis, Lázaro: Three Spanish Aces

Miguel Fleta (Albalate del Cinca 1893 - La Coruña 1938) premiered in 1919 at Trieste in *Francesca da Rimini* and was immediately classified as the typical *tenore espada*. With a warm, sensual timbre soaring to explosive high notes, he was capable of reinforcing or diminishing the volume at any height, as in *Tosca, Aida, Carmen*, or *Turandot* — of the latter Fleta was the first performer at La Scala in 1926 under the baton of Arturo Toscanini.

Notwithstanding his excellent technique, the Spanish tenor was overtaken by a premature decline. Only a decade after his first appearance his voice already presented signs of tiredness and strain, with dangerous inequalities and, towards the end of the thirties, it wobbled uncontrollably. Lauri Volpi says in *Voci Parallele* that he was present at, and heard with great regret and sincere compassion, the last appearance of the great tenor in *Christus* by a young Spanish composer.

Antonio Cortis (Altea 1891 - Valencia 1952) was active from 1919 until 1937 and was applauded in all the major Italian and Spanish theatres in *Pagliacci, Carmen, Aida*, and *Fanciulla del West*. In these operas he was able to exhibit a voice that was well-coloured, extended, sturdy and rounded over the *passaggio* notes, even if not quite resistent enough to confront, unscathed, the verist repertory. In fact, in the long run, his original vocal virtues were overtaken by a certain tiredness and shadowing.

Hipólito Lázaro (Barcelona 1889 - Madrid 1974), had a similar fate. Having tackled the risky works of Mascagni, from *Isabeau* to *Parisina* and *Piccolo Marat* (of these two last works he was the first performer in 1913 and 1921 respectively) he found that the same destiny awaited him as that which had touched Fleta and Cortis, an early withdrawal from the stage. During his golden years, between 1911 and 1920, this Spanish tenor was able to sing with taste and elegance, but above all, with a generous voice (even if affected in the centre by an unpleasant *vibrato*) the operas *Rigoletto, Puritani, Favorita, Elisir d'Amore*, along with *Aida, Cavalleria, Trovatore* and the Mascagni operas we have already mentioned.

It seemed an impossible challenge, but the flexible and brilliant voice of Lázaro overcame every obstacle gloriously. "Remember, you are listening to the greatest tenor in the world!" he would tell the audience, interrupting a performance. Towards the end of the twenties his star began to shine less brightly than in his youthful days, and, bit by bit, it faded completely. His huge and demanding repertory had robbed him of at least another fifteen career years.

Pertile, an Isolated Voice

Aureliano Pertile (Montagnana, Padua 1885 - Milan 1952) was one of the most intelligent and sensitive artists of our century, able to compensate an unattractive vocal colour and physical appearance with a style, variety of phrasing and an emotional participation that totally engaged the public. He sang from 1911 until 1946, when he gave a last performance of Boito's *Nerone* at the Rome Opera. He sang mainly in Italy, at La

Aureliano Pertile *as Canio in* I Pagliacci. *(Historic Archives of La Fenice Theatre of Venice).*

Scala (1918-1937) and all the other principal theatres, but also at the Metropolitan Opera from 1921-22, and at Covent Garden from 1927 until 1931.

His favorite operas were *Carmen, Tosca, Cavalleria, Pagliacci, Manon Lescaut, Lucia, Fedora, Ballo in Maschera, Andrea Chénier, Bohème, Rigoletto, Forza del Destino*, and even *Otello* towards the end of his career. In these operas every word, every note, had its correct weight, its own expressiveness, its own internal meaning.

He was Arturo Toscanini's favourite tenor, and the legendary conductor fully understood and used the huge potential that was contained in that awkward body. (By his enemies Pertile was called "the Hunchback"). In the higher registers his voice reached high b' with ease; but he was often obliged to lower the most difficult arias. Notwithstanding this, the nuances and inflections with which he flavoured each passage he interpreted were such as to overshadow any "theatrical inconveniences".

Caruso's Heir

Giovanni Martinelli (Montagnana, Padua 1885 - New York 1969) was considered Caruso's heir in the United States. The New York Metropolitan adopted him in 1913, the year of his debut in *Butterfly*, until 1945-46, giving him honour and unconditional praise. For about a

decade, between the thirties and forties, this tenor from Padua used his voice, originally clear and soaring, to imitate Caruso, thus enlarging the central notes and darkening the sound. These strainings produced unpleasant slips of intonation and damaged the precious quality of his high notes, apart from robbing him of stylistic flexibility. However Martinelli managed to escape the Caruso experiment relatively unscarred and after 1935 continued to have success all over the world ranging from the verist Puccini repertory to *Norma, Forza del Destino, Gioconda, Aida, Carmen* and *Trovatore*. During the last part of his lengthy career he also sang *Otello, L'Ebrea* and *Tristan* together with Flagstad.

The Dramatic Tenors of the First Three Decades of This Century

Among the dramatic and the *spinto* tenors of the first thirty years of the nineteen hundreds we must not forget **Giulio Crimi** (Paternò, Catania 1885 - Rome 1939) who was a great Puccini singer and took part in the first performances of *Il Tabarro* and *Gianni Schicchi* in New York; the Spaniard **Isidoro Fagoaga** (Vera de Bisadea, Navarra 1895 - San Sebastian 1976) who was famous also as a Wagnerian tenor; **Francesco Merli** (Corsico, Milan 1887 - Milan 1976) a Calaf and Otello with golden high notes and a vibrant and robust voice; the Englishman **Alfred Piccaver** (Long Sutton 1884 - Vienna 1985) whose *legato* was impeccable and his timbre dark, who had easy high notes and flexi-

An exceptional trio: whilst **Maria Jeritza** and **Giovanni Martinelli** sing, Arturo Toscanini accompanies them on the piano. The Venetian tenor retained the power of his high notes even in his old age.

bility in phrasing. He was considered the German Caruso at the Vienna Staatsoper. Added to this list we also have the Canadian **Edward Johnson** (born Edoardo Di Giovanni; Guelph, Ontario 1881- 1959), an acclaimed Chénier between 1912 and 1935. His principal characteristics were the warmth of his timbre and his piercing high notes.

Thill, Roswänge: Ambassadors of Italian Opera in France and Germany

Georges Thill (Paris 1897 - Lorgues 1984) was not really a "dramatic" tenor in the true sense of the word, but rather a *lirico puro* (pure lyric) with exceptional versatility. He was able to sing *Manon, Werther, Faust* and *Lakmé* while at the same time obtaining great results in operas such as *Aida, Turandot, Guglielmo Tell, Fanciulla del West, Carmen,* and even *Samson and Dalila.*

His career began in Paris in 1918, as Don José, and was concluded, once again in Paris, with a farewell concert in 1955.

Taking into account Thill's undoubted natural talent and his training in De Lucia's school it can nevertheless be said that the breadth of his repertory did not help his vocal longevity. The first noticeable signs of his decline were already audible in the 1929 performances of *Turandot* at La Scala. However it is also true that despite his fluid emission and beautiful *mezzavoce,* the French tenor had always suffered from a certain harshness in his high notes especially when singing in a more demanding repertory. His *Werther,* however, remains unsurpassed, equalled only perhaps by that of Schipa.

Helge Roswänge (his real name was Helge Rosenving-Hansen, Copenhagen 1897 - Munich 1972) had an exceptionally long career that began in 1921 (with his debut as Don José at Neustrelitz) and continued until the end of the fifties. He was by then singing exclusively in Berlin and Vienna.

His golden years were, however, between 1926 and 1940. These were years when his voice with its rich timbre, extension up to high d″, and capacity for varied dynamic effects enthused the public in operas by Mozart, Verdi, Puccini, Leoncavallo, Wagner, and Richard Strauss.

Roswänge was actually the first performer of many of Verdi's operas in the German opera theatres during the well-known Verdi revival begun in the 1930's. Some of his interpretations that have remained on record are memorable despite the fact that they are sung in a German translation: from "Vesti la giubba" (*Pagliacci*) to "Ah! Sì, ben mio" (*Trovatore*) without forgetting the perfection of "Giorno di pianto" (*Vespri Siciliani*) where we can admire not only the legato but also the shining high note in the cadenza.

For Roswänge, as for the others, the last part of his career was not particularly happy from a vocal point of view. His voice began to wobble; the various registers began to separate; and even his intonation began to slide as witnessed by recordings made in Vienna between the end of the forties and the end of the fifties. We must not forget his considerable activity in operetta at the Vienna Volksoper where Roswänge was an acclaimed favourite.

Two other excellent protagonists of the world opera scene who belonged to the same generation as that of Thill and Roswänge were **Richard Tauber** (Linz 1891 - London 1948) of whom we have already spoken in the paragraph on Mozart tenors, and **Galliano Masini** (Leghorn 1896-1986), a generous and robust interpreter of so many performances of *Cavalleria, Pagliacci, Aida* and also *Carmen, Andrea Chénier, Turandot, Adriana Lecouvreur,* and, in 1955, *Otello.*

He was from humble origins but gifted with a formidable theatrical instinct. He used to literally terrify his partners with the force of his performances, throwing fiery glances and even real punches at the poor Carmen or Desdemona of the evening.

*"No, no, principessa altera, ti voglio ardente d'amor!" sings **Lauri Volpi** and launches his high c″ to the stars like a luminous comet. This photo depicts the mythical tenor during one of his last performances, a* Turandot *of June 28th, 1958, at the Terme di Caracalla. His partners were Inge Borkh and Onelia Fineschi. (Photo: Oscar Savio. Historic Archives of the Rome Opera).*

The Message Brought by Lauri Volpi

Many do not know that, despite the fact that the role of the Principe Ignoto was first performed by Miguel Fleta, it was actually conceived by Puccini for **Giacomo Lauri Volpi** (stage name of Giacomo Volpi; Lanuvio, Rome 1893 - Burjasot, Valencia 1978). He was a vocal phenomenon without equal, especially from the point of view of his voice, more than his style, which now seems quite old-fashioned.

Between 1919 and 1959 he was the lone Knight of Belcanto, crusader of the old way of singing, and an ideal lover in operas such as *Puritani, Favorita, Les Huguenots, Rigoletto, Manon, Guglielmo Tell*; but he also sang Puccini (*Bohème, Tosca, Fanciulla del West, Turandot*) and Verdi (*Luisa Miller, Rigoletto, Trovatore, Forza del Destino, Otello*).

His voice had three octaves (ranging from low f to the high f″ above high C of *Puritani* which he sang in chest voice), of limpid tone colour and clear enunciation, trained to softly caress before passionately exploding. It was called "the happy man's voice" by Barilli.

This exceptional voice was formed by the great Cotogni, who gave Lauri Volpi lessons, Maria Ros, his wife and also an excellent soprano, but above all, by the determination and intelligence of the artist himself. He was a man of culture and with many interests. He was the author of numerous books: *Cristalli viventi* (Living Crystals), *Voci Parallele* (Parallel Voices), the novel *La prode terra* (The Valiant Earth), the collection entitled *A viso aperto* (With an Open Glance) are the better known examples.

At the summit of his glory and no longer young, the Roman tenor was easily able to perform the difficult phrase "Talor dal mio forziere" (*Bohème*) in *falsettone*, or the high b′ in the Raul — Valentina duet from *The Huguenots*. When he was sixty he was still singing with an incredible vocal freshness in the roles of Calaf, Arturo, Manrico, Poliuto, and Edgardo. Not even the young Corelli managed to perform them all.

To demonstrate the fact that a voice, if well cultivated and trained, never tires and accompanies its owner until death, there were the last concerts of the great Lauri Volpi: Valencia 1971, Barcelona 1972, Busseto 1976 and Madrid 1977. On this last occasion the "golden oldy" (eighty-four years old) sang once again "Nessun dorma" with that final amazing "Vincerò!", which was, to once more quote Barilli, the most beautiful "human message" ever launched towards the moon.

Many could not accept the pompous last century style used by Lauri Volpi. Envious colleagues were very hostile towards him, but he always answered "in key" both orally and in writing. As we listen to his recordings today, however, we must ask ourselves if some of his vocal habits were really necessary, such as the abuse of *falsettone* and *portamenti*, the approximate *solfeggio*, and his not always impeccable intonation.

Giuseppe Lugo (Sona, Verona 1899 - Milan 1980) was considered by the French to be the successor to Thill. He possessed a solid vocal ability at least until the end of the thirties.

He was excellent in parts such as the Duke of Mantua, Rodolfo, Werther, and the French repertory in general, but not so successful in the Italian repertory undertaken after 1936. He found himself in difficulty handling the type of emission used in Italian theatres, and, as a result, his Italian career, although not without its successes, did not last long.

As far as **Mario Filippeschi** (Pisa 1907 - Florence 1979) is concerned, the discussion is different. The former tram-driver had easy high notes but an alternating career which did not last long due to his lack of style and a sloppy interpreta-

On 28 June, 1953, Caracalla opens with Rossini's Guglielmo Tell, featuring three ace cards: the baritone **Tito Gobbi**, in the centre, the bass **Giulio Neri**, and to the right in the extremely difficult role of Arnaldo is **Mario Filippeschi**, famous for his high C's in chest voice. (Historic Archives of the Rome Opera Theatre).

tion of certain operas (*Ballo in Maschera, Tosca, Bohème,* and *Lucia di Lammermoor*). However his high c″'s and c″ sharps launched with generosity in *Trovatore* and *Puritani* were enough to assure him a noteworthy following during the forties and fifties.

The voice and handsome appearance of **Mario Lanza** (the stage name of Alfredo Arnold Cocozza; Philadelphia 1921 - Rome 1959) quickly assured him fame. He was considered the "new Caruso" in the United States, perhaps more so because of his many films (the most famous being, by chance, *The Great Caruso*, made in 1951) rather than because of his voice. His voice did have a pleasant tone-colour, dark and velvety; but it was produced in a way that was often negligent, even rough, lacking in refinement. A sudden heart attack killed him at only thirty-eight years of age, and thus helped to increase the cult following of this son of Italian emigrants who had become rich and famous, thanks to his Carusian voice colour.

Let's consider two past important American tenors, Peerce and Tucker. The first was **Jan Peerce** (born Jacob Pincus Perlemuth; New York 1904-1984) who began his musical career in 1933 as a violinist in a jazz orchestra. Peerce made his debut in 1938 in Philadelphia as the Duca di Mantova in *Rigoletto*. He became a tenor at Toscanini's urging and made many recordings with this famous conductor, among which are those of *Traviata, Ballo in Maschera* and *Bohème*. In his Met career he interpreted a wide variety of Verdi and Puccini roles. And when he was eighty years old, he made a recording which revealed all the old vocal power and high notes!

Richard Tucker (whose real name was Rueben Ticker; New York 1913 - Kalamazoo, Michigan 1975) was encouraged to study by Peerce, who became his brother-in-law in 1936. In 1945 he premiered at the Metropolitan singing Enzo in *La Gioconda* — a role so well suited to him that he favoured it during his entire career. He had excellent vocal gifts, technique, (perfect sound placement, brilliant high notes) and timbre. In Italy he sang in *Pagliacci* and *Ballo in Maschera*, in Rome, Florence and the Arena of Verona.

Tucker's career was mainly based in America, from 1945 until 1975; he frequently sang *Pagliacci, Carmen, Forza del Destino, Tosca, Rigoletto, Lucia, Aida, Ballo in Maschera,* and *Manon Lescaut*. During his thirty years of activity at the Metropolitan he sang over six hundred times in approximately thirty different roles. In 1973 he succeeded in making one of his dreams come true by singing Eléazar in *La Juive* by Halévy at New Orleans.

Mario Del Monaco (Florence 1915 - Mestre 1982) was both the last to follow Caruso and the

Richard Tucker and **Grace Bumbry**. *It is March 1970 and at Rome there is a new production of* Carmen *in the original edition; and with stage sets by Guttuso that were destined to cause scandal. It was the only appearance the American tenor made in the Italian capital apart from a* Manon Lescaut *in 1968. (Historic Archives of the Rome Opera Theatre).*

first of a new school, that of the imitators of Del Monaco, of course. It must be said that his vocal qualities can not be copied; any other vocal or respiratory system would be seriously damaged by imitating his techniques. Already rich and powerful by nature, the voice of this Italian tenor was built on the central tenor notes, which were strengthened and thickened, and on the incredible power of his high notes, which were joined to the middle register by an excellent *passaggio*. The result was a declamatory singing, unique in its incisiveness, but sometimes exaggerated, in difficulty in utilizing dynamic effects and mezzavoce, and with little variety. When guided by a great conductor, such as von Karajan, Del Monaco could adapt to the shadings required by the part; thus he gave the public a superb recording of *Otello*, 1960 (Decca). This Verdi opera was to be his principal role from 1950, when he sang it for the first time at Buenos Aires, until his last performances in the sixties in which his interpretation was based on the power and incisiveness of his high notes.

Thus **Mario Del Monaco** and **Tito Gobbi** close the second act of Otello put on stage at the Palazzo Ducale of Venice in 1960. Del Monaco was the protoganonist of many incredible performances of this, his favourite Verdi opera. Once, at the La Monnaie Theatre in Brussels, he sang the difficult phrase "Dopo l'armi lo vinse l'uragano" all in one breath - an "Esultate" that left the public gasping! (Photo Afi. Historic Archives of La Fenice Theatre, Venice).

Elegant and proud, **Mario Del Monaco** constituted a vocal phenomenon without precedent; his lung capacity, and the brilliance and power of his high notes were exceptional. (Archives of the San Carlo Opera Theatre of Naples. Photo: Troncone).

In I Pagliacci **Mario Del Monaco** used to insert a series of sobs at the end of the famous aria "Vesti la giubba" which were more comical than tragic; and yet one cannot help but be impressed by the drama in his phrase "No, pagliaccio non son". (Historic Archives of the Rome Opera Theatre).

During the first part of his career, from 1941 (he made his debut in *Butterfly*) until 1949, Del Monaco's repertory included *Lucia*, *Rigoletto*, *Tosca* and *Bohème*; it seemed that he might continue as a pure lyric. Then came the vocal tidal waves of *Aida*, *Fanciulla del West*, *Pagliacci*, *Otello*, *Samson and Delilah*, and *Trovatore*. He had made his choice.

Del Monaco did not sing frequently at Covent Garden, appearing for the first time in 1946, on tour with the San Carlo Company from Naples, and once again in 1962 as Otello. He performed regularly at the Metropolitan from 1951 until 1959.

He retired after a series of performances of *Pagliacci* in Vienna in 1976; but when listening to recordings of songs made shortly before his death, we cannot help but be amazed by the vocal metal and the intact vigour of the many high b'flats.

The Del Monaco School

A vocal phenomenon of the strength and fame of Del Monaco was sure to be imitated, all too often with deleterious effects for the singers who tried. In the attempt to imitate the heavy centres and the forceful declamation of the Florentine tenor, gifted singers such as **Flaviano Labò, Pier Miranda Ferraro, Gastone Limarilli, Gianfranco Cecchele**, and **Nunzio Todisco** unnaturally enlarged sounds, forcing their emission, and eliminating all nuances. Thus they gained only a fleeting success and had an early decline. However Cecchele is worth a comment apart. He possessed a beautiful voice colour, and he managed to overcome a critical period at the end of the seventies when he underwent a throat operation.

The story of the cat who thought he was a tiger has repeated itself in the case of the last generation of dramatic tenors: **Franco Bonisolli, Nicola Martinucci** and **Giuseppe Giacomini**. They are all very active in Italy and elsewhere in operas such as *Aida*, *Trovatore*, *Turandot*, or *Andrea Chénier*; but they have done nothing new. Theirs are voices of good quality with facility in high notes, but monotony in phrasing; with few shadings of tone and little respect for the many dynamic signs on the scores. While Bonisolli has continued to gain success by con-

Franco Bonisolli
(Rovereto, Trento
1938) and **Teresa**
Zylis-Gara *in*
Rossini's Guglielmo
Tell *in Nice in 1981.*
Bonisolli is a rather
singular character in
the operatic world: he
is gifted with
excellent high notes
(which reach up to
high e" flat in
falsettone) but is
sloppy and without
style, and forced in
the central notes. He
is renowned for his
exuberant,
unpredictable
character. (Archives
of the Nice Opera).

Pier Miranda Ferraro *(Altivola, Treviso 1924) is a typi-*
cal Del Monaco follower who had a noteworthy career,
distinguished by his professionalism and the constancy
of his vocal renderings. (Archives of the Rome Opera
Theatre).

A "sherpa" version of **Mirto Picchi** together with the mezzo-soprano **Gianna Pederzini** in I Cavalieri di Ekebù, by Zandonai, during a performance in Rome in January, 1954. Picchi gave greatly intelligent and sensitive interpretations of these lesser known parts; giving them equal dignity with those of the grand repertory. (Photo: Oscar Savio. Historic Archives of the Rome Opera).

tinuously hurling high c″ at the public, Martinucci and Giacomini have managed to build sound international careers performing operas that would otherwise have been condemned, unjustly, to oblivion.

1950-1960: Picchi, Poggi, Fernandi: Three Little Men Amongst The Giants

During the period from 1950 until the end of the sixties there was a ferocius competition amongst tenors, especially in the *lirico-spinto* category. Some managed to carve out a small niche by choosing an unusual repertory or by emigrating overseas. **Mirto Picchi** (S. Mauro a Signa, Florence 1915 - Florence 1980) had begun as a *lirico-spinto* in operas performed by Del Monaco, Corelli, and other colleagues who had more vocal weight. He soon decided to employ his particular skills, both vocal and acting, in a rarer repertory and in new works (*La Figlia di Jorio*, by Pizzetti, 1954; *La Sposa Sorteggiata* by Busoni, 1966; *Celestina* by Testi, 1963; *Lorenzaccio* by Bussotti, 1972). In these operas the friendly Tuscan tenor had no rivals.

Gianni Poggi (Piacenza 1921-1989) earned himself widespread fame as Alfredo, the Duca di Mantova, Riccardo, Manrico and as a Donizetti

singer both in Europe and America. His tone-colour was typical and has been accurately described as "fat" — that is, rich and thick. His

Giuseppe Giacomini in Puccini's Turandot.

43

A beautiful close-up of **Franco Corelli**, who looks more like one of Hollywood's stars than a typical opera singer. Just imagine what that spectator felt like when, after having "booed" Corelli in Trovatore he turned round to find the colossal tenor in his very box — furious! — This actually happened in Bologna.

What Escamillo could ever compete with such an enchanting Don José? This photo depicts **Corelli** and **Giulietta Simionato** in the Carmen performed at Venice, 1956. In the final two acts Corelli used to exibit a vigour that has never been surpassed. (Historic Archives of La Fenice Theatre, Venice. Photo: Giacomelli).

Corelli is hardly recognisable in his costume for Canio in Pagliacci at Caracalla in 1953. His voice was robust and metallic, but also able to express even the most delicate nuances. (Historic Archives of the Rome Opera. Photo: Oscar Savio).

When Pier Miranda Ferraro was taken suddenly ill, the management of the Teatro Regio of Parma immediately called **Franco Corelli** to fill the part of Pollione, all in less than one day. It was the 1971-72 season, and thanks to the presence of the great Italian tenor, the performance was a triumph. (Historic Archives of Parma's Teatro Regio. Photo: Montacchini).

high notes were noteworthy for their brilliance and incisiveness.

Eugenio Fernandi (Milan 1926) sang very often in Italy between 1954 and 1960, but emigrated to France where he kept the most strenuous dramatic roles in his repertory. His performances were not always happy ones: his voice was always ready to crack, probably because of some original intonation problems that were never completely resolved. All the same Fernandi was part of many prestigious casts and worked under the direction of many great conductors — of special note, the Salzburg *Don Carlos* of 1958 with Herbert von Karajan.

Corelli: Power and Charm

Like many dramatic tenors, **Franco Corelli** (stage name of Dario Corelli; Ancona 1921) made his debut as Don José at Spoleto in 1951. The first things which were noted about the young tenor were his exceptional good looks, worthy of a Hollywood film star, united with a dark, baritone-like voice of great power and large extension, but affected by a *vibrato stretto* which did not please everyone.

With time and under the precious guidance of Lauri Volpi, he managed to dam the "gushing river" of his voice, rising to the highest notes of the pentagram and gaining a flexible and smooth emission. Thanks to this technical control he was not only able to sing *Pirata, Trovatore, Turandot, Poliuto* and *Les Huguenots* but also *Werther, Faust, Romeo and Juliet* by Gounod, and *Don Carlos*, all major roles, during his long

permanence at the Metroplitan Opera of New York. He retired in 1976, still in perfect condition. One of his typical characteristics was his great insecurity and the panic attacks which would grip him before appearing in public. Quite often friends and colleagues would have to literally "launch" him onto the stage.

The Great Vocal Traditions of Emilia: Gianni Raimondi

Gianni Raimondi (Bologna 1923) showed right from the beginning (*Rigoletto*, Budrio 1947)

Gianni Raimondi as Arrigo (Vespri Siciliani) in the 1973 performance at Turin under the direction of Di Stefano and Maria Callas. (Historic Archives of the Teatro Regio of Turin. Photo: P.G. Naretto).

Carlo Bergonzi during one of his rare performances as the Calaf in Turandot in Naples, 1976. The tenor was never famous for his extension in the high notes but few have been able to equal him in expressiveness. (Historic Archives of the San Carlo Opera Theatre of Naples. Photo: Troncone).

that he possessed very solid vocal means protected by a sound vocal technique. His was a voice with a superb consistency and a timbre that, because of its clarity and transparency, recalled that of Di Stefano.

His exceptional High c″'s and c″ sharps, together with his good taste and elegant stylistic line, made him a belcanto singer in much demand in his time (*Puritani, Favorita, Armida, Mosè, Semiramide, Guglielmo Tell*).

As a pure lyric tenor, Raimondi excelled as Alfredo, Edgardo, Rodolfo, and Cavaradossi, and was engaged by theatres all over the world for these parts. (Let us note one of the many — the La Scala *Bohème* with von Karajan in 1963).

The only criticism we can make, faced with his thirty-five year honourable career, is that he showed a certain laziness in performing. He had to be pushed to perform any extra *mezzavoce* and reminded to avoid monotonous phrasing; he succeeded if he was guided by a good conductor.

The Authentic Verdi Tenor: Carlo Bergonzi

For the first part of his career, from his initial debut as a baritone at Lecce in 1948 and his second debut, this time as a tenor (*Andrea Chénier*, Bari, 1951), until the beginning of the seventies **Carlo Bergonzi** (Vidalenzo, Parma 1924) did not enjoy the same critical acclaim extended to less worthy colleagues. The critics accused him of lacking attractive timbre, of having a voice that was too artificial, with no high notes, little stage

presence; and even his "s" pronounced "sh" in the Emilian way seemed to annoy them. However, few singers in this century can compete with Bergonzi as far as style, breathing technique, and enunciation are concerned.

His perfect *legato* and vigorous accent made him an ideal Duca di Mantova, Riccardo, Radames, Don Alvaro, Canio, and Pinkerton, not to mention his unforgettable Don Carlos. Although he has never had high notes because of his insistence in "covering" (the *passaggio*), Bergonzi overcame even the most arduous vocal passages with incredible breath control: great examples are the aria "Quando le sere al placido" from *Luisa Miller* or the prison scene in *I Due Foscari*; he also possessed a wide variety and imagination in phrasing. In this he is the rightful heir to Aureliano Pertile.

Thanks to his excellent technique, the Italian tenor is still singing in his favourite operas.

Since 1956 Bergonzi has been linked to the Metropolitan where he has performed with great success even in recent years. Especially noteworthy are *La Gioconda, Elisir d'Amore, Lucia*, and a concert performance of *I Lombardi* with Aprile Millo and the New York City Opera in 1986.

Placido Domingo: The Tenor Who Came From the South

Placido Domingo was born in Madrid. His detractors say that his birth date is in 1934 (who knows why?), but his friends say that he was born in 1941. Wisely we propose both dates and leave the decision to the reader. He studied piano and composition during his youth in Mexico City, which gave him a firm grounding as a musician before he began as a singer. A friend persuaded him to attempt a vocal career, which was not altogether an unknown road to him as both his parents had been successful *Zarzuela* singers.

The steps on Domingo's ladder to success can be summarised as follows: 1959 — debut in a small part in *The Dialogues of the Carmelites* in Mexico City 1962 — his first lead part; 1963-65, stable member of the Tel Aviv Opera; 1967, debut at the Metropolitan in *Adriana Lecouvreur*; 1969, Italian debut at Verona and the opening of the La Scala winter season on the traditional 7th December with *Ernani*.

Since then Domingo's presence in the world's major theatres, arenas, squares, stadiums, film sets, recording and television studios has been uninterrupted, almost unbelievable. His repertory has, with time, embraced all the principal tenor roles from Verdi to Donizetti, Puccini, Massenet, Gounod, Wagner; most of these interpretations have been preserved on record.

Until 1975 the Spanish tenor kept the best qualities of his voice intact. Its colour was magnificent, warm and sensual, smooth and caressing in quality, a beautiful *falsettone*, (of which, unfortunately, he has always made little use), penetrating high notes, and a clear but passionate declamation. If to this we add his intelligence and musical brilliance, not to mention his psychological understanding of his roles, his acting ability, his undoubted charm, and his good looks, it would be easy to proclaim Domingo the greatest tenor of our time. But alas, his hyperactivity and monstrous repertory have taken their toll. Since the second half of the seventies his precious voice has begun to suffer: the high notes (even only a' and b' flat) became strained or even worse, as evidenced by the 1977 Vienna *Trovatore*; the *mezzavoce* has become *falsetto*; the breathing is difficult in certain passages; the *legato* lost its polish. These defects are now permanent. We can still admire certain passages in *Tosca, Otello, Fanciulla del West* and *Manon Lescaut* but on the whole recent performances have been tired and monotonous.

After the disastrous earthquake which hit Mexico City in 1985, the tenor generously decided to dedicate an entire year of activity only to charity performances, cancelling all his previous engagements with theatres all over the world.

Among his best recent performances let us remember the wonderful *Lohengrin* at the Vienna Opera, conducted by Claudio Abbado; and *Samson and Delilah* and *Parsifal*, both at the Metropolitan. These operas seem to have been written especially to show off Domingo's best vocal qualities.

The Great Wagnerian Tenors of the Twentieth Century

Giuseppe Borgatti (Cento, Ferrara 1871 Reno, Lago Maggiore 1950) was the apostle of Wagner's music in Italy. Gabriele D'Annunzio wrote of him "that the Wagnerians have found their Saint Paul". In fact, after his debut in *Faust*, at Castelfranco Veneto, 1892, his repertory was almost exclusively Wagnerian. He was the first Lohengrin at Milan in 1894, the first Italian Siegfried during the Scala 1899-1900 season; in the next season, Tristan; and finally Tannhäuser at Buenos Aires in 1901.

Borgatti's vocal means were perfectly suited to the difficult *Heldentenor* roles: he had brilliant high notes, smoothness of emission, and an excellent technique. The Italian operas he most frequently performed were *Andrea Chénier, Tosca, Fedora* and *Iris*; however it appears that in these parts he had considerable difficulty in sustaining the high notes from 1905 on. This was probably the reason why he decided to limit his repertory exclusively to Wagner during the last part of his career — the *tessitura* required by the Wagnerian roles being noticeably central for tenor voice.

From 1904, he was welcomed at Bayreuth, the Wagner temple, where his presence became essential for future editions of the festival. In 1914 he sang his last *Parsifal* at La Scala, in concert form, then he retired because of ill-health. He suffered from glaucoma which gradually caused complete blindness by 1923.

Notwithstanding his advanced age and poor physical condition, his Colombia recordings made in 1928 are amazingly forceful interpretations of the "Ode to Spring" from the *Walküre*, and the finale of *Otello*.

Besides the "Borgatti phenomenon", for whom spreading the Wagnerian *Gesamtkunstwerk* was a true vocation, there were many other great performers.

The first of this illustrious line was **Italo Campanini** (Parma 1845-1896), brother of the famous conductor Cleofonte; he was the first Lohengrin at Bologna in 1871. He was also active in the French *lyrique* and Italian repertories, especially in London and New York. The tenor from Milan, **Ettore Cesa-Bianchi**, was a noteworthy Lohengrin, and was described by Eugenio Gara as having "a voice of silver, just like the hero's armour". **Fiorello Giraud** (Parma 1870-1928) was the first Canio at La Scala in 1892 and was Toscanini's favourite Siegfried, having been chosen by him for this opera at La Scala. **Edoardo Ferrari-Fontana** (Rome 1878 - Toronto 1936) was first an operetta tenor but the great Maestro Tullio Serafin persuaded him to take on roles more suited to him, such as

The tenor **Giuseppe Borgatti** in his hairy costume of Siegfried. It seems that, to train for this role, he kept a hammer and anvil in his hotel room - with much disapproval from the other clients!

those of Tristan or Tannhäuser. In these he triumphed at the Metropolitan of New York.

Amongst the first Germans to champion Wagnerian melodrama in this century: **Heinrich Knote** (Munich 1870 - Garmisch 1953) who was famous for his outstanding diction and his super powerful high notes, which made him very popular as Manrico in Verdi's *Trovatore*. He continued to sing with intact vocal means until 1931.

Another *Heldentenor* of rare quality was **Jacques (Jac) Urlus** (Hergenrath, Aachen 1867 - Noordwiik 1935) whose repertory was incredibly wide; (apart from the main Wagnerian roles he could easily perform Tamino in *The Magic Flute, Faust*, and Raoul in *The Huguenots*). Striking for his robust vocal means and the smoothness and flexibility of his emission, this Dutch tenor was able to diminish or increase sounds even in the high register.

Karel Burian (Carl Burrian) (Rousinov, Rakovnik 1870 - Senomaty 1924) was very popular in the R. Strauss repertory and especially as Herod in *Salome*. He was the first to interpret this part, in 1905 in Dresden. He also distinguished himself in Wagner, Smetana, and in lieder works, displaying a technique and style of rare quality.

After having made his debut as a baritone at Wiesbaden in 1891 **Erik Schmedes** (Gjentofte, Copenhagen 1866 - Vienna 1931) debuted again

as a tenor in 1898 at Vienna, singing the part of Siegfried. He was one of the most acclaimed performers at the Staatsoper during Mahler's management. His biggest successes were *Tristan, Lohengrin*, and *Parsifal*, apart from his lively portrayals in *Otello, Pagliacci, Norma*, and *Carmen*. He was the first Austrian Cavaradossi in 1910.

Leo Slezak: Humourous and Amiable

Leo Slezak (Schonberg, Moravia 1873 - Rottach Egern, Bavaria 1946) remains the greatest *Heldentenor* of this century. He made his debut in *Lohengrin*, at Brno, in 1896; and went on to work mainly in Berlin (1898-99), Vienna (1901-09), and New York (1909-13), and then in Vienna and in German opera theatres until 1934.

He was gifted with vocal chords which were flexible, beautiful in timbre, sturdy, and luminous in the high register, warm and sensual in the middle register. His imaginative phrasing allowed him to range from Mozart, Delibes and Charpentier to the most difficult of Wagnerian roles and Verdi's *Otello*. In the latter he triumphed at the Metropolitan in 1911 under Toscanini's baton. We must not forget his musicality and his polish when singing lieder either, an approach which demonstrated a decided artistic superiority to his Italian colleagues of the time.

Slezak had an imposing appearance, but also a pronounced sense of humour which was often undisciplined. The management of the Metropolitan Opera had to fine him after a performance of *Aida* for the confusion he had caused among members of the chorus. The remark he made during a performance of *Lohengrin* has remained famous. After singing the "Farewell to the Swan" he casually enquired "When does the next one leave?", making everyone collapse with laughter. His book of memories is appropriately titled *The Clown's Song: Memories of a Starving Tenor*.

François Gauthier, in art **Paul Franz** (Paris 1876-1950) spread Wagner's operas in France; after 1908, when he debuted in *Lohengrin* at the Paris Opera, he was clearly one of the most complete dramatic tenors of his generation. He was chosen for many important premiers by composers such as Roussel, d'Indy, Rabaud, and he also participated in Paris performances of *Les Troyens* by Berlioz, *Hérodiade* by Massenet, and *La Juive* by Halévy. He withdrew from the stage on the July 12th, 1938, and then dedicated himself to teaching.

In Russia, and precisely at the Marynskij

Theatre, the German repertory was triumphantly upheld by **Ivan Ers'ov** (Novocerkassk 1867 - Leningrad 1943) from 1895 on. Meanwhile, in the Bayreuth sanctuary shone the bright star of **Alois Burgstaller** (Holzkirchen 1871 - Gmünd 1945). An excellent Sigmund, Siegfried, Erik and Parsifal, he was exiled from the "sacred hill" in 1903 because he was guilty of having sung *Parsifal* in New York before the exclusive copyright had expired.

Melchior, the Giant with the Golden Voice

Lauritz Melchior (Copenhagen 1890 - Los Angeles 1973) had a truly golden voice. A baritone from 1913 until 1917, he became a tenor in 1918 when he made his debut as Tannhäuser. During his first career years he dangerously alternated tenor and baritone roles, putting his voice at great risk. He was saved from ruin by his incredible physical resistance and a period of hard study between 1921 and 1923 under the guidance of several different teachers.

In 1924, having obtained a valuable engagement at Bayreuth, he began his spectacular rise to fame, and even to cult status in America. He

Ivan Ers'ov was a great interpreter of the Russian and Wagnerian repertory. He was exceptional for his total emotional involvement and his stage presence, especially in Lohengrin and Parsifal. (Historic Archives of the Kirov Theatre of Leningrad. Photo from 1910).

sang at the Metropolitan Opera from 1926 until 1950 when he retired.

When listening to some of the recordings made during the span of his long career, what is most striking is the extraordinary consistency and sonority of that voice with a cutting *Sprech-*

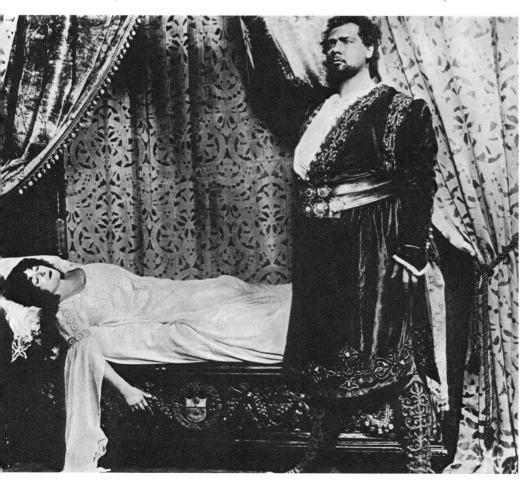

Leo Slezak. Otello, has just strangled *Frances Alda*, Desdemona.

gesang and spear-like high notes. We can, however, also hear a certain difficulty in moulding such vocal bulk in order to respect all the dynamic signs. Sometimes the same difficulty is noticeable in the most treacherous *legato* passages and in held high notes, as is demonstrated in the live recording of *Tannhäuser* made in 1942 at the Metropolitan.

These were defects due, perhaps, to his original beginnings as a baritone and were never completely resolved or camouflaged. As Lauri Volpi accurately noted in his book *Voci Parallele*, "his declamation and sonority were those of a Wagnerian orchestra"; and we might add that his physical stamina was indestructable. Melchior sang Tristan over three hundred times!

A second wave of Wagnerian singers followed the generation of Melchior and Slezak, even if they always remained a step below the level of their immediate predecessors.

Julius Patzak (Vienna 1898 - Tegernsee 1974) was the flag bearer of this new regiment of tenors, being active from 1926 until 1960, par-

ticularly at the Vienna Staatsoper. His voice was neither beautiful nor particularly powerful; his art consisted of a rare musicality and sensivity. Thanks to his uncommon acting ability and his complete stylistic adherence, he made memorable portrayals of Florestan in *Fidelio*, *Palestrina* by Pfitzner, Herod in *Salome*, Mime in *The Ring*, *Lohengrin*, and performed all the most important Mozart roles.

Max Lorenz (Düsseldorf 1901 - Salzburg 1975) started his career in 1927, one year after his colleague, Patzak, in the part of Walther in *The Mastersingers of Nuremberg*. The audiences of Berlin, Vienna, New York, London, Bayreuth, Rome and Milan were able to applaud him until the beginning of the seventies, admiring his passionate declamation and penetrating voice. It is true that his voice had already shown evident signs of tiredness by the fifties: this caused problems in certain roles (Tristan, for example) but it is also true that Lorenz emerged victorious from every performance. He is even remembered in opera annals for that very criti-

"The Great Dane", **Lauritz Melchior***, in the title role of Wagner's* Tannhäuser. *The greatest* heldentenor *of the century.*

50

cised *Tristan* wonderfully performed at La Scala with the mythical conducting by De Sabata in 1948.

Amongst the best Lohengrins and Siegmunds (*Walküre*) between the wars there was **Franz Völker** (Neu Ilsenberg 1899 - Darmstadt 1965), who was also famous as Otello and Canio in German theatres. His "Addio alla madre" (Farewell to the mother) from *Cavalleria Rusticana* is the most beautiful recording of this piece ever recorded.

Set Svanholm (Vasteras 1904 - Stockholm 1964) was another who began as a baritone, having debuted in 1930 as Silvio in *Pagliacci*, and then as a tenor in the role of Radames in 1936. This role was well suited to him despite his average vocal means and the absence of a "physique du rôle". In the immediate post-war period his dramatically intense interpretations created him a reputation as an almost irreplaceable Tristan and Siegfried.

The German tenor **Marcel Wittrisch** (Antwerp 1901 - Stockholm 1955) distinguished himself in both the Wagnerian repertory and in the operettas of Lehar, succeeding in an incredible stylistic cocktail. His career lasted for three decades, from 1925 until 1955.

The Wagnerian Meteors

In the fifties it was a tenor from Chile who excited the custodians of the Holy Grail of Bayreuth. His timbre was dark, his high notes imposing, his enunciation sculptured, his stage presence magnificent. He seemed a fairy-tale Tristan: his name was **Ramón Vinay** (Chillan 1906). Alas the dream did not last long. Unresolved technical problems and a heavy repertoire prematurely wore out Vinay's voice, and his voice was often forced and strained.

In 1962, as a last hope, he returned to his original baritone register; but the parts of Telramondo, Iago, Scarpia, and even Falstaff in no way helped him to find his lost voice.

The same fate awaited the Italian **Gino Penno** (Felizzano, Alessandria 1920), who was endowed with a generous and rich voice but used it badly in operas that were too strenuous for it (*Lohengrin*, *Walküre*, *Turandot*, *Aida*, *Forza del Destino*), sacrificing himself prematurely. During a *Trovatore* at La Scala in 1954 he had to lower the "Pira" by an entire tone! In 1956, following a few performances of *Boris Godunov* at La Scala he withdrew permanently. Almost eighty, but unabashed, **Hans Beirer** (Berlin 1912) continues to perform in the theatres of Berlin and Vienna in the same repertoire he has followed during his fifty years of career; *Tannhäuser*, Erik in *The Flying Dutchman*, and Herod in *Salome*. It is as this

The 1948-49 season: **Ramon Vinay** sings "Dio, mi potevi scagliar" in the third act of Otello. (Historic Archives of the San Carlo Opera Theatre of Naples).

last character that he has always gathered the greatest acclaim.

A master of *Sprechgesang*, with fine, powerful high notes, he is more ill-at-ease in a lighter, delicate style of singing. Beirer has included in his repertory *Otello*, *The Ring*, *Lohengrin*, *Parsifal*, and has sung in many Italian theatres.

Hans Beirer - Siegfried. A photo from at least thirty-five years ago. (Historic Archives of the Rome Opera. Photo: W. Saeger).

The Twilight Of the Gods

After the war of 1939-1945 there were fewer *Heldentenoren*. It was an evident sign of a lack of real voices and the decline of singing schools.

Wolfgang Windgassen (Annemasse, Geneva 1914 - Stuttgard 1974) was, together with Jon Vickers, the last great Wagnerian of our times. He began his activity in 1941, making his debut at Pforzheim as Don Alvaro in *La Forza del Destino*. After a pause during the war years, he started singing again, in the Stuttgart Opera ensemble, and was noticed by Wieland Wagner in 1951. Wagner was favourably impressed by the tenor in the operette *La Belle Hélène*, by Offenbach, and signed him up for the Bayreuth festival.

Soon Windgassen became irreplacable in the roles of the heroic Wagnerian tenor. He demonstrated a timbre, a technique and an interpretive intelligence of absolute excellence. During the fifties and sixties he undertook the difficult roles of the German lyric theatre, refining his characterisations and always giving the public new sensations, especially in the revolutionary productions of Wieland Wagner at Bayreuth. He retired from the stage at Stuttgart in 1972, leaving a fine record as singer, director and artistic manager.

Furtwängler's favourite tenor was **Ludwig Suthaus** (Cologne 1906 - Berlin 1971) who had made his debut, as many of his colleagues before him, in the part of Walther in *The Mastersingers of Nuremberg*, in 1928. Because of his vocal volume, the colour of his voice, and his penetrating high notes, he was considered Melchior's heir, notwithstanding the fact that he had a relatively early decline. The career of this German artist was formed in all the world's major theatres, up to 1967. He was often part of prestigious companies and sang under the batons of such illustrious conductors as von Karajan, Erich Kleiber, and, as we have already mentioned, Furtwängler. His renderings of operas such as *Tristan*, *The Ring*, Strauss' *Elektra*, *Fidelio*, and *Wozzek* were, on the whole, dignified, apart from an early, marked vocal fatigue.

The Canadian tenor **Jon Vickers** (Prince Albert 1926) belongs undoubtedly to the category of Wagnerian tenors, despite the fact that, since 1956, he has also been an excellent Verdi dramatic tenor (*Otello* and Don José in *Carmen*); he performs Samson in Saint-Saëns' opera and Pollione in *Norma*. For all of the sixties and most of the seventies, his voice remained robust and vigorous in the centre, powerful and secure in the high notes, (at least up to b' flat), able to follow all the dynamic indications in a score and creatively vary phrasing.

With the passing of years, his voice has been marred by a certain hard woody sound, a fault

*A close-up of **Peter Hofmann**, the best* Heldentenor *in circulation today.*

which an excellent technique has not been able to remedy, and which has not been helped by his timbre, which has always been poor. However Vickers has continued to be successful, above all in London and in America, thanks to his intelligence and artistic sensibility. Vickers established a long partnership with Covent Garden (beginning in 1957) singing principally Don José, Aeneas, Don Carlos, Radames, Florestano, Siegmund, and a wonderful Peter Grimes.

The New Generation

Hans Hopf (Nuremberg 1916), **Jess Thomas** (Hot Springs, South Dakota 1927) and **Sàndor Kónya** (Sarkad, Hungary 1923), a tenor with a beautiful voice and phrasing, suffered declining careers after the fifties and sixties; but the star of **James King** (California 1925) continues to shine. With his robust vocal means, penetrating emission, and excellent German pronunciation, he has earned a name in many Wagnerian roles, even more fame in Strauss, and the respect of most of the major conductors. Today the destiny of Wagner lies in the voices of **René Kollo** (Berlin 1937) who is a good Parsifal and Lohengrin despite his difficulty in the high register and his tendency to tire easily and **Peter Hofmann** (Marienbad 1945), a teenage idol because of his boyish looks, a singer gifted with a clear, sweet timbre, but not with an adequate technique. However he phrases excellently in *Parsifal*, *Fidelio*, *Tristan* and *Lohengrin*. Some mention must be made of **Reiner Goldberg** (Crostan, Saxony 1939) who gives a discreet rendering of the main parts in *Der Freischütz*, *Tannhäuser*, and *Fidelio*. Unfortunately, **Siegfried Jérusalem** (Oberhausen 1940) is completely inadequate both vocally and stylistically.

Some Other Famous Tenors

At the end of our section dedicated to the best tenors of this century we insert this chronological table in order to include other noteworthy artists. Beside each name we have listed the date, place and opera for the first performance of each singer, plus the principal roles in his repertory and a brief note on his vocal characteristics and career.

NAME	FIRST PERFORMANCE	BASIC REPERTORY	REMARKS
Ahnsjö, Claes (1942) Light lyric.	1969, Stockholm. (*Magic Flute*).	Mozart, *Don Pasquale, Barbiere, Falstaff, Mastersingers* (David).	An appreciated concert artist.
Albanese, Francesco (1912) Lyric.	1942, Venice. (*Cenerentola*).	*Traviata, Bohème, Armida.*	International career. A soft voice of lovely colour.
Alcaïde, Tomaz (1901-1967) Light lyric.	1925, Milan. (*Mignon*).	*Don Pasquale, Traviata, Barbiere, Werther, Faust, Favorita.*	A most polished and refined technique, capable of spinning high and super high notes and sweet and winning mezzevoci.
Aldenhoff, Bernd (1908-1959) *Heldentenor.*	1938, Darmstadt.	Wagner, Strauss.	Good and penetrating timbre, of excellent power.
Alexander, John (1935) Lyric.	1965, Cincinnati.	Mozart, *Norma, Anna Bolena, Traviata, Faust.*	A noted recitalist and oratorio interpreter.
Altmeyer, Theo (1931) Light lyric.	1955, Berlin.	Bach, Handel, Mozart, Beethoven.	Celebrated for his recordings of Bach: Cantatas and Oratorios.
Altschewsky, Ivan (1876-1917) Lyric.	1901, St. Petersburg.	*Romeo and Juliet, Faust, Les Huguenots*, Russian repertory.	Foremost exponent of the great Russian tradition of the early twentieth century.
Alvarez, Albert (1861-1933) *Lirico spinto.*	1886, Geneva. (*Faust*).	*Faust, Thaïs, Navarraise, Romeo and Juliet, Pagliacci, Carmen.*	Noble declamation, purity of vocal line, efficent actor.
Anders, Peter (1908-1954) Lyric.	1931, Berlin. (*La Belle Hélène* by Offenbach).	*Magic Flute, Ariadne auf Naxos, Fidelio, Der Freischütz, Lohengrin.*	First interpreter of *Friedenstag* by R. Strauss at Munich in 1938. Radiant timbre, intense and varied phrasing, magical mezzevoci, a formidable Lieder singer.
Ansseau, Fernand (1890-1972) Lyric.	1913, Dijon. (*Hérodiade* by Massenet).	French lyrique repertory. Puccini.	Active in Belgium and in the French theatres. Fine timbre, secure technique.
Atlantov, Vladimir (1939) *Lirico spinto.*	1962, Leningrad.	*Carmen, Otello, Queen of Spades, Eugene Onegin, Tosca, Pagliacci, Boris Godunov.*	Voice solid and penetrating, phrasing monotonous. From 1977 he has included some baritone roles.
Bassi, Amedeo (1874-1949) *Lirico spinto.*	1897, Castelfiorentino (*Ruy Blas* by Marchetti).	*Aida, Loreley, Girl of the Golden West, Zazà, Parsifal, Walküre.*	A strong voice, luminous in the high register. Acclaimed in the American theatre. Among his students in Florence, Ferruccio Tagliavini.
Baum, Kurt (1908-1990) *Lirico spinto.*	1932, Zürich. (*Der Kreidekreis* by Zemlinsky).	*Aida, Guglielmo Tell, Trovatore*, Wagner operas.	A burnished timbre colour; penetrating, slight technical insecurity. Studied with Edoardo Garbin in Milano.
Benelli, Ugo (1935) Light lyric.	1960, Milan.	*Barbiere, Cenerentola, Don Pasquale, Italiana in Algeri, Matrimonio Segreto.*	Pleasing timbre, soft emission, some excessive use of falsetto.

Berdini, Amedeo
(1920-1964)
Lyric.

1948, Naples.
(*Lucia*).

Lucia, Rigoletto, Butterfly, Duca d'Alba.

Died whilst in the full glory of his career. Considered a valid candidate as Gigli's successor.

Bergamaschi, Ettore
(1884-1975)
Lirico spinto.

1912, Bari.
(*La Forza del Destino*).

Verdi, Puccini, Mascagni.

Called, because of his talent, the "Caruso of South America".

Breviario, Giovanni
(1891)
Lirico spinto.

1924, Pola.
(*Trovatore*).

Norma, Cavalleria, Pagliacci, Trovatore.

He never received in Italy that recognition achieved in other countries.

Brilioth, Helge
(1931)
Heldentenor.

1959, Stockholm (as a baritone); 1965, Stockholm (as a tenor in *Carmen*).

Otello, Siegfried, Tristan, Parsifal, Ariadne auf Naxos.

A shooting star but of short duration. Dominated Bayreuth from 1969 until 1974.

Burrows, Stuart
(1933)
Light lyric.

1963, Cardiff.
(Ismaele in *Nabucco*).

Mozart, *Fidelio, Traviata,* Lieder and oratorio.

Well emitted voice, musical; specialist in *The Damnation of Faust* and the *Requiem* of Berlioz.

Campora, Giuseppe
(1923)
Lyric.

1949, Bari.
(*Bohème*).

Butterfly, Gioconda, Tosca, Simon Boccanegra, Bohème; operetta.

Rich, dark tones, high notes a little forced.

Casellato, Renzo
(1936)
Lyric.

1963, Parma.
(*Elisir d'Amore*).

Pearl Fishers, Elisir d'Amore, Don Pasquale, Sonnambula, Lucia, Traviata.

Richly grained voice, not very agile but well tuned.

Cioni, Renato
(1929)
Lyric.

1956, Spoleto.
(*Lucia di Lammermoor*).

Butterfly, Tosca, Traviata, Rigoletto, Lucia.

Lovely colour, persuasive phrasing, but rigid in expression.

Conley, Eugene
(1908-1981)
Lirico spinto.

Concerts with the N.B.C. Symphony Orchestra in the early forties. From 1948 in the main European theatres.

Puritani, Guglielmo Tell, Faust, Rigoletto.

Exceptionally penetrating high notes, the voice solid and darkened in the centre. Excellent musicality.

Constantino, Florencio
(1869-1919)
Lirico spinto.

1892, Montevideo.
(*Dolores* by Bretòn).

Gioconda, Don Carlos, Otello, Trovatore.

Acclaimed in South America for his strong high notes. Famous for his "death rattle" in the death scene of *Otello*.

Cossutta, Carlo
(1932)
Lirico spinto.

1958, Buenos Aires.
(Cassio in *Otello*).

Otello, Trovatore, Cavalleria, Aida, Tosca, Don Carlos.

His voice was affected by a vibrato and placed under excessive strain in the early part of his caeer.

Crooks, Richard
(1900-1972)
Lyric.

1927, Hamburg.
(*Tosca*).

Tosca, Rigoletto, Traviata, Manon, concerts and oratorio.

Soft, flexible, clean voice, inclined towards a shaded singing without mannerisms or blanching.

Vladimir Atlantov with *Mietta Sighele, in* Carmen, 1984.

Richard Crooks.

Dalmorès, Charles (1871-1939) Dramatic.	1899, Lyon. (Loge in *Das Rheingold*, with his real name, Henri Alphonse Brin).	*The Ring. Lohengrin, Thaïs, Oracolo*, Verdi repertory.	Exceptional volume and strength. An idol in American and German theatres in Wagner operas.
d'Arkor, André (1901-1971) Lyric.	1924, Luttich. (Gerald in *Lakmé*).	*Lucia, Rigoletto, Lakmé, Romeo and Juliet, Faust*.	Shining, secure high notes; his timbre amongst the most beautiful of the interpreters of the French school.
Davies, Ryland (1943) Light lyric.	1964. Welsh Opera. (*Barbiere*).	*Falstaff, Idomeneo, Così fan Tutte, Eugene Onegin*, oratorio.	A voice a little white-washed, but flexible and pleasant in emission.
de Muro Lomanto, Enzo (1902-1952) Light lyric.	1925, Catanzaro. (*Traviata*).	*Rigoletto, Lucia, Traviata, Don Pasquale, Barbiere, Don Giovanni*.	Refined technique, a liking for shading in the phrasing. Between 1929 and 1932 he was married to Toti Dal Monte.
di Palma, Piero (1916) Light lyric.	Towards the end of the thirties with La Scala company.	Over two hundred roles of comprimario and secondary parts.	A fixed presence in major opera theatres for almost fifty years. Memorable his Malatestino on record.
Dvorsky, Peter (1951) Lyric.	1972, Bratislava. (*Eugene Onegin*).	*Lucia, Rigoletto, Bohème, Traviata, Elisir d'Amore, Manon Lescaut*.	Radiant timbre, strong high notes, clear diction; but his phrasing lacks variety, and this has harmed his recent experiences in a more *lirico-spinto* repertory.
Dyck, Ernest van (1861-1923) Heldentenor.	1883, Paris. (soloist in the cantata *Le Gladiateur*, by Vidal).	*Lohengrin, Parsifal, Siegfried, Tannhäuser*.	He was the first *Werther* in 1892, but the recording of his "Pourquoi me réveiller" is deluding.
Erb, Karl (1877-1958) Light lyric.	1907, Stuttgart.	Mozart, Pfitznert, Lieder and oratorio.	Great musicality and style, flexibility and smoothness.
Escalaïs, Léon (1859-1941) Lirico spinto.	1883, Paris. (*Guglielmo Tell*).	*Trovatore, Robert le Diable, Les Huguenots, Faust*.	Impressive incisiveness and powerful high notes.
Figner, Nikolai (1918) Lyric.	1882, Naples. (*Philémon et Baucis* by Gounod).	*Queen of Spades, Iolanthe, Ernani, Sonnambula, Rigoletto, Carmen, Les Huguenots*.	Exceptionally eclectic. Voice very penetrating and sweet.
Filacuridi, Nicola (1922) Lyric.	1945, Alexandria (Egypt) (*Cavalleria Rusticana*).	*Manon, Traviata, Adriana Lecouvreur, Werther*.	A young, fresh timbre, a caressing emission, some forcing in the highest notes.

Enzo de Muro Lomanto *in* The King *by Giordano.*

Léon Escalais.

Fisichella, Salvatore (1945) Light lyric.	1970, Spoleto. (*Werther*).	*Rigoletto, Puritani, Favorita, Faust.*	A voice which is not powerful but excellently projected; easy high notes reaching high F.
Fusati, Nicola (1882) *Lirico spinto.*	1907, Rome.	*Ernani, Norma, Aida, Trovatore, Otello.*	Exceptional power in the high notes, wide and full central register.
Gibin, Joao (1929) *Lirico spinto.*	1954, Winner, as a baritone in the competition "Mario Lanza".	*Lucia, Andrea Chénier, Turandot, Don Carlos, Fanciulla.*	Nasal sounding emission, and difficulty in singing the mezzavoce.
Gilion, Mario (1870-1914) Lyric.	1901, Monza. (*L'Africana*).	*Huguenots, Guglielmo Tell, Robert le Diable, Faust.*	Easy, and penetrating high notes, even if his recordings don't justify his fame.
Giorgini, Aristodemo (1879-1937) Light lyric.	1903, Naples.	*Bohème, Sonnambula, Don Pasquale, Mefistofele.*	Voice marked by a vibration and mannerisms typical of "Liberty-style" singers.
Giraudeau, Jean (1916) Light lyric.	1947, Paris. (*Pearl Fishers*).	*Barbiere, Thaïs, Les Troyens, Faust.*	Nice vocal colour, smooth and caressing singing, fine sound in the falsettone.
Grassi, Rinaldo (1885-1946) *Lirico spinto.*	1904, Novara. (*Bohème*).	*Mefistofele, Tosca, Butterfly, Cavalleria Rusticana, The Girl of the Golden West, Faust.*	A notable dramatic temperament and passionate acting.
Häfliger, Ernst (1919) Light lyric.	1942, in concert.	*Don Giovanni, Fidelio, Magic Flute, Oedipus Rex.*	Excellent singing school, perfect diction, grace and style.
Hislop, Joseph (1884-1977) Lyric.	1914, Stockholm. (*Faust*).	*Lucia, Rigoletto, Bohème, Traviata.*	One of the best Anglo-Saxon tenors for correct technical positioning and fluid singing.
Hollweg, Werner (1936) Light lyric.	1962, Vienna Chamber-opera.	All Mozart; Lieder and oratorio.	Rich middle register, but some problems in the high register.
Ilosfalvy, Robert (1927) Lyric.	1953, Budapest. (*Hunyadi Laszlo* by Erkel).	*Butterfly, Manon Lescaut, Traviata, Rigoletto.*	Splendid natural means governed by an excellent technique. Inexplicable his lack of fame and the absence of this great singer in Italy.
Imbart de la Tour, Georges (1865-1911) *Lirico spinto.*	1890, Geneva. (*Les Huguenots*).	*Aida, Carmen, Faust, Tannhäuser.*	Major exponent of the French school of singing at the end of the nineteenth century.
Jagel, Frederick (1897) Lyric.	1924, Leghorn in *Bohème*, with the name of Federico Jeghelli.	*Traviata, Bohème, Aida, Peter Grimes.*	Very equal voice over all the range, with a solid centre and easy high notes.
Jörn, Karl (1873-1947) *Heldentenor.*	1896, Fribourg. (*Martha*).	*Faust, Carmen, Parsifal, Tristan and Isolde.*	Stable member of the Metropolitan Opera until 1914; noted as an exceptional Wagner singer.
Kiepura, Jan (1902-1966) Lyric.	1924, Lwow. (*Faust*).	*Bohème, Traviata, Rigoletto;* operetta.	Handsome appearance, pleasant voice. Famous for the films made together with his wife, the soprano Martha Eggerth.
Knote, Heinrich (1870-1953) *Heldentenor.*	1892, Munich, Bavaria. (Georg in *Waffenschmied* by Lortzing).	*Tristan and Isolde, Rienzi, Trovatore, Lohengrin, Queen of Sheba.*	Rivalry with Caruso at the Met at the beginning of the century.
Koslowski, Ivan (1900) Lyric.	1920, Poltawa.	*Sadko, Werther, Orfeo, Lohengrin, Romeo and Juliet, Eugene Onegin.*	A sweet timbre and smooth emission. At seventy years of age he was still amazing his U.S.S.R. public.
Kozma, Lajos (1938) Light lyric.	1962, Budapest.	Lieder and oratorio. *Lucia, Così fan Tutte,* contemporary repertory.	Lovely timbre, warm, not particularly extended, flexible.

56

Kozub, Ernest (1925-1971) *Heldentenor.*	1950, Berlin. (*Zar und Zimmermann* by Lortzing).	*Siegfried, Aida, Mastersingers, Die Frau ohne Schatten, Flying Dutchman* (Erik), *Carmen.*	Some slight technical problems in the *passaggio* hindered a varied phrasing. His natural means, however, were of excellent quality.
Krenn, Werner (1943) Light lyric.	1966, Berlin. (*The Fairy Queen* by Purcell).	*Don Giovanni, La Clemenza di Tito, Lucio Silla, Il Re Pastore,* Lieder and oratorio.	First bassoon player of the Vienna Symphony for three years. Noted as a good Mozart interpreter in innumerable productions.
Kullmann, Charles (1903) Lyric.	1929, American Opera Company (*Madama Butterfly*).	*Così fan Tutte, Die Entführung aus dem Serail, Don Giovanni, Oberon, Faust.*	Fine timbre, perfect technique. He was a star at the Met. between 1935 and 1962.
Labò, Flaviano (1927-1991) *Lirico spinto.*	1953, Piacenza. (*Tosca*).	*Aida, Forza del Destino, Turandot, Don Carlos.*	A worthy protagonist of innumerable productions worldwide, for over thirty years.
Lavirgen, Pedro (1930) *Lirico spinto.*	1964, Mexico City. (*Aida*).	*Carmen, Trovatore, Turandot, Aida, Tosca.*	Splendid natural voice ruined by technical problems and a tendency to "push" the high notes.
Lemeshew, Sergei (1902-1977) Lyric.	1920, Moscow. (*Eugene Onegin*).	*Werther, Rigoletto, Romeo and Juliet, Traviata.*	Excellent singing school. *Mezzevoci* and *smorzature* of high quality; good high notes.
Lewis, Richard (1914) Light lyric.	1939, Carl Rosa Opera Company. (*Barbiere*).	*Don Giovanni, Peter Grimes, Così fan Tutte, The Rake's Progress,* Lieder and oratorio.	Interpreter of many first-ever performances in England, gifted with enormous musicality.
Luccioni, José (1903-1978) *Lirico spinto.*	1931, Rouen. (*Tosca*).	*Carmen, Otello, Aida, Samson and Delilah, Esclarmonde.*	Incisive, fiery, penetrating and passionate voice, which, however, never exaggerated. Chiselled enunciation and formidable stage presence.
Malipiero, Giovanni (1906-1970) Lyric.	At the end of the twenties in small provincial theatres.	*Lucia, Mefistofle, Bohème, Favorita, Romeo and Juliet* (Zandonai).	An authentic specialist in the role of Faust, be it that of Boito or Gounod. He knew how to sing with taste and feeling.
Mazaroff, Todor (1907-1975) Dramatic.	1935, Sofia. (*Prince Igor*).	*Aida, Forza del Destino, Guglielmo Tell.*	An idol of the Vienna State Opera from 1937 until 1953. Noted for the power and beauty of his voice.

Karl Jörn
in Faust.

**Heinrich
Knote** *in*
Otello.

Melandri, Antonio (1891-1969) *Lirico spinto.*	1924, Novara.	*Isabeau, Fedora, Turandot, Cavalleria, Ernani.*	His voice resembled that of Aureliano Pertile. A singer very much appreciated at the Colòn in Buenos Aires.
Merighi, Giorgio (1939) *Lyric.*	1962, Spoleto. (*Ballo in Maschera*).	*Tosca, Adriana Lecouvreur, Butterfly, Manon Lescaut, Rigoletto.*	A clear, lyrical timbre directed to a repertoire excessively dramatic. His worthy stage presence compensated the monotony of his phrasing.
Minghetti, Angelo (1889-1957) *Lyric.*	1911	*Bohème, La Fiamma.*	First performer of *La Fiamma* in 1934 at Rome. Because of technical problems he was already in decline in the thirties.
Nash, Heddle (1894-1961) *Light lyric.*	1924, Milan. (*Barbiere*).	*Don Giovanni, Mastersingers* (David), *Così fan Tutte,* oratorio and recitals.	Studied with Borgatti at Milan and was a singer of impeccable and gracious style.
Nessi, Giuseppe (1887-1961) *Light lyric.*	1910, Saluzzo. (*Traviata*).	All the most important *comprimario* and support roles of the popular repertory.	A support fixture at La Scala Opera Theatre from 1921 until his death. He took part in the first-ever performances of *Turandot* and *Nerone.*
Ochman, Wieslaw (1937) *Lyric.*	1959, Bytom.	*Eugene Onegin, Tosca, Vespri Siciliani, Boris Godunov, Lucia, Idomeneo, Anna Bolena, Salome.*	An exceptionally wide repertoire, ranging from the Baroque to contemporary opera. Present in many recordings.
Oncina, Juan (1925) *Light lyric.*	1946, Barcelona. (*Manon* by Massenet).	*Cenerentola, Matrimonio Segreto, Comte Ory, Don Pasquale, Barbiere.*	A dark and caressing voice.
O'Sullivan, John (1878-1948) *Lirico spinto.*	1909	*Les Huguenots, Guglielmo Tell, Trovatore, Otello.*	Certainly to be contested the phrase "Tenor of only two notes" coined by Carelli to describe O'Sullivan. The middle voice was rich and with a lovely colour, but he was a bit lazy in interpretation.
Paoli, Antonio (1870-1946) *Lirico spinto.*	1899, Paris. (*Guglielmo Tell*).	*Trovatore, Otello, Samson and Delilah, L'Africana, Pagliacci.*	Lightning-like high notes, great scenic temperament.
Pattiera, Tino (1890-1966) *Lirico spinto.*	1915, Dresden. (A sentinel in *The Magic Flute*).	*Andrea Chénier, Tannhäuser, Queen of Spades, Ariadne auf Naxos, Forza del Destino.*	Very active in the "Verdi Renaissance" in Germany in the '20-'30 s.
Pauli Piero (1898-1967) *Lyric.*	1929, Trieste. (*Faust*).	*Bohème, Mefistofele, Gianni Schicchi, Traviata, Falstaff, Carmen, Tosca.*	An interpreter of great possibility, sicure and homogeneous over all the scale.
Pears, Peter (1910-1986) *Light lyric.*	1942, London. (*Tales of Hoffmann*).	*Peter Grimes, The Rape of Lucretia, Billy Budd, Death in Venice, Acis and Galathea.*	The favourite singer of Benjamin Britten and the first interpreter of all his most important compositions. Voice inclined towards falsetto, but with good taste.
Piccaluga, Nino (1890-1973) *Lirico spinto.*	1918, Novara.	*Tabarro, Francesca da Rimini, Romeo and Juliet.*	Very esteemed by Zandonai, who wanted him as principal singer in many of his operas. He had to interrupt his career in 1935 because of illness.
Poncet, Tony (1921-1979) *Lirico spinto.*	1955, Luttich.	*La Juive, Pagliacci, Guglielmo Tell, Carmen, Aida, L'Africana, Trovatore, Faust.*	Easy high notes and tone-coloured, full middle register, but little inclination for expressive shadings.
Prandelli, Giacinto (1914) *Lyric.*	1942, Bergamo. (*Bohème*).	*Bohème, Traviata, Lucia, Rigoletto, Peter Grimes, Adriana Lecouvreur, Francesca da Rimini, Mefistofele.*	A cordial and homogeneous voice, very clear in enunciation. He has a repertoire of over fifty roles.

Prevedi, Bruno (1928-1988) *Lirico spinto.*	1958, Milan. (As a baritone, Tonio in *Pagliacci*); as a tenor in 1960.	*Don Carlos, Norma, Macbeth, Aida, Carmen, Ernani, Trovatore.*	Some problems in the *passaggio*, never completely resolved, but a beautiful colour and an intense participation in his roles.
Riegel, Kenneth (1938) Light lyric.	1965, Santa Fe. (*König Hirch* by Henze).	*Don Giovanni, Così fan Tutte, Die Entführung aus dem Serail, Elisir d'Amore, Traviata, Lulu.*	A vast repertory with alternating results; good in contemporary operas but bad in the great works in which he couldn't compete with voices of better quality and placement.
Rogatschewsky, Joseph (1891-1985) Lyric.	1922, Toulouse.	*Manon, Rigoletto, Traviata, Eugene Onegin, Werther.*	Elegance, expressive variety, a liking for vocal nuances, secure technique.
Salvarezza, Antonio (1906) *Lirico spinto.*	1935	*Guglielmo Tell, Turandot, Tosca, Rigoletto, Puritani.*	An idol in America and South America, but his star didn't shine brightly for long.
Scaramberg, Emile (1863-1938) *Lirico spinto.*	1893, Paris. (*Richard Coeur de Lion*, by Crétry).	*Lohengrin, Werther, Faust, Romeo and Juliet.*	Above all active in the principal French theatres until the end of the first decade of this century, when he suffered a vocal decline.
Schmidt, Joseph (1904-1942) Lyric.	1928, Berlin. (*Idomeneo* - a concert performance for the radio).	Concerts all over Europe, North America, Mexico and Cuba. Many recordings, and films with celebrated arias.	Crystalline timbre and outstanding high notes, with a capacity for effortless phrasing at high level. Extremely short of stature, he could never appear on stage. He died in a concentration camp.
Schock, Rudolf (1915) Lyric.	1937, Braunschweig.	*Magic Flute, The Mastersingers, Carmen, Fidelio, Lohengrin, Tiefland, Tosca, Fra Diavolo*; also operetta by J. Strauss and Lehár.	Connected to the great German tradition; very ecclectic; excellent phrasing. Protagonist of many famous films.
Schreier, Peter (1935) Light lyric.	1957, Dresden. (*Matrimonio Segreto*).	*Magic Flute, Don Giovanni, Così fan Tutte, Mastersingers* (David), *Das Rheingold* (Loge), *Capriccio.*	A noteworthy musician, a voice which was not particularly beautiful but based on a good techinique. Excellent phrasing, a superb concert singer in the oratorios of Bach. A good Lieder singer. Also orchestra conductor.
Sénéchal, Michel (1930) Light lyric.	1952, Winner of the Geneva Competition.	*Platée, Comte Ory, Dame Blanche, Thaïs.*	A full flexible voice, gracious *falsettone*, controlled emission. Excellent in many character roles.
Shirley, George (1932) Light lyric.	1960, Spoleto. (Herod in *Salome*).	*Così fan Tutte, Idomeneo, Barbiere, Traviata, Bohème,* Lieder and oratorio.	Active and appreciated at the Met, London, and Glyndebourne during the '60-70's.
Simoneau, Léopold (1918) Light lyric.	1943, Montreal. (*Mignon*).	*Magic Flute, Così fan Tutte, Don Giovanni, Idomeneo, Ifigenia in Tauride, Orfeo, Traviata.*	A Mozart interpreter, smooth and *sfumato*, caressing timbre; an excellent recitalist.
Smirnoff, Dimitri (1881-1944) Lyric.	1903, St. Petersburg. (*Camorra* by Esposito).	*The Demon, Rigoletto, Tabarro, Lakmé, Fedora, Traviata, Sadko, Butterfly.*	Rival of the great Sobinov, he fared best in more lyrical roles.
Spiess, Ludovico (1938) *Lirico spinto.*	1962, Galati. (*Rigoletto*).	*Tosca, Carmen, Aida, Dalibor, Turandot, Fidelio, Boris Godunov.*	Although gifted with an interesting voice, he had a brief career.
Stolze, Gerhard (1926-1979) Light lyric.	1949, Dresden. (Augustin Moser in *The Mastersingers*).	*Mastersingers* (David), *Magic Flute* (Monostatos), *Elektra* (Egisto), *Salome* (Herod); contemporary repertory.	An unequalled singing-actor in Wagner and Strauss operas.

59

Heddle Nash.

Alessandro Ziliani *in* Madama Butterfly.

Léopold Simoneau.

Francisco Vignas *in* Aida.

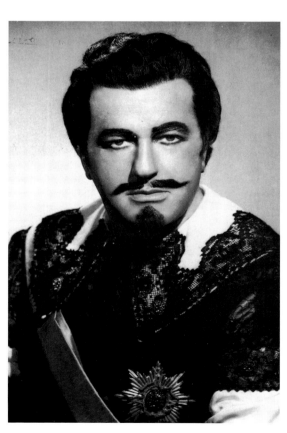

Taccani, Giuseppe (1885-1959) *Lirico spinto.*	1905, Bologna. (*Andrea Chénier*).	*Trovatore, Aida, Forza del Destino, Nerone, Fedora.*	Dazzling high notes, burnished middle register, great temperament.
Tappy, Eric (1931) Light lyric.	1964, Paris. (*Zoroastre*, by Rameau).	*Magic Flute, Pelléas et Mélisande, Oedipus Rex, Orfeo.*	Great elegance and taste, very smooth emission.
Treptow, Günther (1907-1987) *Heldentenor.*	1936, Berlin. (*Der Rosenkavalier*).	*Siegfried, Tristan, Fidelio, Otello, Tannhäuser, Mastersingers.*	An inferior artist in respect to his more famous colleagues, but a good professional and an intense interpreter.
Uhl, Fritz (1928) *Lirico spinto.*	1950, Graz.	*Das Rheingold* (Loge), *Flying Dutchman* (Erik), *Salome* (Herod), *Elektra* (Egisto), *Tristan, Antigonae.*	Very, very good in the minor roles of the Wagner and Strauss repertory.
Unger, Gerhard (1916) Light lyric.	1947, Weimar.	*Mastersingers* (David), *Die Entführung aus dem Serail* (Pedrillo), *Butterfly* (Goro), *La Finta Giardiniera, The Barber of Bagdad.*	An exceptional *Spieltenor* and singer of Masses, concerts, and oratorio (Bach, in particular).
Uzunow, Dimiter (1922) *Lirico spinto.*	1946, Sofia.	*Otello, Forza del Destino, Pagliacci, Aida, Boris Godunov.*	Stylistically not convincing; but gifted with dazzling high notes.
Valero, Fernando (1854-1914) Lyric.	1878, Madrid. (*Fra Diavolo*).	*Faust, Pearl Fishers, Cavalleria Rusticana, Rigoletto, Favorita.*	He studied with the famous Tamberlick and was one of the last singers of the legendary school of the eighteen hundreds. His recordings are therefore useful in helping us decipher that style.
Vesselovsky, Alexander (1885-1964) Lyric.	1917, Moscow.	*Manon Lescaut, Kovantchina, Traviata, Rigoletto, Fedora, Lohengrin.*	Called by Toscanini to La Scala in 1925 to interpret *Kovantchina.* He was one of the best Russian singers of this century and one of the best of his generation.
Vezzani, César (1886-1951) Lyric.	1911, Paris. (*Richard Coeur de Lion* by Grétry).	*Faust, Carmen, Pagliacci, La Juive, Trovatore, Guglielmo Tell, Werther, L'Africana.*	An extraordinary voice and temperament, solid as steel. He died during a rehearsal at Toulon, still in full form vocally.
Vignas, Francisco (1863-1933) *Lirico spinto.*	1888, Barcelona (*Lohengrin*).	*Cavalleria Rusticana, Carmen, Lucia, Tristan, Tannhäuser.*	Considered the successor of the great Gayarre, he had unforgettable triumphs at the Met, at Covent Garden and at La Scala.
Villabella, Miguel (1892-1954) Lyric.	1918, Poiters (*Tosca*).	*Lakmé, Bohème, Manon, Barbiere, Tosca, Traviata, Rigoletto, Don Giovanni.*	World Champion Rollerskater. He was a student of Lucien Fugère. His voice was clear and crystalline.
Winbergh, Gösta (1943) Light lyric.	1971, Göteborg. (*Bohème*).	*Don Giovanni, Don Pasquale, Così fan Tutte, Barbiere, Traviata;* Lieder and oratorio.	Engaged by important record companies and esteemed by illustrious conductors, however he has obvious unresolved technical problems, especially in the high register.
Zanelli, Renato (1892-1935) Dramatic.	1916, Opera of Chile. (Valentino in *Faust*, as a baritone); 1924, Naples (Raoul in *Les Huguenots*, as a tenor).	*Otello, Lohengrin.*	One of the most beautiful "natural" voices there has ever been. His brother, Carlo Morelli, has considerable success as a baritone.
Ziliani, Alessandro (1906-1977) Lyric.	1928, Milan. (*Butterfly*).	*Gioconda, Traviata, Tosca;* operetta.	Very popular in America and Germany. He was the first interpreter of many operas of Peragallo, Pannain, Pedrollo, Respighi, and Wolf-Ferrari.

The French coloratura soprano **Lily Pons**, as Lucia di Lammermoor. *She was a Met star from 1931 until well into the 1950s.*

THE SOPRANOS

The Soprano Voice: Extension and Emission

The soprano voice is the highest of the female voices. Its ideal tessitura goes from g′ to g″, and the full extension usually reaches from c′ up to c‴ or d‴.

The dramatic soprano can reach down to an a′ or an a′flat while a coloratura soprano easily surpasses high f‴. The mythical Lucrezia Agujari, called "la Bastardella", ranged from g′ up to c⁗, according to Mozart's testimony; whilst in more recent times Mado Robin could exhibit high a‴ and b‴flats, without any apparent effort (and could reach high d⁗flat when vocalising!).

The Different Soprano Categories

During this century the soprano voice has been divided into various categories: *coloratura soprano*, or *soprano leggero* (a union of the eighteenth century soprano *à roulades* with the *soprano sfogato* voice), a voice suited for virtuoso roles such as *Barbiere, I Puritani, Rigoletto, Lucia, Sonnambula, Traviata, Ariadne auf Naxos* and *Le Rossignol*. The *pure lyric soprano* (who stands exactly between the late-Verdi *soprano di forza* and the *virtuoso soprano*) whose voice is not greatly extended but who must continually sing on the first high notes with a passionate and vehement phrasing; ideal for the operas of Massenet, Puccini (*Butterfly, Suor Angelica*, and Liù in *Turandot*) and those of the Verist composers in general (Mascagni's *Iris*, Cilea's *Adriana Lecouvreur* and Leoncavallo's *Zaza*). The *soprano lirico spinto* is suited to the heavier Verdi operas (*Forza del Destino, Don Carlos, Aida*), Puccini (*Turandot, Tosca*), and the early Wagner and Strauss roles. The *dramatic soprano* (*dramatischer-Sopran*) has solid, powerful vocal means that can overcome the huge orchestral complexes in the operas of Wagner (Brünnhilde in the *Ring*, Kundry in *Parsifal*, Isolde in *Tristan and Isolde*), and Strauss (*Salome, Elektra, Die Frau ohne Schatten*). Finally, there is the *soprano soubrette* for the parts of the cunning little maid servants in the comic opera of the seventeen hundreds (Despina in *Così fan Tutte*, Susanna in *Nozze di Figaro*).

THE COLORATURA SOPRANO IN THE NINETEEN HUNDREDS: THE EMPEROR'S NIGHTINGALES

At the beginning of our century there was an extraordinary flourishing of *coloratura soprani*, coming mainly from Spain. The song of these phenomenal nightingales, however, was not immune from the vices and licences of the Liberty style then in vogue. Alongside high notes of crystalline purity they alternated exaggerated *cadenze* and decorations which were, at times, even annoying. What's more, their limited volume in the middle and lower registers and their mechanical stage presence seriously detracted from roles originally written for the *soprano drammatico d'agilità*.

Amongst the historical singers of the first half of the twentieth century we must remember **Maria Barrientos** (Barcelona 1883 - St. Jean de Luz, Low Pyrenees 1946) who made her debut at only fifteen years of age and was active in all the world's major theatres until about 1920. With her great flexibility, soaring high notes and crystalline timbre, she formed a mythical duo with Hipólito Lázaro, and was widely acclaimed as Elvira in *Puritani*, Lakmé, and Amina in *La Sonnambula*.

Amelita Galli-Curci was Italian (Milan, 1882 - La Jolla, California, 1963). She made her debut

Amelita Galli-Curci in Traviata. *In order to better show-off her vocal extension she often transposed the arias a tone higher. She was forced to retire because of a throat illness. After an operation in 1935 she tried to return to the stage with La* Bohème *at Chicago; but the results convinced her to renounce any further career.*

as Gilda in *Rigoletto* (1907) and remained faithful to this role until the mid-twenties when she was primarily singing in North American theatres. Thanks to the brilliance of her high notes and the precision of her *roulades* she was able to compete with her Spanish rivals, Pareto, De Hidalgo, Barrientos, Galvany, and Capsir, and shared the favour of the public with Tetrazzini.

Luisa Tetrazzini (Florence 1871 - Milan 1940) had a very long career, spanning from 1890, when she made her debut in Florence in Meyerbeer's *L'Africana*, until her last American concerts in 1932.

She made use of an almost transcendental virtuosity built on pyrotechnical trills, *picchiettati*, breath-taking melismic passages, and giddy *cadenze*. Often the Florentine singer exaggerated, exceeding the expressive limits of some

roles. Let us consider, for example, her recording of Oscar's aria from *Il Ballo in Maschera* where, in the finale, Tetrazzini inserts a long *cadenza*, which was frankly out of place.

Antonietta Meneghel, in art **Toti Dal Monte** (Mogliano Vento, Treviso 1893 - Pieve di Soligo, Treviso 1975) was by far the most important coloratura soprano before the revolutionary advent of Maria Callas.

Having completed her studies with Barbara Marchisio and Antonio Pini-Corsi she made her debut at La Scala in 1916 as Biancofiore in *Francesca da Rimini*. During the whole of her career (she retired in 1943), she successfully alternated the lyric repertory (*Butterfly, La Rondine, Bohème, Lodoletta*) with true coloratura roles (*Lucia, Barbiere, Rigoletto, Mignon*), succeeding in gaining the approval of a world-wide public and of one of music's "gods", Arturo Toscanini.

Toti's best quality was the colour of her voice: light, almost infantile in certain inflexions, ethereal. It had a timbre which, united with the luminescence of her high notes, was able to bewitch her listeners, so that they literally held their breath. To demonstrate we need only listen to her Mad Scene from *Lucia* or Gilda's "Caro Nome" from *Rigoletto*. They have remained unsurpassed. However the Venetian soprano can be accused of a lack of psychological depth in decisive roles such as Violetta, Mimì or Butterfly; she had a tendency to resolve such difficulties merely with the beauty of her voice.

The beautiful and gifted Alice Joséphine Pons, in art **Lily Pons** (Draguignan, Cannes

Mercedes Capsir Tanzi (Barcelona 1895 - Suzzara, Mantova 1969). Here photographed as Butterfly, she had a notable interpretative temperament as well as a voice of absolute excellence. In counterbalance to colleagues more adventurous and powerful in the higher octave she offered an impressionable elegance of phrasing and softness of tone. (Historic Archives of the Rome Opera Theatre).

A beautiful photograph of **Toti Dal Monte** in the costume of Gilda, a role which remained associated with her name for many years. The La Scala performances in 1922 with Toscanini on the podium were unforgettable. It was Toscanini who chose her for "his" Rigoletto, after she had sung with him in the Beethoven Ninth Symphony at Turin. With the end of her lyric career, and after a period on stage again as a prose actress, 'Totina' dedicated her life to teaching.

1898 - Dallas 1976) also belongs to legend. She made her debut in *Lakmé* in 1927 (she had already made a concert debut in 1917) and continued her activity at the Metropolitan for over thirty years, (from 1931 until 1961) as well as performing in many other important theatres.

Apart from having a particularly attractive appearance, nature had also given her an agile voice which extended above high f''', ideal for the acrobatic passages contained in *Lakmé*, *Dinorah*, *Lucia*, *Tales of Hoffman*, and *Barbiere*.

Pons' timbre was neither beautiful nor powerful; but she knew how to govern her breath, completely controlling the vocal stream at will. Thus she obtained dynamic effects without effort, interminable *filature*, resonant high notes and all the true virtues of belcanto.

Her first vocal successes were in France (Cannes, Deauville, Montpellier). But once discovered by Zenatello and recommended to Casazza, Director of the Met, she was brought to New York and began her Met career in 1931 in *Lucia* by Donizetti. She continued with the Met until 1959. Married to the conductor André Kostelanetz, she made many recordings and was particularly sought-after for films, as she was a lovely woman as well as a fine singer.

Among the coloratura sopranos active in the Russian, French, German, and Italian repertory there were also: **Lidia Lipkovska** (Babino, Bessarabia 1880 - Beirut 1955); **Antonia Nejdanova** (Kryvoje Balka, Odessa 1875 - Moscow 1950); **Eidé Norena** (Norten, Oslo 1884 - Lausanne 1968); **Graciela Pareto** (Barcelona 1889 - Rome 1973); **Olimpia Boronat** (Genoa 1867 - Warsaw 1934); **Fritzi Jokl** (Vienna 1895 - New York 1974); **Frances Alda** (Frances Davies; Christchurch, New Zealand 1883 - Venice 1952) who was able to sing both Gilda and Leonora from *Trovatore* but with a dubious technique as her high notes were whistling and unsustained, and her timbre was light and colourless; **Regina Pacini** (Lisbon 1871 - Buenos Aires 1965); **Irene Abendroth** (Lemberg 1872 - Weidlind, Vienna 1932); **Ada Sari** (Wadowice, Krakow 1886 - Kriowoshnek 1968); **Miliza Korjus** (Warsaw 1907 - Culver City, California 1980); **Emma Luart** (Brussels 1892 - 1968); the amazing **Mado Robin** (Yseures-sur-Creuse, Tours 1918 - Paris 1960); **Wilma Lipp** (Vienna 1925); **Anneliese Rothenberger** (Mannheim 1924); **Erika Köth** (Darmstadt 1927 - 1989); **Selma Kurz** and **Frieda Hempel** (whom we will discuss in the chapter dedicated to the lyric soprano); and, finally, **Maria Ivogün** (Ilse von Gunther; Budapest 1891 - Beatenberg, Switzerland 1987). The latter was the first Zerbinetta in the newer version of *Ariadne auf Naxos* by Strauss, which was performed in Vienna in 1916. She was active in the lyric and coloratura repertories of Italian , French, and German opera between 1913 and 1933. Elizabeth Schwarzkopf was one of her students.

Between 1927 and 1956 the star of **Lina Pagliughi** (Brooklyn 1907 - Rubicone 1980) shone brightly, on an international scale. Hers was one of the purest and best-placed voices ever heard in the roles of Gilda, Lucia or Amina. Hampered by her physique Pagliughi could not compete with her more attractive colleagues as far as stage presence is concerned, but outclassed them in musicality and vocal emission. In *Traviata* she revealed a temperament and passion which was not common, as witnessed by her recordings — both the official and the "pirate" ones.

Sharing the favours of the public in the vocal pirouettes of Lucia, Amina, Gilda, and Violetta in the Sixties were **Roberta Peters** (New York 1930) and **Anna Moffo** (Wayne, Pennsylvania 1935), the latter being also attracted to a more lyric repertoire. (Cio-Cio-San, Mimì).

Peters amazed her audiences with her precise agility and her extension beyond high f′′′ whilst Moffo enchanted the public with her fascinating and elegant appearance as well as her voice (which was, however, always considered small and more suited to the recording studio than the opera theatre). With her show-girl looks and gifts as as actress, she often participated in movies.

In 1965 **Cristina (Engel) Deutekom** (Amsterdam 1934) appeared, for the first time, as the Queen of the Night — the part which would consign her to musical history. At last the terrifying role of the Mozart queen was taken away from the peeky chirpings of the small voiced sopranos and returned triumphantly to a true *soprano drammatico d'agilità*. Alas, with the passing of time and with the difficult repertory chosen (*Puritani, Norma, Armida, Lucia*) Deutekom's voice became worn and uneven in the various registers. Her vocal agility is in the Tryol Yodel style, hers being a unique compromise between legato and aspiration of the notes.

The Contemporary Coloratura Soprano: Serra, Gruberova, Devia

Two singers have taken the place of Toti dal Monte and Lily Pons. They are **Luciana Serra** (Genoa 1943) and **Editha Gruberova** (Bratislava 1946).

The first was active for years at Teheran, where she performed as the "Shah's nightingale" and can truly be defined as Toti's heir. Serra has many similarities with the famous Venetian singer: a clear, child-like voice, a perfect legato, a silvery high register, a rare perfection in high passages and in agility in general. Her intonation is not always perfect; but when she is at her best she can evoke with surprising emotion all the ghosts of *Lucia*, the legends of *Lakmé*, the clockwork acrobatics of Olimpia in the *Tales of Hoffmann*, and Amina's painful love in *Sonnambula*.

Editha Gruberova was born in Bratislava, but she is pure Viennese in formation. She has been a stable member of the Vienna State Opera ensemble for years, where she regularly triumphs in operas such as *Lucia, Traviata, Die Entführung aus dem Serail, The Magic Flute, Rigoletto* (she was the first to perform the critical edition conducted by Riccardo Muti), and especially *Ariadne auf Naxos*: the elegance and security with which she performs Strauss's terrifying melismas whilst amiably twirling Zerbinetta's parasol cannot be equaled. Her voice is sweet and flexible, richer in harmonics than that of Serra; she easily performs *smorzature* and *rinforzandi* and reaches up to high f′′′. During these last years Gruberova has directed her repertory towards the Italian early romantic composers with a natural preference for Donizetti: her recent debut in *Maria Stuarda* and her engagements in *Anna Bolena* and *Roberto Devereux* demonstrate the intelligence of this artist and her knowledge of her own vocal capacity.

We must not forget these other important presences in the belcanto coloratura repertory; the Welsh soprano **Norma Burrowes** (Bangor 1944), who has been a regular member of the English National Opera since 1971 and

*A photo showing the suffering of Lucia, here interpreted by **Luciana Serra**. (Historic Archives of the Teatro Regio of Parma).*

renowned Blondchen, Despina, Zerlina, Fiorilla in *Turco in Italia*, and Nannetta in *Falstaff*; **Ruth Welting** (Memphis, Tennessee 1949) made her debut in the part of Blondchen in New York in 1970, and since then she has performed in all the major international theatres in the roles of Zerbinetta, Gilda, Lucia, the Queen of the Night, Adele in *Die Fledermaus*, and has sung in a vast repertory of Lieder and oratorio; The Italians **Alida Ferrarini** and **Patrizia Pace** — who specializes in an extraordinary characterisation of the page Oscar; and, above all, **Mariella Devia** (Imperia 1950) who with fluent virtuosity and a pleasant vocality-reproduces the lunar heroines of Bellini (Amina, Giulietta, Elvira) as well as singing in lesser known Rossini and Donizetti operas while maintaining an intense activity in oratorio.

The Lyric Sopranos of the Twentieth century

The long list of the greatest lyric sopranos of this century starts with **Emma Carelli** (Naples 1877 - Montefiascone, Viterbo 1928), one of the most intense and fiery singing actresses to have trod the lyric stage.

Her interpretations of *Zazà*, *Wally*, *Bohème*, *Siberia*, *Adriana Lecouvreur*, and *Arlesiana* deeply moved the public, even to tears, and frequently it was the soprano from Naples who was the first to be thus moved, crying on stage and beginning the tradition of the sobbing Verist *primedonne*.

Right from her debut in *La Vestale* at Altamura in 1895, her voice was not particularly beautiful or widely extended; so Carelli had to make her way using her passionate temperament and "the sweetness of her heart" — as Eleonora Duse, one of her great admirers, chose to put it. It was Carelli who invented the solemn rites that conclude the second act of *Tosca*, immediately after Scarpia's death. Those well-studied movements send a shiver up your spine and have been copied by every other soprano. From 1912 until 1926 she and her husband managed the Costanzi Theatre of Rome, earning esteem as theatrical agents who discovered many new singers.

One of the most important Massenet and Puccini performers was **Rosina Storchio** (Venice 1872 or 1876 - Milan 1945). She made her first

Mariella Devia *at the end of the "Mad Scene" from Lu-cia di Lammermoor, presented in Bologna in 1986.*

lirica in operas such as *Barbiere* and *Traviata*.

Geraldine Farrar (Melrose, Massachusetts 1882 - Ridgefield 1967) possessed a magnificently forceful voice. Agile, despite some problems in the high register, she was one of the most acclaimed interpreters of *Butterfly*, *Zazà*, and *Manon*, especially in the theatres of North America. Her popularity was enormous, even among the younger generation, to the extent that every one of her performances was attended by flocks of *Gerry-Flappers*. Farrar had first sung at ten years of age in a Christmas pageant where she played the part of Jenny Lind. She made her second debut at the Hofoper of Berlin in 1901 as Marguerite in *Faust*. In 1906, after a perfection course with Lilli Lehmann, she made her way into the Metropolitan Opera and stayed there until 1922, singing five hundred performances of twenty-nine different operas. She was the first to perform Mascagni's *Amica* (1905), *Madame Sans-Gêne* (1915), and *Suor Angelica* (1918). Geral-

appearance in Milan in *Carmen* as Micaëla in 1892. Her voice was essentially small; but it was very penetrating and animated by an exceptional artistic spirit. She gave the right expressive value to each note, to every accent, every movement, even those that were apparently insignificant. Storchio created extremely dramatic portrayals. Her Butterfly (she was the first-ever performer), her unequalled Violetta, Iris, Zazà, Manon and Mimì will never be forgotten. She retired after a final *Butterfly* in Barcelona in 1923. Puccini wrote that hers was "the sweet little voice that comes from the soul".

Another historic performer in the French repertory, from Massenet to Debussy (of whom she was a great friend) was **Mary Garden** (Aberdeen 1874 or 1877 - 1967), the first to perform *Pelléas et Mélisande* in 1902. She was beautiful, ethereal and misty like Debussy's harmonies; careful, like few others, to analyse the phrasing and detail of the spoken word even more than the sung note. The Scottish soprano created the title role of Louise in Charpentier's opera in 1900, and was a wonderful interpreter of Massenet (*Chérubin*, *Thaïs*, *Manon*), Leroux (first to perform *La Reine Flammette* in 1903) and Erlanger (*Aphrodite*). She continued to sing at the Chicago Opera until 1913, and retired after a final performance of *Carmen* in an open-air theatre in Cincinnati.

A reference is due to **Fanny Heldy** (Liège 1888 - Paris 1973) who was chosen by Toscanini to sing Louise and Mélisande at La Scala. She was gifted with a lovely timbre and a notable virtuosity which made it possible for her to emerge (during the arc of years that goes from 1913 to 1939) both in the French *lyrique* and the Italian

Emma Carelli *in the role which made her famous - Floria Tosca. Her farewell to the stage was in Rome in 1924, with a memorable Iris. She was a shrewd business-woman and theatrical agent, having learnt very well from her husband, Walter Mocchi, who ran the Rome Opera and the Colòn of Buenos Aires. (Historic Archives of the Rome Opera Theatre).*

The beautiful **Carmen Melis**, who was able to prepare her Minnie with the help of Puccini himself. "Vibrant, exquisite, very beautiful" raved Puccini; captivated by the excellence and beauty of this exceptional singer-actress.

Zazà by Leoncavallo: sitting one in front of the other are the baritone **Mario Sammarco** and the soprano **Rosina Storchio** a famous Butterfly, Violetta, Mignon, Mimì. She retired in 1923 in Barcellona after a last Butterfly. (Historic Archives of La Fenice Theatre, Venice).

dine also wrote a delightful autobiography, *Such a Sweet Compulsion* (1938), and made at least a dozen successful films.

Carmen Melis (Cagliari 1885 - Longone al Segrino, Como 1967) boasted a rich voice, docile in modulation, together with an attractive physical appearance and a superior ability as actress. From 1905 until the year of her withdrawal from the stage in 1935 she was an exceptional Manon (both in Massenet's opera and Puccini's), a fantastic Salome, Minnie (*La Fanciulla del West*), Nedda (*Pagliacci*) and Thaïs. Renata Tebaldi was one of her pupils.

Favoured by Puccini who wanted her as the first performer of Magda in *La Rondine* (1917), Suor Angelica and Lauretta in *Il Trittico* (1919) and Liù in *Turandot*, **Gilda Dalla Rizza** (Isola della Scala, Verona 1892 - Milan 1975) was a magnificent *Traviata* under Toscanini's baton; she was guided by a stage instinct which has few comparisons. She made her debut at Bologna in 1910 as Charlotte in *Werther* and retired with a final *Suor Angelica* at Vincenza at the 1942 Puccini celebrations.

Salomea Krusceniski (Kruszelnicka; Tarnopol 1872 - Leopoli 1953) had a superb figure, a passionate temperament and a perfect singing tech-

Gilda Dalla Rizza in Act IV of Traviata. Puccini composed La Rondine for her. Gilda Dalla Rizza was also the first performer in Italy of Suor Angelica and Lauretta.

nique. She was the fabulous Butterfly who brought the opera to success at Brescia in 1904 after the original failure at La Scala. The flexibility and expressive possibilities of her voice made her so suited to both the lyric and dramatic repertory that it is impossible to give a precise definition of the Polish soprano.

In his book *Voci Parallele* (Parallel Voices) Lauri Volpi defined Krusceniski's voice as an isolated one: "Amazingly beautiful sound, - perfect technique and stylistic correctness".

In the Italian and above all the German repertory, the most applauded lyric sopranos were Frieda Hempel and Selma Kurz. **Frieda Hempel** (Lipsia 1885 - Berlin 1955) could pass nonchalantly from singing the Marschallin in *Der Rosenkavalier* to the Queen of the Night; from Rosina and Eva in *The Mastersingers* to Oscar in *Un Ballo in Maschera* and Euryanthe. **Selma Kurz** (Biala, Galizia 1874 - Vienna 1933) became a super-star because of her trills and her incredible versatility. (Between 1895 and 1927 she sang Wagner, Donizetti, Verdi and even Puccini). Her favourite aria was "Lockruf" from *The Queen of Sheba* (Goldmark) which contained her mythical, inimitable trill.

It is our duty to mention some other important exponents of the pure lyric voice in the early part of this century: **Angelica Pandolfini** (Spoleto 1871 - Lenno, Como 1959); **Emma Eames** (Shanghai 1865 - New York 1952); **Lina Cavalieri** (Rome 1874 - Florence 1944) who was applauded in many Verist operas, more for her beauty than for her vocal gifts; **Bessie Abbott** (Bessie Pickens; New York 1878 - 1919), famous as Juliette and Mimì at the Met; **Maria Kuznetsoya** (Odessa 1880 - Paris 1966), one of the most authoritative Russian singers specialised in the roles of Tatyana, Juliette, Mimì, Marguerite in *Faust*, Elsa and Carmen; **Miura Tanaki** (1884 - 1946) was the most important Japanese soprano, with successful performances in the roles of Mimì, Manon, Iris, and Santuzza; **Germaine Lubin** (Paris 1890 - 1979); **Maria Zamboni** (Peschiera del Garda 1895 - Verona 1976); **Rosetta Pampanini** (Milan 1896 - Corbola 1973); **Marthe Chenal** (Paris 1881 - 1947); **Alma Gluck** (Bucarest 1884 - New York 1924); **Joan Cross** (London 1900); the sweet **Ninon Vallin** (Mantalieu-Vercien 1886 - Lyon 1961); **Cesira Ferrani** (Turin 1863 - Pollone, Biella 1943) who was the first *Manon Lescaut* and Mimì at the Regio Theatre of Turin; **Adelaide Saraceni** (Rosario, Argentina 1895); **Josefina Huguet** (Barcelona 1871 - 1951); **Margaret Sheridan** (County Mayo, Ireland 1889 - Dublin 1958) a respected Puccini singer and a specialist in the part of Mimì; **Lotte Schone** (Vienna 1891 - Paris 1977); **Maggie Teyte** (Wolverhampton 1888 - London 1976), whose voice was flexible and delicate.

Before the revolutionary advent of Maria Cal-

las, towards the end of the forties, many lyric sopranos with beautiful voices appeared on the scene. All of them were incredibly gifted, but still tied to the oldfashioned way of singing — a style of singing which would soon be swept away by the philological rigor of the great Maria, and by the belcanto revival.

Voices like those of **Licia Albanese** (Bari 1909), a legendary Violetta and Butterfly at the Metropolitan (until 1966); **Mafalda Favero** (Portomaggiore, Ferrara 1905 - Milan 1981), a refined Mimì and Manon; and **Iris Adami-Corradetti** (Milan 1907), world famous interpreter of *Francesca da Rimini* and of almost all the roles created by Wolf-Ferrari. They were rich voices, guided by noteworthy artistic talent; but often they were tempted by verist excesses that were beyond the limits of good taste.

It is a different story for the Brazilian **Bidù Sayao** (Baldwina de Oliveira; Rio de Janeiro 1899) who studied with the legendary Jan De Reszké. Between 1926 and 1958 she distinguished herself as a moderated and sensitive performer of Manon, Mimì, Juliette (Gounod), Mélisande, Zerlina, Gilda, Violetta and Susanna: all her performances were characterised by artistic taste and elegance.

And we cannot forget: **Margherita Carosio** (Genoa 1908); **Jarmila Novotná** (Prague 1907), active at the Metropolitan from 1939 till 1954

It is difficult to resist a Salome so seductive: **Salomea Krusceniski**, *perhaps inspired by her name, knew how to captivate her audience with her vibrant voice and sinuous movements.*

Mafalda Favero, here photographed as Cio-Cio-San, first sang, as Liù, in Parma in 1927. During a long career she was much appreciated as Mimì, Manon, Adriana Lecouvreur, Thais. (Historic Archives of La Fenice Theatre of Venice. Photo: Camuzzi).

Intelligent and versatile, **Iris Adami-Corradetti** had a repertory of about eighty operas and had a particular fondness for the works of Wolf-Ferrari. Among her students - **Katia Ricciarelli**. (Historic Archives of La Fenice Theatre of Venice. Photo: Giacomelli).

as an unforgettable Donna Elvira and Manon; **Dame Joan Hammond** (Christchurch, New Zealand 1912), who studied with Dino Borgioli and possessed a smooth and caressing voice ideal for Puccini's operas; **Dorothy Kirsten** (Montclair, New York 1917) sang at the Met from 1945 until 1975 and specialized in the roles of Louise (which she studied with Charpentier), Manon Lescaut, Minnie, and Cio-Cio-San; **Janine Micheau** (Toulouse 1914 - Paris 1976); **Grace Moore** (Jellicoe, Tennessee 1901 - Copenhagen 1947) had a sensitive personality and a delightful vocality and was active in a double repertoire, the lyric and the light lyric; **Onelia Fineschi** (Florence 1924) had a brief but exciting career; whilst **Ilva Ligabue** (Reggio Emilia, 1932) gave a consistent rendering over a vast repertory.

Art Is Ageless: Magda Olivero

Madga Olivero (Saluzzo 1910) was a rare bird for her time, and she prepared the ground for Maria Callas. Even without possessing exceptional vocal means, especially as far as timbre and volume were concerned, she outclassed all of her colleagues in style and vocal longevity. As well as having an incredible technique (right up until the end of her career she was able to perform *filandi* and *diminuendi* with ease) she proved herself to be an artist of great sensitivity and intelligence, always involved in her roles, acting passionately but never "hamming". She made ner debut in 1933 at Turin, as Lauretta in *Gianni Schicchi*, and in the first career years she sang the light-lyric repertory with success (Gilda, Zerlina, Violetta). In *Traviata* she easily reached a high e''' flat, and exhibited an acrobatic series of *vocalizzi* that were nothing short of amazing.

In 1941 she abandoned the stage, having married, only to return in 1951, having changed to the verist repertory. Her intense renderings of *Adriana Lecouvreur*, *Tosca*, *Manon Lescaut*, *Francesca da Rimini*, and *Butterfly* are unforgettable. In a crescendo of emotion she would alternate from cutting, burning phrases to estatic or melancholic moments of incomparable intensity. She was able to do this thanks to her complete command of breath control.

Thanks to her technique, Olivero continued her career into the eighties (*La Voix Humaine* by Poulenc at Verona in 1981; and a concert at Voghera during that same year where she performed a perfect "Pace, pace, mio Dio" from *La Forza del Destino*). In 1990, at Cosenza, she sang the aria "Adieu, notre petite table" (*Manon*) and the finale of *Butterfly*, closing with a b'' flat that would make a thirty year old green with envy; and in late 1991 she is planning a solo recital.

An elegant **Tito Gobbi** (Sharpless), **Magda Olivero** (Cio-Cio-San) and the tenor **Gianni Poggi** (Pinkerton) - principals of a *Rome* Madama Butterfly. (Historic Archives of the Rome Opera Theatre).

The 1959-60 season at the San Carlo Opera (Naples) opened *with* Adriana Lecouvreur. **Giulietta Simionato** (Princess of Bouillon) hugs **Magda Olivero** (Adriana) who, at the last moment, splendidly replaced an ill Renata Tebaldi. (Historic Archives of the San Carlo Theatre, Naples).

An Angel's Voice

Renata Tebaldi (Pesaro 1922) is still defined by every opera lover as a *voce d'angelo*, that is, "the voice of an angel". It is difficult to find even one amongst any of her colleagues, past or present, who can equal the smooth, velvety quality of her voice: a precious instrument formed by the great school of Carmen Melis and Ettore Campogalliani.

She made her debut in 1944 at Rovigo as Elena in *Mefistofele*; and from then on, but especially following 1946 (after Toscanini had asked her to participate in the concert that re-opened La Scala after the war), Tebaldi became a legend in the greatest theatres and in a wide repertoire which reached its highest peaks in the roles of Desdemona, Mimì, Tosca and Maddalena di Coigny. She was especially loved in Italy and in America. She sang at Chicago from 1955 until 1969 and at the Metropolitan from 1954 until 1973, leaving behind her indelible memories.

During the years in which Callas represented a blazing return to a proto-romantic vocality, Tebaldi, virtuoso and radiant (but always profoundly expressive), incarnated the typical post-verist soprano: a large, beautiful voice that unfolded sumptuously over a melody by Puccini or Verdi, a luminous timbre, and a warm, forceful phrasing.

This was the context in which one can talk of rivalry between the two *primedonne*: Callas and Tebaldi. Not because there existed any actual disagreement between the two divas; but because they conceived vocal interpretation from two completely opposing viewpoints. On one hand there was dramatic agility and analytic phrasing (Callas), and on the other the pure luxury of sound, the ecstatic abandonment to melody, the dulcet sound of a Stradivarious without equal (Tebaldi).

It is not easy to make a judgement about Victoria Lopez, in art **Victoria De Los Angeles** (Barcelona 1923) which will satisfy everyone. She is a singer who has been either idolized (especially in Anglo-Saxon countries) or harshly protested. Her debut took place in her native city as the Countess in *The Marriage of Figaro* in 1945; but her repertory, during her lengthy

Renata Tebaldi in the La Forza del Destino, an opera particularly adapted to her vocal means. (Historic Archives of La Fenice, Venice).

Tebaldi in full sail in the first act of Tosca under the gaze of **Mario Del Monaco**. (Historic Archives of the Rome Opera Theatre. Photo: Savio).

This time **Tebaldi's** partner is **Franco Corelli**, in an Adriana staged in 1959. (Historic Archives of the San Carlo Theatre of Naples).

But just look how the applause of the audience has made **Giangiacomo Guelfi's** Scarpia as poised as a court dandy and **Tebaldi's** Tosca as coy as Musetta. (Historic Archives of the Rome Opera Theatre).

career, numbered a huge variety of roles, ranging from Elsa (*Lohengrin*) to Rosina, Cenerentola, Carmen, Violetta, Manon, Mimì, and Marguerite (*Faust*), as well as including an almost obsessive Lieder activity. All these varied opera roles were characterised by a refined interpretation, aided by a noteworthy stage presence and great musicality; but they were hampered by precise technical limits. For example, her usual rise to the high register was not correctly breath sustained, thus rendering the sound hard and strained and any modulation impossible.

Northern Charm

Three sopranos from three different generations, each with a vast repertory, deserve a special mention: **Hilde Güden** (Vienna 1917 - 1989), **Elizabeth Söderström** (Stockholm 1927) and **Anja Silja** (Berlin 1940).

Güden was a light-lyric soprano of enormous possibilities. She swept easily from Mozart to Lehar, from Strauss's "King of the Waltzes" to Richard Strauss (her Sofia in *Rosenkavalier* was wonderful), without excluding Verdi and some modern operas.

Söderström did not have a pure and crystalline voice like that of Hilde Güden; but she was an intelligent and versatile artist. She was noted for her elegant singing of Mozart and Strauss (superb her Countess in *Capriccio*); and she kept close ties with contemporary composers (Berg, Britten, Henze).

Beautiful and alluring, Anja Silja was launched in public whilst still an adolescent. Her years of glory went from 1956 (the year of her debut as Rosina at Berlin) until the second half of the seventies when she sang, without respite, *Lulu, Turandot, Die Entführung aus dem Serail, The Flying Dutchman, Fidelio, The Ring, Elektra, Salome*, and many contemporary works. Then came her vocal decline, and the spell was broken; the wobbling and harshness of her high register could not be compensated even by her exceptional stage presence.

Price and Freni: Two of von Karajan's Pupils

Leontyne Price (Laurel, Mississippi 1927) had cleanliness and brillance in her high register, but also a purity that few other sopranos have ever been able to boast. It compensated for the fact that she was never able to overcome a certain opaque quality in her middle register, which was often annoying. The beautiful American took her diploma at the Julliard School of Music in 1952, and then began her prestigious career as a typical lyric and *lirico-spinto* soprano.

Leontyne Price, *a gorgeous Donna Anna in Mozart's* Don Giovanni - *a role approached with exemplary precision.*

Although she is principally identified with *Aida*, Price is also a great Elvira in *Ernani*, *Butterfly*, Leonora in *Trovatore* and in *Forza del Destino*, showing a style and a brilliance which was rare even in the greatest sopranos of the century.

It seems impossible to believe, but over thirty-five years have passed since **Mirella Freni** (Modena 1935) made her debut as Micaela in a *Carmen* staged at Modena in 1956. Freni has a solid technique and an uncommon intelligence. With a scrupulous respect for the score and its expressive signs, she first emerged as Susanna in *The Marriage of Figaro*, Zerlina in *Don Giovanni* and Marie, in *La Fille du Régiment*; then she introduced parts into her repertory that were more suited to her vocality, such as Mimì, Liù, Marguerite in Gounod's *Faust*, Adina in *Elisir d'Amore*, *Puritani* (Rome, 1971) and even an unjustly protested *Traviata* at La Scala in the 1964-65 season.

Under the guidance of exceptional *Maestri* such as von Karajan, Carlos Kleiber, and Abbado, Freni has sung some perfectly characterised roles over the last twenty years: Amelia in *Si-*

La Scala, *on tour in Japan, performed* La Bohème *with* **Peter Dvorsky** *and the best Mimì of today,* **Mirella Freni**. *(Photo: Bunka Kaitan, Tokyo. September, 1981).*

Leontyne Price: *A noble Aida of the purest vocal line. (Historic Archives of the Rome Opera Theatre. Photo: Mélançon).*

Another photo of the Scala Bohème *in Japan with* **Mirella Freni**. *Here we are in the third act. (Bunka Kaitan, Tokyo. September, 1981).*

A singing lesson for **Mirella Freni**, *a pleasing Maria in* La Fille du Régiment. *(Historic Archives of the Teatro Comunale of Bologna).*

mone *Boccanegra* which opened La Scala in 1971-72 (directed by Strehler, conducted by Abbado), Elisabetta in *Don Carlos*, Desdemona and Aida at Salzburg with von Karajan as mentor — thus managing to succeed in a repertory that seemed beyond her means. Lately Freni has been able to include the roles of Manon Lescaut, Adriana Lecouvreur, Tatyana in *Eugene Onegin* and Lisa in *The Queen of Spades* in her vast repertory with surprising results, thanks to her intelligent evolution.

Raina Kabaivanska (Burgas, Black Sea 1934) is another fine example of vocal longevity. Her official debut was in 1959 when she sang in a

Tabarro staged at Vercelli. Despite being employed by major theatres and applauded by public and critics, the soprano from Bulgaria did not initially manage to make the "big-time". However, from the seventies on, Raina has won herself a place in the heart of the opera public. Her repertory is wide, going from Verdi to Puccini's masterpieces (*Tosca*, *Butterfly*, and *Manon Lescaut* in the lead), from *Pirata* and *Beatrice di Tenda* (Agnese and Beatrice) by Bellini to *Fausta* and *Roberto Devereux* by Donizetti, up to the Verists (*Francesca da Rimini*, *Adriana Lecouvreur*) and Strauss (*Capriccio*); she has also made a recent excursion into the comic field and operetta

In 1980, invited and expressly encouraged by Karajan, **Freni** *attempted the perilous role of Aida and emerged victorious. Supported by von Karajan's authoritive conducting of the orchestra the soprano overcame every difficulty and gave the role of the Ethiopian slave a lyrical flow and sweetness which very few dramatic sopranos have been able to achieve. (Archives of the Salzburg Festival).*

(*Merry Widow* 1989, in Naples, Venice and Rome). Because of her talent as an actress and certain obvious timbrical and technical similarities (*filature, rinforzandi*, and a liking for expressive nuances), Kabaivanska can be considered a worthy heir of Magda Olivero. Nowadays she is one of the most popular opera singers with the general public.

There are other important names on the opera billboards of the fifties and sixties. **Clara Petrella** (Milan 1914 or 1919 - 1989), for example, who was not called the "Duse of the singers" for nothing. She was a sensitive and intelligent in-

terpreter of a very vast repertory. **Herva Nelli** (United States 1923) was chosen by Toscanini for the now famous recordings of *Aida, Ballo in Maschera, Otello, Falstaff*, and *Requiem*; she sang mainly in important American theatres. **Virginia Zeani** (Bucarest 1928) studied with Lipkovska in her homeland and with Pertile in Italy. She was versatile to the point of being able to perform Rossini's *Zelmira* and *Otello* whilst singing equally well in *Manon Lescaut, Bohème* and *Lohengrin*, and she managed a fantastic portrayal of the *three* heroines in *The Tales of Hoffmann*, which she sang with her husband, the

bass Nicola Rossi Lemeni. **Rosanna Carteri** (Verona 1930) was attractive and precise in the roles of Liù, Adina, Mimì and Violetta. **Antonietta Stella** (Perugia 1929) was considered Tebaldi's heir because of the natural beauty of her voice; but she retired early - a victim of bad choice of repertory. **Marcella Pobbe** (Montegaldo, Vincenza 1927) was active in many operas of the lyric and *lirico-spinto* repertory, the best of which were *Faust, Otello*, and *Adriana Lecouvreur*.

In the following generation we find **Margherita Rinaldi** (Rome 1935) one of the best and most refined Italian singers; she possessed a warm and homogeneous voice ranging over two octaves. She was active in the classic light-lyric repertory, with a few interesting escapades into the lyric repertory and an intensive oratorial and concert activity (*Le Prophète* by Meyerbeer at the RAI in 1970 is amongst her best realisations). We must not forget the Puccini singer **Mietta Sighele** (Rovereto 1944), one of the most applauded Liùs, Butterflys, and Mimìs of recent decades. She is a singer who is technically and musically well prepared, giving an intimate portrayal of each character.

Beautiful Katia

A favourite of the greatest conductors and directors, **Katia Ricciarelli** (Rovigo 1946) has already more than twenty years of career behind her, having made her debut at Mantua in 1969. Her repertory reaches from Rossini to Puccini, even if her pure timbre and delicate emission make verist exaggerations little advisable. The abstract, ecstatic abandon of Bellini's and Donizetti's melodies are perfectly suited to her vocal means. Let one example stand for all: that of her *Anna Bolena* at the Regio Theatre of Parma during the 1976-77 season. The final aria "Al dolce guidami castel natio" was performed by the Venetian soprano with surprising *pianissimo* effects and an impeccable legato, proof of the great school of Iris Adami-Corradetti.

Thanks to her ease in fast vocalizing passages, her fluid emission of trills and *roulades* (especially if sung at *mezzavoce*) Katia Ricciarelli has been able to alternate performances of *Tosca, Ballo in Maschera, Trovatore*, and *Aida* with Rossini's lesser known and now finally rediscovered

Rosanna Carteri started her career in 1949, after having won a competition on the Italian national radio. She was very musical and versatile and was often protagonist of first-ever performances: Ifigenia by Pizzetti, Flavia in Prosperina e Lo Straniero by Castro, Natasha in the European premiere of War and Peace by Prokofiev. (Historic Archives of La Scala. Milan. Photo: Piccagliani).

A refined stylist, in possession of a rich voice, ranging from warm deep notes to the most luminous filatura, **Jessye Norman** amazed the Roman audience in a splendid performance of Dido and Aeneas by Henry Purcell. The perfection of her phrasing, the moving intensity of her expression, make her one of today's great artists. (Photographic Archives of Philips. Photo: Z. Dominic).

operas: *Donna del Lago*, *Tancredi*, *Armida*, *Assedio di Corinto*, *Semiramide*, and *Gazza Ladra*. The critics have accused the singer of overlooking the authentic Rossini virtuosity *di forza* in favour of an emission almost exclusively performed at *mezzavoce*, noticing signs of fatigue in the soprano's voice. However, for all opera lovers Katia remains the sweetest and most beautiful Desdemona to have appeared on the scene. This is fully confirmed by Zeffirelli's film, which is masterfully brought to life by Ricciarelli and Placido Domingo.

In the Mozart repertory, the lieder repertory, and in a few of Verdi's operas (especially in *Aida*) Jessye Norman and Margaret Price have made their mark.

Jessye Norman (Augusta, Georgia 1945) has an extended and expressive voice and is one of the greatest concert artists of our time.

She studied at Harvard University in Baltimore and at the University of Michigan, making her debut in Berlin in 1969 as Elizabeth in *Tannhaüser*. In 1973 she made her debut in Paris at the Salle Pleyel in *Aida*.

Her performances incited great enthusiasm among the opera public. We note *Hippolyte et Aricie* by Rameau in 1983 and *Ariadne auf Naxos*

One of the rare operatic appearances of **Jessye Norman** - an outstanding Phèdre in Hippolyte et Aricie by Rameau at Aix-en-Provence. It was during her studies at Michigan University with Pierre Bernac, a legendary French chansonnier, that Norman became interested in German Lieder and especially in the beautiful songs of Poulenc, Fauré, and Satie. (Giandonato Crico Collection).

by Strauss in 1985 in Aix-en-Provence, and, at the Metropolitan *Les Troyens* by Berlioz (1983) and Wagner's *Parsifal* (1991). She shines in oratorio and Lieder concerts, of which there are numerous recordings.

Margaret Price (Blackwood, Wales 1941), an exceptional Pamina, Fiordiligi, Donna Anna, and Countess in *Marriage of Figaro* is also active in German theatres performing in Italian operas such as *Norma, Otello*, and the above mentioned *Aida*.

She made her debut in 1964 as Cherubino at Covent Garden, and she seemed destined for a career in Mozart roles. At the end of the seventies, however, she attempted a Verdi repertoire, with much less success. Nor did she excell in Bellini's *Norma, Adriana Lecouvreur*, or Strauss' *Ariadne auf Naxos*. She remains an unbeatable Lieder singer, especially in Schubert and R. Strauss.

During the last few years Jessye Norman, perhaps the best loved singer today on an international level, has shown her great talent in a restricted group of operas: from Purcell (*Dido and Aeneas*) to Berlioz (*Les Troyens*), from Mozart to Rameau, Wagner (*Die Wallküre, Lohengrin* and *Parsifal*), Strauss (a memorable *Ariadne auf Naxos*) and Stravinsky (*Oedipus Rex*), with a parallel activity in the oratorio and Lieder field, which is truly praiseworthy. Price has attempted further excursions into the Verdi terrain, sometimes with happy results, but she would be better off keeping to Mozart where she is a first class performer.

We must mention, amongst the youngsters, ·**Daniela Dessì**, the best Italian soprano of her generation, **Fiamma Izzo d'Amico**, who shows some promise, **Anna Caterina Antonacci**, an intense, agile and beautifully coloured voice, and **Maria Dragoni**, who should be more careful in her repertory choice.

And here is a Susanna par excellence: **Irmgard Seefried**, darling of all the great conductors in the last forty years. In her final years, before her recent death, the Viennese artist became interested in prose theatre.

Mozart Lyric Sopranos

Three important names open the section on the most famous and acclaimed Mozart sopranos of this century: **Maria Cebotari** (Chisinau, Bessarabia 1910 - Vienna 1949), **Elisabeth Grümmer** (Diedenhofen, Alsace-Lorraine 1911) and **Rita Streich** (Barnaul 1920 - Vienna 1987).

The beautiful and ill-fated Cebotari could not continue her luminescent career as Susanna, the Countess, Donna Anna, Salome, and Sophie (Der Rosenkavalier) because she was killed by a tragic illness when only thirty-nine years old. She sang from 1931 until 1949, and was the first to perform the parts of Aminta in R. Strauss' *Die Schweigsame Frau* (1935) and Lucilla in *The Death of Danton* by Einem (1947). She also par-

ticipated in several important first performances of works by German composers.

Elisabeth Grümmer had a refined and highly musical voice, with a beautiful timbre. Her only handicap was that of having the same repertory as the great Elizabeth Schwarzkopf, thus being faced with a fearful rival in operas such as *Così fan Tutte* and *Don Giovanni*, without forgetting Wagner (*Lohengrin, The Mastersingers*). She did, however, find a space of her own, remaining an unsurpassed Agathe in *Der Freischütz*. From 1941 until the sixties she sang in Berlin, Vienna, London, Bayreuth and Hamburg; she was often conducted by Furtwängler, who had a particular appreciation of her vocal and scenic talents.

As for Rita Streich, we need only say that she was taught, in Berlin, by Maria Ivogün, Erna

*The beautiful Swiss soprano **Lisa Della Casa**, as the Countess Rosina in Mozart's* Le Nozze di Figaro.

Berger, and Willy Domgraf-Fassbänder: a formation that made her an acclaimed Mozart singer (Queen of the Night, Costanza) and Strauss singer (Zerbinetta, Sophie) over a long period of time and in many famous theatres.

The beautiful **Lisa Della Casa** (Burgdorf, Bern 1919) was a famous Strauss and Mozart singer. Her artistic beginnings were very precocious. She was part of a theatrical company when seven years old, performing Shakespeare and Shaw; in the meantime her vocal studies were directed by Margaret Haeser. After her debut as Butterfly in 1941 at Solothurn-Biel, Lisa Della Casa commenced a brilliant career which included her memorable *Arabella, Nozze di Figaro, Don Giovanni* (Donna Elvira and Donna Anna), *Der Rosenkavalier* (in the roles of Sophie, Octavian and the Marschallin), *Così fan Tutte* (Fiordiligi) and *Ariadne auf Naxos*, performing in the world's major theatres: the Staatsoper of Vienna (State Opera), the Metropolitan, Covent Garden, La Scala, Salzburg, and the Colon of Buenos Aries. The best vocal characteristics of the Swiss soprano were her superb legato, her equality between registers, and her soft, sweet timbre; her elegant appearance accentuated her charm.

Let us just mention a few of the other important Mozart sopranos of our century: **Minnie Nast** (Karlsruhe 1874 - Füssen im Allgäu 1956); the great **Elisabeth Schumann** (Merseburg 1888 - New York 1952) who was also an excellent lieder singer; **Maria Stader** (Budapest 1911); **Suzanne Danco** (Brussels 1911); **Jo Vincent** (Amsterdam 1898); **Audrey Mildmay** (Murstmonceaux, Vancouver 1900 - Glyndebourne 1953); and **Aulikki Rautawaara** (Vassa, Finland 1906). And we must not forget the great **Edda Moser** (Berlin 1941) who enjoyed a brief, but magical moment as an unbeatable Queen of the Night and Donna Anna.

Eleanor Steber (Wheeling, W. Virginia 1916 - Zanghorne, Pennsylvania 1990) deserves a paragraph apart for her luminous and intense voice. In her vast and ecclectic repertory, some brilliant highlights came in her Mozart roles of The Countess, Fiordiligi and Donna Anna. She made her debut at the Met in 1940 as Sophie in *Rosenkavelier*, and she remained a bright and active star there until 1970. Thanks to an enormous vocal talent, reinforced by a solid technique and an extraordinary expressive capacity, she was able to sing Puccini, Wagner, contemporary operas (she was the first interpreter of Samuel Barber's *Vanessa* in 1958) and Strauss (the first American Arabella).

Eleanor Steber; a Met star from 1940 on, she created the title role in Barber's Vanessa.

Four Queens of Song: Seefried, Schwarzkopf, Stich-Randall and Jurinac

Irmgard Seefried (Kongetried, Baviera 1919 - Vienna 1989) was a sensitive and extremely refined performer especially in the Mozart repertory, where she shone as one of the best Susannas of the post-war period. She began in the small part of the priestess in *Aida* conducted by von Karajan at Aquisgrana in 1938. Until the second half of the sixties she performed in all the principal theatres of the world, with, however, a decided preference for the Vienna State Opera and Salzburg, where, until recently, she continued to sing in acclaimed *Liederabende*.

Amongst her characteristics were her spicy, good-humored stage presence, her innate musicality, and her excellent vocal technique - the result of continuous study.

The uncontested queen of Lieder and German opera is **Elizabeth Schwarzkopf** (Jarocin, Poznan 1915). After her beginnings as a light-lyric soprano (Flower maiden in *Parsifal*, Berlin 1938) she immediately emerged as a lyric soprano of great worth: in Mozart and in Strauss (her Marschallin in *Der Rosenkavalier* is unforgettable); in Verdi (*Falstaff, Requiem*) and Puccini; she also performed many contemporary composers. (She was, for example, the first Trulove in Stravinsky's *The Rake's Progress*, Venice, 1951).

After 1947 Schwarzkopf's star began to shine in all the most important European and international theatres. From 1947 until 1951 she sang regularly at Covent Garden, where she returned in 1959 for a triumphant *Rosenkavalier*. She was acclaimed at La Scala between 1948 and 1963, at San Francisco in 1955, in Chicago in 1959, at the Metropolitan between 1964 and 1966. She made her farewell to the stage after a last, moving performance of the Marschallin in Brussels in 1972.

An intelligent and cultured artist, Schwarzkopf never over-looked one note or one phrase in an entire performance, giving each its true expressive value. This was also made possible by her sound technique which permitted her to give colouring and shadings and to easily overcome all the difficulties of perilous tessituras.

Another refined Mozart interpreter was **Teresa Stich-Randall** (West Hartford, Connecticut 1927). She made her debut as Aida at the age of fifteen. In 1952 she was engaged at the Vienna Staatsoper, where she was immediately given the title part in *Traviata*. From then on her activity extended to all the major operatic theatres, mainly in America, England and Italy.

Among her favourite operas were *Rosenkavalier* (Sophie), *Così fan Tutte* (Fiordiligi), *Don Giovanni* (Donna Anna), *Magic Flute*

Elizabeth Schwarzkopf *refined her interpretive art with the help of her husband, Walter Legge, general manager of a big international recording company. Every new recording was prepared with meticulous care - every nuance, every note, each single inflexion which added to the psychological insight of the character was studied and cultivated and nothing left to chance. The Marschallin of* Der Rosenkavalier *(photo) was one of the most successful results of this exacting work, both on stage and in recordings. (San Francisco Opera: Collection Giandonato Crico).*

Teresa Stich-Randall *in* Ariadne auf Naxos *by Richard Strauss; a photo taken in 1963. (Giandonato Crico Collection).*

(Pamina) and *Ariadne auf Naxos* which she performed with a crystalline voice and instrumental purity.

We must not forget **Sena Jurinac** (whose real name is Srebrenka, born at Travnik, Jugoslavia 1921), an exceptional Cherubino, Fiordiligi, Ilia (*Idomeneo*), Donna Elvira, Donna Anna, Pamina, and the Countess of Almaviva. Her voice was pure and she had a beautiful legato. Thanks to her noteworthy extension she was an excellent Octavian in *Der Rosenkavalier*, Marschallin in the same opera (second only to that of Schwarzkopf) and also successful as the Composer in *Ariadne auf Naxos*, Desdemona, Butterfly, Elisabetta in *Don Carlos*, Mimì, and Suor Angelica.

Two singers who have had a long career and who have distinguished themselves for their versatility, style, and flexible voices, are the Spanish soprano **Pilar Lorengar** (Saragozza 1929) and the German **Gundula Janowitz** (Berlin 1937). The former made her debut in Barcelona in 1949 and spread her repertory over Verdi, Puccini, and various contempory composers; but she obtained her best results with Mozart. Janowitz performs most frequently in Mozart (Countess, Fiordiligi, Donna Anna) often adding Wagner (Elsa, Eva, Senta, Sieglinde) and Strauss (Marschallin, Ariadne, Arabella) and has often sung at Salzburg under the baton of von Karajan. At times her voice is a little whistling; but her timbre is sweet and penetrating.

Looking at some other great Mozart interpreters, the first in time is **Graziella Sciutti** (Torino 1927), an unforgettable protagonist of innumerable Neapolitan comic operas as well as an unparalleled Mozart soubrette (Despina, Zerbina, Susanna). She made her debut in Rome in 1948 in Mozart's *Oca del Cairo*, demonstrating an innate musical talent, even though her voice was not particularly extended nor very strong. From 1958-1962 she sang regularly at Covent Garden, from 1958-1966 at Salzburg, and at the Glyndebourne Festival from 1954-1959, having become an indispensable part of the great comic repertory. From the mid 1970's on she turned to music teaching and opera directing as her main interests, being particularly involved with Neapolitan opera, Mozart and Poulenc (she had been an unexcelled interpreter of *La voix humaine*).

Dame Kiri Te Kanawa (Gisborne, New Zealand 1944), a magnificent Donna Elvira in *Don Giovanni* and Countess in *The Marriage of Figaro*, and the United States. Te Kanawa made her debut at Camden in 1969 as Elena in Rossini's *Donna del Lavo*. Since 1970 she has been tied to Covent Garden, where she is acclaimed and loved in her wide repertory.

Dame Te Kanawa began her music studies as a mezzo-soprano, with Vera Rosza at the London Opera Centre. Richard Bonynge first suggested her move to the soprano range and a Mozart specialisation. With a fascinating *portamento*, a light and delicate timbre, Te Kanawa has been applauded worldwide. Hers is a truly vast repertory which includes the roles of Mimì, Desdemona, Arabella, the Mareschallin in *Rosenkavelier*, Manon Lescaut and even Violetta Valéry. However, she achieves greater success in Mozart than in Verdi or Puccini, since her vocality is a bit too limited for the latter repertory. In Lieder concerts Te Kanawa receives enthusiastic acclaim, either live or on records.

Ileana Cotrubas (Galati, Romania 1939) has been a sensitive interpreter of so many Susannas, Paminas, and Mélisandes (Debussy). She has been applauded both for her exquisite vocal technique and her expressive and emotional acting. She made her debut in Bucharest as Yniold in *Pelléas* in 1964 and was a major performer until 1990 when she retired after a series of performances of *Werther* in Lisbon and Vienna. Without doubt, she preferred Mozart roles (Susanna, Pamina, Konstanze). But she was also able to create a sensitive, exciting Mimì at the Scala in 1979 with Kleiber conducting. Kleiber insisted on having her as Violetta Valéry in the Deutsche Grammonphon recording. Cotrubas has also earned due fame as a concert and oratorio performer.

Kiri Te Kanawa *can be considered the heir of Lisa Della Casa in repertory as well as in vocal characteristics; she has a sweet and soft timbre, perfect legato, and extension. She began her studies as a mezzo-soprano, but on the advice of the celebrated conductor, Richard Bonynge, she changed to a soprano. Her first important success came in December, 1971, when she sang the role of the Countess in a new production of* The Marriage of Figaro, *conducted by Colin Davis, at Covent Garden. (Giandonato Crico Collection).*

Barbara Hendricks, *an American soprano especially popular in France. Her Lieder concerts are widely acclaimed.*

Emmy Loose (Ustìnad Labem, Bohemia 1920 - Vienna 1989) belonged to the "bright and breezy" category of *soubrette* sopranos. She was a regular member of the Vienna State Opera from 1943 on. She was applauded there as Zerlina, Despina, Musetta, Norina, Gilda, and, above all, as Adele in *Die Fledermaus*. **Erna Berger** (Cossebande, Dresden 1900 - Essen 1990) gave performances in the Austrian and German theatre that remain unforgettable. She was one of Furtwängler's favourites. Her voice was small but well positioned and sweetly coloured, enabling her to interpret Gilda, Rosina, and Zerbina with grace and elegance. **Reri Grist** (New York 1935) was a spirited Despina, Susanna, and Zerlina; but also famous as Zerbinetta, Sophie, and Rosina in *Barbiere*.

Before closing this chapter let us mention just a few more names which were often printed on the billboards of the great theatres over the last twenty years. **Edith Mathis** (Lucerne 1936); **Judith Blegen** (Missoula, Missouri 1943); **Helen Donath** (Corpus Christi, Texas 1940); **Christiane Eda-Pierre** (Port de France, Martinique 1940); **Barbara Hendricks** (Stephens, Arkansas 1948); the young **Kathleen Battle** and the very young **Elisabeth Norberg-Schulz**, both of whom are favoured by the great conductors for their Mozart performances.

The Ambassadors of the Russian Repertory

Galina Vichnevskaya (Leningrad 1926) gave magnificent La Scala performances of Tchaikovsky's *Eugene Onegin* and Prokofiev's *Semyon Kotko* on tour with the Bolshoi in 1973. She had splendid vocal means - incisive in the dramatic phrases, soft and caressing in the *mezzavoce*.

These gifts made her insuperable in the Russian repertory, and also in chamber music, so much so that Shostakovich (and he was not the only one) dedicated his seven *Romanze* op. 127 to her voice.

We do not want to leave out **Tamara Milashkina** (Astrakhan 1937), a regular member of the Bolshoi of Moscow during the sixties and seventies, interpreting the great Russian repertory (Tchaikovsky, Rimsky-Korsakov, and Borodin) as well as having a valid activity in some Italian operas and being excellent in Lieder.

Elly Ameling (1938) is an exceptional Lieder singer but is rarely present on the operatic stage except for some rare and precious Mozart performances. Finally, **Lucia Popp** (Bratislava 1939), gracious and refined as Pamina, Sophie in *Der Rosenkavalier*, Zerlina, Zerbinetta, Marcellina (*Fidelio*), Rosalinde in *Die Fledermaus*, and wonderful in a wide Italian light-lyric repertory (Norina, Gilda, Musetta) and, naturally, in Lieder, ranging from Mozart to Mahler. Lately, following a normal evolution towards heavier roles, Popp has included in her repertoire roles such as that of the Marschallin, the Countess in *Figaro*, Eva in *The Mastersingers of Nuremberg* and Elsa in *Lohengrin*.

THE *LIRICO-SPINTO* SOPRANOS OF THE TWENTIETH CENTURY

Emmy Destinn (Ema Kittlovà; Prague 1878 - Ceské Budejovice 1930) dominated the stage during the full Verist era, not only because of her vocal power, but also because of her stylistic gifts, her moderation, and the expressive intensity with which she played the roles of Tosca, Salome, Butterfly, Santuzza, and especially Minnie in *The Girl of the Golden West* (of which she was the first interpreter at the Metropolitan in 1910, with Toscanini).

She began her singing career at Dresden in 1897 in *Cavalleria Rusticana*, and retired in 1921, already in full vocal crisis; her cutting high c‴ and her impeccable polish were severely compromised. Only the art and the intelligence of the great artist remained.

"La divina" **Claudia Muzio** (Pavia 1889 - Rome 1936) was a singing actress of insuperable bravura in the parts of Violetta, Tosca, Desdemona, Manon Lescaut, and Leonora in *Trova-*

Rosa Ponselle *as Elvira in Verdi's* Ernani, *one of the many notable revivals organised especially for her. She starred at the Met from 1918 to 1936.*

tore - all characters veined with a subtle melancholy, pushed by fate to their tragic end, involved in impossible loves. In these roles Muzio demostrated an artistic temperament without comparison in our century (with the exception of Maria Callas).

Despite the fact that she possessed a voice that was limited in extension, agility, and volume, she was able to resolve every moment of her performances with the variety of her colouring and shading, an intense and imaginative phrasing, and her passionate acting and good stage presence.

She sang from 1910 until 1934, when she died of heart disease (although tuberculosis and suicide were also spoken of). Her most sublime creation was that of *Cecilia*, by Refice, at the Rome Opera.

Rosa Ponselle (R. Ponzillo; Meriden, Connec-

Claudia Muzio *crowned with laurel. (Historic Archives of the Rome Opera Theatre).*

ticut 1897 - Baltimore 1981) was a lucky discovery made by Enrico Caruso. In 1918 the famous tenor heard her by chance and suggested that she should study opera. Only six months of lessons with the teachers Thormez and Romani were necessary, and then the young Rosa made her debut by Caruso's side, at the Metropolitan, in *La Forza del Destino*.

She sang until 1937, emitting one of the softest and velvety voices in the history of opera. Although her voice was flexible and equal in all registers, being resonant in the first high notes, she had precise limits in her extension, not being able to reach high c‴ with ease. Her stylistic quality, the noble composure of her singing, and her physical beauty compensated for these defects and helped create the legendary interpretations of *Ernani*, *Trovatore*, *Aida*, *Gioconda*, and *Norma* during the 1920's and 1930's.

A belcanto expert during a period that was little inclined towards variations and vocal decorations: **Giannina Arangi Lombardi** (Marigliano, Naples 1891 - Milan 1951). She was the first true *soprano drammatico d'agilità* of this century, preceding Callas.

After her debut as a mezzo-soprano in 1920 in Rome she went on to sing Aida at La Scala in 1925 and from then on was the star of many splendid performances of *Gioconda*, *Trovatore*, *Lucrezia Borgia*, *La Vestale*, and even Rossini's *Mosè* (Florence 1935), and Bellini's rediscovered *Beatrice di Tenda* (Catania 1935).

It was not a coincidence that she withdrew from the stage with *Vespri Siciliani* at Palermo in 1937 - the role of Elena has all the characteristics of the *drammatico d'agilità*.

Arangi Lombardi was also an excellent singing teacher at the Conservatorium of Milan, from 1947 on teaching at Ankara, Leyla Gencer being one of her prized students there.

The heir of Arangi Lombardi, as far as beauty and fullness of voice was concerned, was **Maria Caniglia** (Naples 1906 - Rome 1979), one of the most famous applauded performers in *Tosca*, *Andrea Chénier*, *Traviata*, *Adriana Lecouvreur*, *Trovatore*, *Forza del Destino*, *Ballo in Maschera* and *Aida* during the two decades from 1930 - 1950. Caniglia's best characteristic was the natural capacity of her voice to expand in the central register and in the first high notes, like a river of sonority ("Io son l'umile ancella" in *Adriana* and "Amami Alfredo" in *Traviata*). The only thing which occasionally ruined her singing style was her fiery temperament, for it often led her into excesses in the climactic moments of the Verist operas. She was unforgettable when coupled with Beniamino Gigli, especially in *Tosca*, *Traviata*, and *Fedora*.

Gabriella Gatti (Rome 1908) was an impeccable stylist and a refined singer in an era which was still tied to the powerful and exuberant verist voices. She began distinguishing herself in 1934 (the year of her debut in Monteverdi's *Orfeo*), becoming an irreplaceable interpreter of new and rare operas. She sang in first-ever performances by composers Robbiani, Malipiero, Frazzi, Casella, Alfano, Gnecchi, and also in Busoni's *Turandot*, *Wozzek*, *Enfant Prodigue*, *Rinaldo*, *Der Freischütz* (Agata), *Oberon* (Rezia), *William Tell* (Matilde), whilst also singing the more normal repertoire of the *lirico-spinto* soprano: *Tosca*, *Traviata*, *Forza del Destino*, *Norma*, *Tannhäuser*.

Let us look at some other great *lirico-spinto* sopranos. **Margherita Grandi** (Hobart, Tasmania 1894) a famous Lady Macbeth and Tosca; **Margarete Teschemacher** (Cologne 1903 - Bad Wiesse 1959); **Celestina Boninsegna** (Reggio Emilia - Milan 1947), much acclaimed in *Trovatore* and *Aida*; **Dusolina Giannini** (Philadelphia 1902 - Zurich 1986); **Ester Mazzoleni** (Sebenico, Dalmazia 1883 - Palermo 1982), a great Medea and Giulia in *La Vestale*; **Rosa Raisa** (Bialystok 1893 - Los Angeles 1963) first to perform *Turandot* and *Francesca da Rimini*; **Giannina Russ** (Lodi 1873 - Milan 1951); **Yvonne Gall** (Paris 1885 - 1972); **Maria Nemeth** (Kormend, Hungary 1897 - Vienna 1967) a wonderful Tosca and Amelia in *Ballo in Maschera*, but also able to sing the Queen of the Night; **Ina Souez** (Windsor, Colorado 1908), famous in the Mozart repertory; **Rose Bampton** (Cleveland 1908): from 1932 until 1950 she was a diva at the Metropolitan Opera in a wide repertoire - she went from mezzo-soprano roles to the parts of Donna Anna, Kundry, and Sieglinde; **Lucrezia Bori** (Gandia, Valencia 1887 - New York 1960) - prima donna at the Met from 1912 until 1936; **Lina Bruna Rasa** (Milan 1907 - 1984); **Maria Farneti** (Forli 1877 - 1955); **Eugenia Burzio** (Milan 1872 - 1922); **Bianca Scacciati** (Faenza 1894 - Milan 1948), a powerful Turandot and Tosca; **Eileen Farrell** (Wilmantic, Connecticut 1920) one of the most sought after singers for the roles of *Medea* and *Gioconda* during the years when Maria Callas was already dominating the scene.

The splendid **Dame Eva Turner** (Oldham 1892 - London 1990) was one of England's most extraordinary voices. Hearing her sing, Toscanini brought her to La Scala where she debuted in 1924 as Freia in *Rheingold*. From that time on her career was crowned with one success after another, especially when she sang *Turandot*, *Aida* or Amelia in *Ballo in Maschera*, roles which she regularly performed from 1928-1948 at Covent Garden, in Chicago, Buenos Aires and Lisbon, to name but a few of the world's most famous opera theaters where she shone. Her voice had excellent emission, a beautiful colour, and a famous capacity to achieve equality among notes in a more than two octave range.

Nearer to our times, **Martina Arroyo** (New

York 1935), gifted with magnificent vocal means; but her rise to the high notes was never well resolved. Excellent in *Aida*, *Ballo in Maschera*, *Tosca*, *Macbeth*, and *Forza del Destino*. **Anna Tomowa-Sintow** (Stara Zagora, Bulgaria 1941) was one of von Karajan's favourites, and an excellent Elsa (*Lohengrin*), Leonora in *Forza del Destino*, and *Aida*.

The best Verdi voices of today deserve a quick mention. They are the British **Rosalynd Plowright**, who has serious problems in the high register; the American **Leona Mitchell**, who has a lovely voice colour but lacks flexibility; **Susan Dunn**, also American, has a flexible and well emitted voice up until the first high notes when she runs into difficulty (she has given good results in *Vespri Siciliani*, *Forza del Destino*, and *Giovanna d'Arco*); finally the most solid of them all is **Aprile Millo**, capable of modulating her vocality, and exhibiting *pianissimi* and good high notes (up to high e‴ flat as in the final of the second act of *Aida* at the Arena of Verona). Finally we must mention **Cheryl Studer**, who studied with Hans Hotter; she is famous in Anglo-Saxon Countries and favoured by Riccardo Muti in Italy.

The Lirico-Spinto sopranos of the German repertory

Lotte Lehmann (Perleberg, Brandenburg 1885 - Santa Barbara, California 1976) was a great interpreter of Wagner and Strauss. Her solid preparation and her sensitive acting allowed her a long career which stretched from her appearance at Hamburg in *The Magic Flute* (Third Boy) in 1909 until her last concerts in America in 1951 (she withdrew from the stage in 1946 in Los Angeles, performing the Marschallin in *Der Rosenkavalier*). Her declamation was impetuous and dramatic; her voice was sweet and delicate in the elegiac passages, elegant and sensual in the love scenes. Lotte Lehmann was the best performer of *Rosenkavalier*, *Fidelio*, *Lohengrin*, and *The Mastersingers of Nuremberg* between the years 1920 - 1940, as well as being the first to interpret many of Richard Strauss's operas (the Composer in *Ariadne auf Naxos* in 1916, the wife of Barak in *Die Frau ohne Schatten* in 1919, Christina in *Intermezzo* in 1924). She was also much acclaimed in *Manon Lescaut*, *Tosca*, and *Suor Angelica*.

Maria Jeritza (born Mimi Jedlitzka; Brno, Moravia 1887 - New York 1982) had an exceptional vocal and physical attraction and was the perfect incarnation of Salome and Thaïs, both enchanting women bursting with sensuality. Her interpretation of the Dance of the Seven Veils and the Kiss Scene in *Salome* have remained legendary. Strauss himself wanted Jeritza

Elisabeth Rethberg, German soprano, as Sieglinde in Wagner's Die Walküre.

as the first performer of *Ariadne auf Naxos* in Stuttgart in 1912, and of *Die Frau ohne Schatten* (as the Empress) in Vienna in 1919.

Hers was a voice with a good timbre and resonance, sustained by a noteworthy technique. She was able to perform in many operas by Wagner and Puccini, gaining great success in *Tosca*, *Butterfly*, and *Turandot*. Her scenic follies in *Cavalleria Rusticana* and *Carmen* have remained proverbial (the Americans went crazy over them): in Bizet's opera Jeritza used to chew on an apple in a deliberately vulgar way during Don Jose's imploring aria, whilst as Santuzza she would launch the curse "A te la Mala Pasqua" after having rolled down all the stairs of the church.

Elisabeth Rethberg (born Lisabeth Sättler; Schwarzenberg, Saxony 1894 - Yorktown Heights, New York 1976) sang from 1915 (when she made her debut in Johann Strauss' *Gypsy Baron* at Dresden) until 1944, stunning the American and Central European audiences with her rich and well modulated voice, able to confront over one hundred roles. Due to the homogeneity of her sound and her stylistic fidelity she was a divine Aida, Desdemona, Brünnhilde, Mimì, Elisabeth in *Tannhäuser*, Leonora in *La Forza del Destino*, Amelia in *Un Ballo in Maschera*, and also the first to sing in Richard Strauss' *Ägyptische Helena* at Dresden in 1938.

Giuseppina Cobelli premiered in 1924, at Piacenza, in La Gioconda; *but her career really took off the next year when she sang Sieglinde at La Scala. Wagner and other modern composers were a fixture in her repertoire. She was the first to sing* La Fiamma, *by Respighi, and* La Notte di Zoraima, *by Montemezzi. (Historic Archives of the Rome Opera Theatre).*

A certain frigidity was noticed in her — an incapacity to transmit deep emotions to the public, perhaps because of her majestic stature which made her little inclined to dynamic acting. However her relative scenic weakness was amply compensated by her style and the purity of her timbre, individualised by her typical German "r".

The beautiful **Giuseppina Cobelli** (Salò, Brescia 1898 - 1948) spread the Wagnerian message throughout Italy in the twenties and thirties. She was a wonderful Isolde and Sieglinde but also a superb Fedora, Minnie, Adriana Lecouvreur and the first to perform Respighi's *La Fiamma*.

She studied with Germaine Lubin and was active in a very wide repertoire from Mozart to Wagner - her name: **Régine Crespin** (Marseille 1927). She made her debut in *Lohengrin* (1950) and specialised immediately in the roles requiring a dramatic vocality (Leonora in *Fidelio*, Kundry, Brünnhilde, Tosca, Fedora, Fedra by Pizzetti, the Marschallin) until, towards the end of her career, she demonstrated a fantastic comic verve (*La Périchole*, *La Belle Hélène*, *La Grande-Duchesse de Gerolstein*) and an incredible dramatic intensity shown in her noteworthy characterisation of the old Mother Superior in Poulenc's *Di-*

alogues of the Carmelites. During the golden years of her career she performed with brilliant sound and intelligent, psychologically detailed acting.

Let's look at a list of possibly secondary but still important sopranos active in the German *lirico-spinto* repertory. **Meta Seinemeyer** (Berlin 1895 - Dresden 1929) was unforgettable protagonist of the Verdi revival in Germany. She died of leukaemia; **Florence Austral** (Richmond, Victoria, Australia 1894 - New Castle, N.S.W. Australia 1968); **Sophie Sedlmair** (Hannover 1857 - 1939); **Lucie Weidt** (Troppau, Bohemia 1879 - Vienna 1940); **Margarethe Siems** (Breslau 1879 - Dresden 1952) excellent in the R. Strauss repertory; **Florence Easton** (Middlebrough 1884 - New York 1955) was able to range over a wide repertory (from Carmen to Brünnhilde) in a total of eighty-eight different roles; **Rose Pauly** (born Rose Pollak; Eperjes 1894 - Tel Aviv 1975) a famous *Elektra* much loved by Strauss; **Giulia Tess** (born Giulia Tessaroli; Verona 1889 - Milan 1976) acclaimed as Salome and Elektra and in the works of Wolf-Ferrari; **Martha Fuchs** (Stuttgart 1898 - 1974); **Nanny Larsén-Todsen** (Hagby, Sweden 1884 - Stockholm 1982); **Elisabeth Ohms** (Arnheim, Holland 1888 - Marquardstein, Bavaria 1974); **Hilde Konetzni** (Vienna 1905 - 1980) and her sister **Anny Konetzni** (Ungarisch-Weisskirchen 1902 - Vienna 1968); **Suzanne Juyol** (Paris 1920) famous Isolde and Kundry in France; **Johanna Gadski** (Anklam, Pomerania 1872 - Berlin 1932); **Germaine Lubin**, already mentioned; **Viorica Ursuleac** (Czernowitz, Rumania 1894 -

Régine Crespin, one of the most important French lyric singers in this century.

Ehrwald, the Tryol 1985) favoured by Strauss, who conducted her many times; **Helen Traubel** (St. Louis 1898 - Santa Monica, California 1972), star of the American theatres and famous also in operetta; **Maria Reining** (Vienna 1903 - London 1991); **Tiana Lemnitz** (Metz 1897) who had a vast repertory thanks to her perfect technique; **Sylvia Fisher** (Melbourne 1910) who was active at Covent Gerden from 1949 until 1958, especially in her favourite roles of the Marschallin, Leonora in *Fidelio*, and Sieglinde. Closer to our times there are **Ingred Bjoner** (Kraakstad, Norway 1928); **Gré Brouwenstijn** (Den Helder, Holland 1915); **Catarina Ligendza** (Stockholm 1937); **Helga Dernesch** (Vienna 1939); **Hildegard Behrens** (Varel, Oldenburg 1946); **Jeanine Altmeyer** (Pasadena, California 1948); and **Marita Napier** (Johannesburg, South Africa 1939); **Josephine Barstow** (Sheffield 1940) has sung regularly at Covent Garden since 1969, and is also active in the contemporary English repertoire; **Elizabeth Connell** (Johannesburg 1946) is known especially for her performances of *Medea*, Lady Macbeth, and Ortrude (*Lohengrin*); **Rita Hunter** (Wallasey 1933) studied with Eva Turner and is memorable for the extraordinary power and incisiveness of her voice.

The Dramatic Sopranos of the Twentieth Century

Among the historic dramatic sopranos we must first of all remember **Olive Fremstad** (born Olivia Rundquist; Stockholm 1868 - Irvington, New York 1951). She made her debut as a contralto in 1895 (Azucena at Cologne), and became a soprano in 1903 after her Sieglinde in *Die Walküre* at the Metropolitan. She was one of the most applauded performers of Isolde, due to the metallic brilliance of her high notes and her dramatic impetus. At the end of her farewell performance (*Lohengrin* at the Met in 1914) she received nineteen curtain calls and over twenty minutes of applause.

Another wonderful Isolde, Kundry, Brünnhilde, and Sieglinde was **Melanie Kurt** (Vienna 1880 - New York 1941) who made her debut as a singer in 1902 after having begun her artistic career as a pianist.

Anna Mildenburg-Bahr (Vienna 1872 - 1947) and **Gertrude Kappel** (Halle 1884 - Munich 1971) both had piercing high notes, robust central and lower registers, great temperaments and stage presence. They were "two ace cards". The latter was an exceptional Elektra and Marschallin during the two decades between 1910 and 1930.

"A true vocal hurricane" is the only way to describe **Félia Litvinne** (St. Petersburg 1866 - Paris 1936), the famous Wagnerian soprano in

An imposing stance taken by **Olive Fremstad**, a powerful and spirited Brünnhilde.

French theatres in which she was the first to perform Isolde and Brünnhilde in the *Ring*. Her recordings, alas, do not give the right idea of what one of the most potent and incisive voices of the time must really have been like. They do, however, bring to light some of her blatent

Helen Traubel, as Brünhilde in Wagner's Götterdämmerung. After Flagstad left the Met in 1941, she was regarded as its leading Wagner soprano. In 1953 she stopped singing there because its director, Rudolf Bing, objected to her performing in night clubs.

Frieda Leider *began at Halle in 1915, singing Venus in* Tannhäuser. *She continued to sing until the forties, having a repertoire ranging from Wagner, Strauss and Verdi to 18th Century works such as* Armida *and* Don Giovanni. *(Historic Archives of the Rome Opera Theatre. Photo: Pieperhoff).*

stylistic blanks (her "Ho -jo- to- ho" is proof).

Showing far more good taste in style and equally prestigious vocal means, **Maria Müller** (Theresienstad, Bohemia 1898 - Bayreuth 1958), had smooth extension, equal in each note, with lightninglike high notes, and a magnificent consistency. From 1930 until 1944 she was a corner stone of the Bayreuth "Temple".

Frieda Leider (Berlin 1888 - 1975) had very few rivals in parts like Brünnhilde or Isolde during the period stretching between the two wars. Her full, warm and luminescent voice was also flexible enough to be able to sing operas such as *Don Giovanni, Trovatore, Aida,* and *Tosca,* all parallel with her Wagnerian repertoire.

The artistic story of **Kirsten Flagstad** (Hamar, Oslo 1895 - Oslo 1962) was exceptionally long and triumphal. Her debut was in 1913 in *Tiefland* by Albert, whilst her farewell was given in December, 1953, in Oslo. In 1955, her vocal means still intact, Flagstad went on a long concert tour and recorded Gluck's *Alceste* for the B.B.C. We cannot recall any other female singer in the history of opera who has had such a powerful and incisive voice, but a voice which was always contained within the limits of an absolutely secure technique. The most stunning thing about this operatic "Berta Krupp" (as she was defined by Riemens) was her fluidity of emission and the equality of her registers, which per-

sisted through the years despite the fact that she constantly exposed herself to the risks of a perilious repertory.

Isolde, Brünnhilde, Leonora in *Fidelio,* Kundry, Elsa, and Elisabeth are roles which are all associated with Flagstad's voice, as well as being those which she mostly performed with Melchior and Svanholm.

Gina Cigna (Paris 1900) was on stage from 1927 until 1947, but still amazing for her style and vocal state in some chamber arias recorded towards the end of the seventies. She was, by antonomasia, *Gioconda, Norma,* and *Turandot,* imposing powerful and silvery sounds on a merciless tessitura.

Due to her technical and stylistic virtues she could include in her repertoire Bellini's *La Straniera,* Donizetti's *Lucrezia Borgia,* Gluck's *Alceste* and Monteverdi's *Incoronazione di Poppea,* even if this last may very well have made a philologist's hair curl.

Great fame as a *lirico-spinto* soprano was gained by **Zinka Milanov** (Kunc, Zagreb, 1906 - New York 1989), exceptional in the operas of Verdi (*Trovatore, Forza del Destino, Ballo in Maschera, Aida*), and in *Gioconda, Tosca, Fanciulla del West,* and even in Wagner (Sieglinde) and Richard Strauss (the Marschallin). After her debut at Lubiana in 1927, she sang at Zagreb from 1928 until 1935, then she moved to Prague and the Metropolitan of New York, where she became uncontested diva over the successive twenty years. Her voice was extraordinarily robust and penetrating, technically solid enough to resolve Verdi's many dynamic indications (legato singing, *pianissimi, smorzandi, rinforzandi*). However during the fifties her voice became somewhat fatigued, with the inevitable loss of flexibility which this implies.

Majorie Lawrence (Melbourne 1909) was a divine Wagnerian, intense and shining as Brünnhilde, Elisabeth in *Tannhäuser, Tosca,* and *Thaïs.* Struck by poliomyelitis in 1941, she had to abandon the stage and dedicate herself exclusively to oratorio. However she did perform a much acclaimed *Elektra* in Chicago in 1947 in concert form.

The heir of Flagstad towards the end of the sixties was **Astrid Varnay** (Stockholm 1918), gifted with a magnificent vocal instrument but not protected by a sufficently solid technique; from 1941, the year of her debut at the Metropolitan as Sieglinde, until half way through the sixties, she relentlessly sang all the most difficult Wagnerian roles, especially Brünnhilde. Then came the vocal decline: her high notes began to wobble, her various registers split apart; and her beautiful vocal polish tarnished completely.

After twenty years of superb Strauss characterisations (Clytemnestra, Herodias, and the

Nurse in *Die Frau ohne Schatten*) Varnay today still sings the tiny part of Mamma Lucia in *Cavalleria* in German theatres; but of those high notes which seemed like golden comets there remains not the slightest, most pitiful little shadow.

Birgit Nilsson (West Karup, Sweden 1918) had, as opposed to her colleague, Varnay, great control over her musical instrument, managing to continue to hurl her vocal lightning bolts up until 1979-80 in some memorable performances of *Elektra* and *Die Frau ohne Schatten* at the Vienna State Opera. Because of the enormous possibilities of her voice, Nilsson was able to keep all the most complex Wagnerian and Strauss roles in her repertoire as well as *Tosca*, *Aida*, *Don Giovanni*, *Macbeth*, *Fidelio*, *Oberon*, *Fanciulla del West* and, above all, her legendary *Turandot*.

In the part of the Ice Princess the Swedish artist launched her incredible vocal spears in theatres all over the world, often singing together with Franco Corelli.

Miss Nilsson made her debut in Stockholm as Agathe in C.M. von Weber's *Freischutz*. Her

The riddle scene of Turandot. The Ice Princess is **Birgit Nilsson**. At her side an unusual Calaf, **Carlo Bergonzi**. This photo was taken during a performance in Naples in 1976. (Historic Archives of the Teatro San Carlo of Naples. Photo: Troncone).

Marjorie Lawrence, Australian soprano: she was notably athletic, riding her horse into the scenic flames when performing Brünhilde in Götterdämmerung.

The mighty **Astrid Varnay** captured in a dramatic moment. She's singing the part of Herodias in Richard Strauss's Salome at Nuremberg in 1973. (Historic Archives of the Opera Theatre of Nuremberg. Photo: Bischof and Broel OHG).

*A dramatic expression for **Martha Mödl** as Maria in Wozzek by Berg. (Düsseldorf, 1947). She was an excellent actress as well as a singer of sound vocal ability.*

Fidelio. But she was showing signs of vocal tiredness and harshness as early as 1955.

Even if she lost ease in the high register, Mödl gained even greater acting skill (with the passing of time). She continued to walk the boards in Germany and to gather profuse applause.

Nowadays, after almost fifty years of career, she continues to sing frequently in the part of the Mother in *Bluthochzeit* by Fortner and in some contempory works, preferably in her home-town theatre in Nuremberg. In 1989 she performed in the role of the Countess in the *Queen of Spades*, much to everyone's amazement.

One of the most beautiful and sensual Salome's of our century was **Ljuba Welitsch** - her real name was Ljuba Velickova (Borissova 1913). During her golden years, between 1936 and 1960, she boasted a pure but penetrating voice, with brilliant high notes, like lightning bolts, and an acting skill worthy of a true professional: a lioness of the stage.

She sang Donna Anna, Butterfly, Tosca, Aida, Amelia; but her favourite, and the public's favourite as well, was the perilous role of Salome. She studied it with Richard Strauss himself in 1944. The final scene, as demonstrated by her recordings of the role (especially the

career continued in Swedish theatres where she sang her preferred operas: *Macbeth, Tannhäuser, The Flying Dutchman* and *Don Giovanni.* It was her Elsa in a 1953 *Lohengrin* at Bayreuth that launched her international fame. Public and critics were stunned by her powerful voice and penetrating high notes, and further amazed to note with what ease this voice adapted to even the most delicate *mezzevoci.* Nilsson sang frequently at Covent Garden from 1957 on, but her strongest ties were to the Metropolitan (1959-1975) and the Vienna Staatsoper, where she performed until 1982.

Today her dynamic personality and extraordinary technical command are on display in her celebrated Master Classes, for which she has an enthusiastic and faithful following.

Martha Mödl (Nuremberg 1912), after making a late debut as Cherubino in *The Marriage of Figaro* in 1942 at Remscheid, alternated mezzo soprano and dramatic soprano parts during all her career. She possessed a fine voice that was particularly extended and of ambiguous colour, somewhat steely, and suited especially to "demoniac" parts (Lady Macbeth, Clytemnestra in *Elektra*, and Kundry). She sang in all the most important theatres worldwide, gaining great acclaim as Isolde (for her detail and melancholic rendering), Brünnhilde (for the variety of her vocal and physical performance) and as Leonora in

Ljuba Welitsch here as Butterfly a role in which she enchanted the public with her penetrating high register, but even more so with her physical beauty - blue eyes, fiery red hair, sensuous movements.

*The splendid Salome of **Gwyneth Jones**, engrossed in the dance of the seven veils. (Giandonato Crico Collection).*

live one conducted by Fritz Reiner), took on a truly apocalyptic aspect when performed by the Austrian red-head. Her high "Ich habe deinen Mund geküsst" (I have kissed your mouth) would triumph radiantly over the storming orchestra. It expressed both the frenzy of the victory and the realisation of her own necromancy.

Welitsch continued to sing small parts at the Vienna Staatsoper until the beginning of the eighties.

We must include in our list of the greatest Wagnerian sopranos the powerful and resonant voices of **Gertrud Grob Prandl** (Vienna 1917), active during the forties and fifties and a wonderful Isolde, Leonora and Turandot; **Amy Shu-**

ard (London 1924 - 1975), one of the most impressive voices heard at Covent Garden between 1954 and 1974, was famous as Turandot, Aida, Amelia, Santuzza, Brünnhilde, Elektrá, and Jenufa; **Leonie Rysanek** (Vienna 1926) made her debut at Innsbruck in 1949 and is still in full activity in Vienna and American opera theatres because of the force and purity of her high notes which easily overcame the Wagner and Strauss orchestras. Recently, Rysanek has had great success in character roles, performed with expressive intensity: Clytemnestra, Herodias, Kostelnicka (*Jenufa*), Kabanikha (*Katya Kabanova*), the Countess (*The Queen of Spades*). The German **Inge Borkh** (Mannheim 1917), was a torrential voice for all the most difficult roles in the German repertory. She had a soft spot in her heart for *Elektra* and *Salome*, which she tackled with fiery vocal temperament. **Gwyneth Jones** (Pontypool, Wales 1936) began as a contralto but became a dramatic soprano in 1964 and specialises in the parts of Brünnhilde, Senta, Kundry, Turandot, and, above all, Salome, in which her perfect interpretation is helped by her superb figure. Her recent Elektra was imposing. **Eva Marton** (Budapest 1943) has been the rival of Ghena Dimitrova over the last ten years in the roles of Turandot, Tosca, Aida; but she is also active in the Strauss repertory.

Today the dramatic soprano section is suffering a serious crisis which is only partially compensated by the imposing vocal presence of **Ghena Dimitrova** (Pleven, Bulgaria 1941). Her formation was Bulgarian, and she began her climb upwards in the Central European theatres during the sixties, improving year by year; initially her voice seemed like a huge machine for producing high notes, with a few problems in the *passaggio* and in more intimate singing. But a strict self discipline and much study made her vocality more homogeneous and pliable, bending to all the subtleties required by scores such as *Turandot, Nabucco, Tosca, Ballo in Maschera, Macbeth*, and *Don Carlos*.

CALLAS AND THE BELCANTO DIVAS

What can be described as "the Callas era" began in the summer of 1947 when, at the Verona Arena, there was a new production of *Gioconda*, featuring a young soprano making her debut in Italy: **Maria Callas** (born Mary Anne Kalogeropoulos; New York 1923 - Paris 1977).

Right from that very first evening her unusual vocal structure and exceptional performing gifts were obvious. Callas's voice was divided into three well defined registers, ranging from the corpulent low notes of the mezzo-soprano (she reached low a') up to the high notes of a coloratura soprano (in Proch's *Variazioni* she reached f‴), all of which was held together by a refined technical knowledge and by the varied, imaginative and authentic phrasing of a virtuoso.

With her "voices" Callas had a virtually unlimited repertoire, recalling the famous divas of the '700s and the '800s: She could resurrect Rossini's *Armida* (Florence 1952) with its pyrotechnical virtuosity, or create grand classical figures such as Medea, Norma, Giulia (*Vestale*), divining the true tragic accent. Or yet again she could overcome all the difficulties of parts once entrusted to the *soprani drammatici di agilità*, such as Lady Macbeth, Elena (*Vespri Siciliani*), Amina, Violetta, Imogen (*Pirata*) and Lucia.

Combined with her vocal gifts, which not everyone appreciated, Callas offered an unequalled acting and scenic skill: her gestures, her visual expression, every tiny movement, contributed to her portrayal of character, from the demoniac Lady Macbeth to the neurotic Violetta, from Norma's noble grandeur (her "Teneri figli" is unforgettable) to the wild arrogance of Abigaille, and then to her wonderful Tosca, so real and so female.

Callas was also famous for the unexpected 'gifts' with which she would surprise the audience: at the end of the second act of *Aida* in Mexico City in 1951 she launched a fantastic high e‴ flat not included in the score.

Her perfect voice placement in the facial mask

8th January, 1953. A pre-thin **Maria Callas**: a gorgeous doll wrapped in metres and metres of spotted taffeta, with the tenor **Francesco Albanese**, in the second act of Traviata. The sublime artist delineated in a unique way phrases such as "Dite alla giovane", "Alfredo, Alfredo, di questo core", "Teneste la promessa...". (Historic Archives of La Fenice Theatre, Venice).

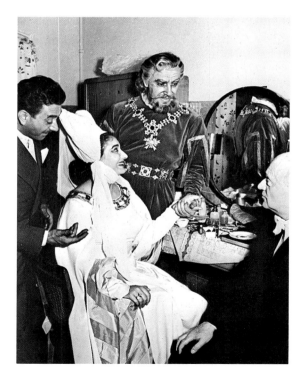

Another photo of historic value. The 1951 Vespri Siciliani in Florence, with conducting by Erich Kleiber (at right in the photo), and with **Maria Callas**, the baritone **Mascherini** (standing), and the tenor **Kokolios**. It was a performance of great interpretative importance, despite the numerous cuts in the score. (Historic Archives of the Teatro Comunale of Florence).

The legendary Armida *created in Florence in 1952 by* **Maria Callas**. *The Rossini opera proposed by Francesco Sicilia-ni, artistic director of the Florence May Festival and by Maestro Serafin, was greeted with general scepticism. Thanks to the extraordinary presence of the Greek artist, in striking vocal form, the choice fired the public's enthusiasm. Scenes and costumes by Alberto Savinio, conducted by Serafin, the performance featured tenors such as Filippeschi, Raimon-di and Albanese. All contributed to the triumphal and historical success of that evening. (Historic Archives of the Teatro Comunale of Florence).*

allowed her full control of the high register and super high register as well as an extremely precise and beautiful legato.

There has been much said about the precocious decline of Maria Callas: in truth the Greek artist had twenty years of fabulous career, having made her debut in *Cavalleria Rusticana* in Athens in 1938, and she possessed all her best vocal prerogatives until 1958, the year in which her real decline began. Her voice did not only suffer from her much famed diet; it was worn by the terribly stressful repertoire she had tackled for two decades. She lost the homogeneous quality of her voice and became ever more wobbly in the high register. However Callas's myth was not at all damaged by her decline. Her last *Norma* at the Paris Opera in May, 1965, and her triumphal concerts with Giuseppe Di Stefano in 1973 - 75 were acclaimed by delirious ovations, which shows that the public (more than some critics) had understood the greatness of this irreplaceable last diva.

The advent of Callas determined the reproposal of many belcanto operas which had been forgotten in the bottom drawer during the verismo boom, and a return to a more correct approach to interpretation.

Joan Sutherland: the Australian Nightingale

The foremost amongst Callas's successors was **Dame Joan Sutherland** (Sydney 1926). She was the centre of the rediscovery and renaissance of the great Baroque operatic repertory (with Handel in the lead) and divine in the protoromantic belcanto operas (Bellini, Donizetti).

Her debut was in *Dido and Aeneas* by Henry Purcell in 1947; but she was really launched in 1957 with a triumphal performance of Handel's *Alcina* at the London Opera Society. Sutherland's voice is not particularly attractive in timbre (if you exclude her radiant high register); but she is armed with an awe-inspiring technique — long breaths, tight trills of exceptional consistency, high notes (up to e''') of rare brilliance, a taste for variations and expressive modulations. These are characteristics that are ideal for roles such as Lucia, Amina, Gilda, Elvira in *Puritani*, Norma, Alcina, Lucrezia Borgia, and Semiramide, finally taken away from the chirpings of the coloratura sopranos and returned to the *soprano drammatico di agilità*.

Because of the importance of her voice, as well as her technique, Sutherland was able to perform Desdemona (Verdi's *Otello*), Eva in *The Mastersingers of Nuremberg*, and even Adriana

95

Maria Callas sings "Teneri figli" from Norma. The famous diet has already had its effect, giving the singer an enviable silhouette. We are in the second half of the fifties and Callas is already a living legend. During a procession for Carnival in Switzerland you could see dozens and dozens of people masquerading as Maria Callas. (Historic Archives of the Rome Opera Theatre. Photo: Reale).

Medea, 22nd June, 1955. An expression typical of **Callas**, a singer capable of revealing all the depth of a character with a look or a slight inflexion of the voice. (Historic Archives of the Rome Opera Theatre. Photo: Savio).

15th January, 1953. **Maria Callas** and **Francesco Albanese** together for Traviata. Few know that during a concert in Greece, in the forties, Maria Callas sang a passage from Otello by Verdi, and immediately after (prophetically anticipating the Rossini revival) she sang a scene from Rossini's Otello. The strange thing was that the young singer didn't perform in the Rossini work as Desdemona but as Otello. For the "Willow Song" by Verdi she wore a white dress, whilst for the part "en travesti" she wrapped herself in a large red cloak. (Historic Archives of the Rome Opera Theatre. Photo: Savio).

This is a historical photo. It depicts **Anton Dermota** during the interval of The Magic Flute at the Vienna Opera which went on stage on the 24th January, 1982. On that occasion Dermota sang the role of Tamino, which he had been singing for over thirty years, for the last time. (Photo G. Zerbes. Vienna).

On the preceding page: **Luciano Pavarotti**, without doubt the most famous tenor on the current world opera scene. Here he sings in Tosca with **Raina Kabaivanska**, at the Rome Opera Theatre, 1990.

Carreras yes or Carreras no? On one hand his passion and incomparable polish, on the other forced high notes and little interpretative imagination. The public is divided over the Spanish tenor as it was years ago over Di Stefano. In the photo are **José Carreras** and **Galia Savova** during Tosca at Ravenna, 1981.

Jaime Aragall is an elegant Don Carlos in the love duet with the Bulgarian soprano *Ghena Dimitrova*. (Photo Romano, Archives of the San Carlo Theatre of Naples).

Veriano Luchetti in one of his favourite roles: that of Macduff in Verdi's opera, Macbeth. *He has recently made his debut as Radames in* Aida *and made a great success as Don Alvaro in a* La Forza del Destino *with Sinopoli conducting. It seems clear that he has decided to orient himself in the* lirico-spinto *direction. (Photo L. Romano. Archives of the San Carlo Theatre, Naples).*

Werther's death. We
recognise **José
Carreras** and **Lucia
Valentini Terrani**.
(Photo: Calosso).

Viorica Cortez *(Carmen)*
and **Veriano Luchetti**
*(Don José) at the Arena
of Verona. (Photo:
Passerini).*

Rockwell Blake and *Leo Nucci* in Il Barbiere di Siviglia *at Modena. The American tenor always performs the difficult aria "Cessa di più resistere" in the finale, which is usually cut. (Photo: Arletti).*

Francisco Araiza in a 1985 Traviata in Houston.

Under the austere tunic of Ferrando in Donizetti's La Favorita, **Alfredo Kraus** sings the aria ''Spirto gentil'' which contains a famous, frightening high c″. However, as we well know, the tenor from the Canary Isles does not fear the top of the pentagram: we need only listen to how, even today, he launches his high c″ and d″'s with bravura.

Kraus, looking like Prince Charming from a fairy tale. Actually the elegance and composure of the famous tenor fears very few comparisons in our century.

The three great tenors — **Pavarotti**, **Carreras** and **Domingo** — on stage together in a concert destined to make history in the annals of opera; at the Terme di Caracalla in Rome, July 1990 (Photo C.M. Falsini).

Mario Del Monaco had the habit of designing his own magnificent costumes for Otello. He was also known for his love of fur coats, luxury cars, and beautiful women. A real ''divo''.

There is no doubt about **Placido Domingo**'s ability as an actor, nor his complete command of the stage. He is an artist of rare musicality and intelligence; but he has never resolved his technical problems. Here we see him in his costume for Andrea Chénier during a production at Vienna in May, 1981.

Nicola Martinucci (Calaf)
and *Cecilia Gasdia* (Liù) in
Verona, *during one of the
many* Turandot *performances
of the Italian tenor. Martinucci
is known for his penetrating
voice and his reliability in
some of the most difficult
repertory. (Photo: G.
Passerini).*

Giuseppe Giacomini as Dick
Johnson in The Girl of the
Golden West. *After a difficult
beginning and an inconsistent
rendering, Giacomini has
gained a position as one of
the best* spinto *tenors of his
generation. (Photo: De Rota).*

Mario Del Monaco as
*Andrea Chénier.
(Photo: Sedqe Le
Blanq).*

*A scene from the film of
Otello, produced by Canon,
with the direction of Zeffirelli.
Otello (**Domingo**) embraces
Desdemona (**Katia
Ricciarelli**) with tenderness
during the duet "Già nella
notte densa". (Photo:
P. Ronald).*

Peter Dvorsky as
*Edgardo in a film version
of Lucia di Lammermoor
in 1983. The
Czechoslovakian tenor has
distinguished himself over
the last years as an
excellent interpreter of lyric
roles, with a few
excursions into lirico-spinto
parts. (Manon Lescaut,
Adriana Lecouvreur, and
even Forza del Destino
and Aida).*

Placido Domingo during the "Esultate". Domingo has removed the verist encrustations that had covered the difficult part of the Moor for over a century, and high-lighted the lyrical aspect. However the Spanish tenor lacks security in the high notes — the ace card for any self-respecting Otello. (Otello. Direction, F. Zeffirelli; Production, Canon. Photo: P. Ronald).

Placido Domingo receives an ovation at the Arena of Verona at the end of Turandot. To the left of the photo is the conductor Patanè. (Photo: G. Passerini).

Dallas, 1982. **Ruth Welting** in the ''Mad Scene'' of Lucia di Lammermoor. *(Photo: H. Kuper).*

Graziella Sciutti *in the Rossini role of Donna Fiorilla in Turco in Italia. (Giandonato Crico Collection).*

Raina Kabaivanska *in* Butterfly; *a favourite opera of the Bulgarian singer, who, however, always states that the labels of Verist Singer or Puccini Singer are too limiting. In her repertory, in fact, are* Fausta *by Donizetti, Spontini's* La Vestale, *and Verdi's* I Vespri Siciliani.

110

The beautiful **Katia Ricciarelli** (Desdemona) in the second act of the film, Otello, directed by Franco Zeffirelli and produced by Cannon.

Sparkling eyes, silk ribboned bonnet, parasol: **Editha Gruberova** is an ideal Zerbinetta, performing often in Vienna and Salzburg. In the Mozart arias she reaches g‴, singing the highest notes without any apparent effort.

Gruberova is an astral Queen of the Night in a Magic Flute at Vienna in 1977.

The exquisite, mature femininity of **Sena Jurinac**, for over thirty-five years a mainstay of the Vienna Opera (Staatsoper). This is a portrait of her in one of the roles played in her mature years - the Marschallin in Der Rosenkavalier. (Photo: Fayer).

The ritual of the autograph: **Gwyneth Jones**, a Wagner and Strauss singer of great esteem, photographed in her dressing room after a concert at the RAI in Rome. (Photo: Giandonato Crico).

After more than forty years of career, **Leonie Rysanek** is still an extraordinary interpreter of dramatic roles. The photo portrays her in the role of Chrysothemis in Richard Strauss' opera Elektra. Rysanek sang the main role for a film version, whilst recently she has also sung Clytemnestra. (Photo: Dresse).

Tosca is the character most closely identified with **Raina Kabaivanska**. She endows this role with a complete emotional participation so irresistible that the public bursts into spontaneous applause even after a simple phrase in Act I such as ''Io piango'' (I cry). In Act II Raina renders ''Vissi d'arte'' in the authentic belcanto tradition, producing extraordinary emotional shadings without even glancing at the orchestra conductor.

Lella Cuberli, an excellent interpreter, at the side of **Marilyn Horne** in Handel's Orlando at La Fenice Theatre, Venice, in 1985. Miss Cuberli has always shown a stylistic authority and phrasing which have made her indispensable in the belcanto renaissance (operas by Handel, Rossini, the comic Neapolitan works, and even Bellini and Donizetti). (Historic Archives of La Fenice Theatre of Venice).

At the end of her recital at the Teatro Malibran at Venice in 1981 **Joan Sutherland** smiles at the well-deserved applause. The first lessons of the great soprano were with her mother, an ex-mezzo who had studied with a student of Matilde Marchesi, legendary teacher of Melba, Eames and Calvé. (Giandonato Crico Collection).

Beverly Sills, an elegant Norina in Don Pasquale by Donizetti. When she retired from the stage in 1980, she

had over seventy different roles in her repertoire, which she performed using an almost exaggerated belcanto style. Her "madness" in Lucia was a fireworks display, which found a worthy competitor only in Joan Sutherland. The Assedio di Corinto at an excited La Scala in 1969 is considered a mile-stone in the history of Rossini interpretations. As for the mythical Roberto Devereux by Donizetti at the New York City Opera, the audience were more than once on their feet during the performance, giving Sills an ovation which few of her predecessors have enjoyed. (Metropolitan Opera Guild. Collection Oreste Musella).

*After the tension of the performance **Lucia Popp** has a happy smile for her admirers. A Mozart and Strauss specialist, she is particularly loved by the Vienna Opera public. (Photo: Giandonato Crico).*

__Kiri Te Kanawa__ in one of her most famous roles; Arabella, by Richard Strauss. The nickname "Arabellissima" was coined for Lisa Della Casa but has been revived to refer to Kiri (Giandonato Crico Collection).

The unmatched elegance of __Elizabeth Schwarzkopf__ in the role of the Countess in Capriccio by Richard Strauss. (Photo: Fayer, Vienna).

Montserrat Caballé and **José Carreras** in Tosca, Ravenna, 1981.

A famous Lucia: **June Anderson**, who is also successfully involved in the revival of Rossini's serious operas. (Photo: Tabocchin).

On the opposite page: **Ghena Dimitrova** during a recent Turandot presented at the San Carlo Opera in Naples. (Historic Archives of the San Carlo Theatre, Naples).

Eva Marton in the candid gown of Brünnhilde, a role she dominates with enormous security. Besides her Wagnerian and Strauss repertoire, Marton sings many Puccini and verist roles. (Giandonato Crico Collection).

Agnes Baltsa and **Thomas Allen** in Il Barbiere di Siviglia. (Photo: C. Barda).

Renato Bruson with **Jeanine Altmeyer** in Verdi's Macbeth-Bruson's favourite role. It is the scene of the appearance of Banquo's ghost. (Historic Archives of the San Carlo Theatre of Naples. Photo: L. Romano).

Leyla Gencer looking extremely elegant in her costume for the opera Prova di un'Opera Seria *by Gnecco, performed at La Fenice in Venice together with the tenor* Luis Alva. *It was her last operatic appearance. It is an opera well-suited to Gencer, an artist both ironic and intelligent, ever ready to criticize her fellow singers, even the most famous. (Historic Archives of La Fenice Theatre, Venice).*

Among the many roles interpreted by Caballé *there is also* Armida *by Gluck, an opera requiring an enormous commitment in acting and in expressive declamation.*

119

The Hungarian soprano, **Eva Marton**, as Turandot. She and the Bulgarian soprano **Ghena Dimitrova** *are the best interpreters of this role. (Oreste Musella Collection).*

Tosca lost in prayer. **Montserrat Caballé** *particularly loves this character, even if her vocal style is far from that required for the verist repertory. Her "Vissi d'arte", for example, sung completely in a heavenly pianissimo, lacks the internal fire of Tebaldi, Callas, Olivero and Kabaivanska.*

Sesto Bruscantini (Falstaff) amiably courts **Raina Kabaivanska** (Alice) during a recent staging of the Verdi masterpiece in Naples. Despite his intelligent and refined interpretation of the chubby knight, the baritone has not had many opportunities to perform it. (Historic Archives of the San Carlo Theatre of Naples. Photo: L. Romano).

The role of Ford in Falstaff allies perfectly with the vocality of **Leo Nucci**. After a long apprenticeship, the likeable singer is now established world-wide. (Historic Archives of the San Carlo Opera Theatre of Naples. Photo: L. Romano).

The favourite opera of **Lucia Valentini-Terrani** is Cenerentola, performed in every great opera theatre of the world. One of the most beautiful and amusing productions is that by Ponelle, well known for the last twenty years. (Historic Archives of the Teatro Comunale of Bologna).

*An intensely dramatic expression of **Fiorenza Cossotto** in her role of Azucena, sung for over twenty-five years in all the most important theatres. (Photo: A. Tabocchini).*

*Isabella (**Marilyn Horne**) and her "boys" in L'Italiana in Algeri by Rossini, for years her favourite role. (Historic Archives of La Fenice Theatre, Venice. Photo: G. Arici and M.E. Smith).*

*An attitude which reveals the determination of **Marilyn Horne** in "pants" roles. Here she is shown in Handel's Orlando, revived in Venice in 1985. (Historic Archives of La Fenice Theatre, Venice. Photo: G. Arici and M.E. Smith).*

Sherrill Milnes in Simon Boccanegra, *one of his most applauded characterisations at the Metropolitan Opera.*

Piero Cappuccilli sings Nabucco at the Teatro Ducale at Parma, the Regio being closed for restoration. Almost all this Trieste baritone's greatest colleagues recognise that he is a master of breathing technique. (Historic Archives of the Teatro Regio of Parma. Photo: Montacchini).

Giuseppe Taddei: Thanks to his strong ties with and affection for Austria and his interpretative gifts, Taddei has linked his name to many, many Mozart performances, thus holding high the Italian flag in this repertory, with the help of Sesto Bruscantini and Rolando Panerai.

125

Cecilia Bartoli (Rosina) and **Alfonso Antoniozzi** (Don Bartolo) in Il Barbiere di Siviglia. (Photo: A. Arletti).

A group photo of Italiana in Algeri *put on at Venice: from the right* **Domenico Trimarchi** *(Taddeo),* **Samuel Ramey** *(Mustafà) and* **Marilyn Horne** *(Isabella). (Historic Archives of La Fenice Theatre, Venice. Photo: G. Arici and M.E. Smith).*

The 1982-83 season. It is the climax of Semiramide, *by Rossini: an opera which was hardly ever performed, it was monopolised by the tandem Sutherland-Horne; but it is now more popular than Bohème, and within the competence of all the best belcanto singers of today. In the photo we can see* **Lucia Valentini-Terrani** *whilst she is being crowned at the end of the opera. (Historic Archives of the Teatro Verdi of Trieste).*

Another image from Don Quichotte *by Massenet. Beside **Raimondi**, we see Dulcinea, the mezzo-soprano **Margarita Zimmermann**. (Historic Archives of La Fenice Theatre, Venice. Photo: G. Arici and M.E. Smith).*

***Enzo Dara** sings "Miei rampolli femminini" in* Cenerentola *(Rossini). His execution of the aria "Sia qualunque delle figlie" is almost unique for his verbal precision and speed. (Historic Archives of the Teatro Comunale of Bologna).*

Lecouvreur. On recordings she has created a belcanto style *Trovatore*, an astral *Turandot*, and a *Suor Angelica* that is perhaps a little too cold and antiseptic.

Forty years after her debut, Sutherland still preserved an enviable vocal form, to the point of being able to keep almost all of her signature roles in her repertoire (from *Norma* to *Semiramide*), often performing with Marilyn Horne at her side. In October 1990, Sutherland retired from the stage with a final series of performances of *Les Huguenots* in Sydney, where she was farewelled with interminable ovations.

Queen Leyla

Leyla Gencer (Istanbul 1928) was another belcanto specialist, interpreting many important Donizetti operas (*Roberto Devereux, Caterina Cornaro, Maria Stuarda, Belisario*, and *Les Martyrs*); she had a wide repertoire, including Gilda, Lucia, Violetta, Elvira, Lucrezia in *I Due Foscari*, Aida, Leonora (*Trovatore* and *Forza del Destino*), Elisabetta (by Rossini), Liù, Suor Angelica,

Joan Sutherland.

The young **Sutherland** in the costume of the sorceress, Alcina. Handel's opera was performed in Venice during the 1959-60 season. Due to her particular singing technique, the Australian artist succeeds in obtaining mysterious echo effects in the difficult aria ''Tornami a vagheggiar''. (Historic Archives of La Fenice Theatre, Venice).

Odabella, Donna Anna, and many, many others, including her satanic Lady Macbeth.

Her best years were from 1950 to 1970, years in which she could reach high e''' flat, alternate different shadings, hold precious *filatura*, overcome with ease bravura variations, use a phrasing that had a great sense of text and dramatic expression. An exceptional example is her furious ''Figlia impura di Bolena'' in *Maria Stuarda*. These characteristics belonged to a voice which was neither powerful nor beautiful in the classical sense, but rendered flexible by constant study. In recent years Gencer has mainly dedicated herself to concert activity, very successfully. There have been many regrets about the injustice of the recording market since her great performances are not on discs. Many memorable Gencer evenings have, however, been preserved on pirate recordings, and for this we must be very grateful.

The duet Norma - Adalgisa in the second act of Bellini's opera. Singing are the soprano **Joan Sutherland** and the mezzo soprano **Margareta Elkins**. In the role of the Druid priestess Sutherland has restored a belcanto of absolute purity typical of nineteenth century prima-donnas. (Archives of the Australian Opera. Photo: W. Mosely).

"Or tutti sorgete, ministri infernali". A demonic Lady Macbeth, **Leyla Gencer** has represented the difficult Verdi character better than any other soprano since Callas. The photo comes from a performance on 8 April, 1969 at the Rome Opera, with Bruno Bartoletti conducting and De Lullio directing; scenes by Pizzi. (Historic Archives of the Rome Opera Theatre).

We are in her dressing room at the Metropolitan Opera in 1964 and **Joan Sutherland** is preparing for Lucia di Lammermoor, an opera of which she has been the undisputed star for over twenty-five years. (Photo: Ermete Marzoni).

Montserrat Caballé's Silver Song

Montserrat Caballé (Barcelona 1933) is on a level similar to that of Gencer; but not identical. The rare polish and the clear timbre, the pearly glow of her *pianissimi*, and her light and delicate emission make her singing ideal for Bellini and Donizetti, where estatic and dreamy passages dominate the score. For such a sweet and seductive timbre the Verdi and Verist repertory should be impossible: yet, thanks to her perfect technique, the Spanish singer performs right, left, and centre the roles of *Tosca, Adriana Lecouvreur, Forza del Destino, Bohème,* and even *Turandot* (the title role), giving us unforgettable moments (let us recall the *messa di voce* at the beginning of Leonora's aria "Pace, pace, mio Dio" and the amazing abstraction of "Poveri fiori" in *Adriana*, a magic string of *filato* notes). Nevertheless, she remains fundamentally estranged from the dramatic character of these roles.

In Rossini and Handel, which she often performs (*Semiramide, Julius Caesar*), we find the advantages of a fast vocalisation and an extremely sound technical backing for every kind of embellishment; but we also find her limited by a singing technique which is too involved in the beautiful sound of the *pianissimo* it is producing. Caballé really abuses them. To eliminate the *agilità di forza* and replace it with vocal acrobatics performed in *mezzavoce* or in falsetto means denying the composer his vocal style. We can say that Caballé's best years were from 1956 until 1976, and that her most unforgettable performances were tied to the proto-romantics: *Lucrezia Borgia, Roberto Devereux,* and above all *Maria Stuarda* by Donizetti. Who could forget her performances in Rome in 1970? And she was, of course, a great Norma - it will be difficult to equal her open-air rendering at the Festival of Orange in 1973.

After 1976 a marked decline began: her high notes became metallic; she no longer enunciat-

January 1982, after Liù, **Caballé** *attempted the perilous role of Turandot, presenting a credible character, thanks to her excellent technique and her interpretative intelligence. (Archives of L'Opéra of Nice).*

"Questo è il bacio di Tosca!" **Caballé** *has just plunged a knife into the unfortunate Scarpia (the baritone* **Juan Pons**) *during a performance in April, 1980. The Spanish soprano is very much appreciated in France. (Archives of L'Opéra of Nice).*

A fairy-tale Lucia with **Renata Scotto, Renato Bruson** (Enrico) and **Luciano Pavarotti** (Edgardo). The orchestra was conducted by Bruno Bartoletti; the director was Aldo Vassallo; scenes and costumes by Franco Zeffirelli. It was a production of April, 1968. The photo shows a moment during the famous sextet: "Chi mi frena". (Historic Archives of the Teatro Massimo of Palermo. Photo: Allotta).

ed the words in the difficult passages; she abused *pianissimo* in the high register; and she took blatent refuge in *filatura* and extremely long breaths to save her skin.

What is more, Caballé has never excelled in artistic discipline, often skipping rehearsals and forgetting (or changing) the words. (What a mess she made of that *Barbiere* in Nice in 1980).

Side by side with her operatic work the Spanish soprano has a noteworthy concert activity, with extraordinary results in Richard Strauss Lieder.

After the Callas comet, the incarnation of the *soprano drammatico di agilità* was **Renata Scotto** (Savona 1934). She started in 1952 in *Traviata* and is still active in all the major theatres, in a wide repertory which has, from her original parts in *Lucia, Sonnambula, Rigoletto,* and *Elisir d'Amore,* extended gradually to *Norma, Ballo in Maschera, Tosca, Macbeth, Nabucco* and *Manon Lescaut,* with results which have been sometimes questionable to say the least. The most important factor in Scotto's vocality is her extreme stylistic correctness, her ability to find the right colour for every phrase, the correct expressive shading. In addition to this virtue, the Italian artist adds a solid technical support which allows her to use trills and fluid vocalising, intense *mezzavoci,* and an extension reaching to high e'''flat (even though it is not securely launched).

These gifts remained almost intact until halfway through the seventies when her vocal organ began to suffer from her far too ambitious repertoire. The high register paid the greatest price.

It became wobbly and screeching, whilst her characterisations became ever more refined (let us remember her wonderful Elena in *Vespri Siciliani* at the Florence May Festival in 1978, or

Renata Scotto sings Sonnambula *in Rome in 1960. One of her great passions is to put herself in spiritual contact with the great divas of the past, such as Giuditta Pasta and Maria Malibran, perhaps with the secret intent of receiving some precious advice from them. (Historic Archives of the Rome Opera Theatre. Photo: Savio).*

December, 1968. A beautiful edition of La Straniera *by Bellini on stage, sung by* **Renata Scotto** *(centre),* **Renato Cioni** *(left), and the baritone* **Domenico Trimarchi** *(right). (Historic Archives of the Teatro Massimo of Palermo. Photo: Allotta).*

Renata Scotto *and* **Alberto Rinaldi** *(Sharpless) — a baritone valid in the Rossini and eighteenth century repertory — in Puccini's* Butterfly, *in a 1975 production. Scotto is in open argument with the Italian opera theatres, which are guilty of having bad organisation and a lack of respect for artists; so she almost always sings elsewhere, especially at the Metropolitan in New York, where she has performed in an impressive variety of roles. (Historic Archives of the Rome Opera Theatre).*

Beverly Sills as Maria Stuarda, one of the many belcanto works she helped revive internationally.

her *Manon Lescaut* at the Metropolitan with Domingo, sung with great passion but without exaggerations).

Another three sopranos rightly belong to the list of the truly great belcanto singers. All three are American. The first is **Beverly Sills** (Brooklyn, New York 1929), active between 1946 and 1981 in a wide repertory that saw her triumph in *Lucia, Traviata, Rigoletto, Puritani*, and *Thaïs*, until she crowned her successes with a triumphal *Assedio di Corinto* by Rossini at La Scala in 1969. Sills' vocal technique originates from the mythical school of Mathilde Marchesi, one of the most famous teachers at the turn of the century. It is a vocality which privileges an intricate coloratura, pyro-technics, tight trilling, and spectacular *cadenze* whilst timbre and homogenity go in second place. This gave rise to her noted virtuoso ability, paid for by a lack of vocal beauty. Sill's renderings were, therefore, technically masterful (let's not forget her recording of *Lucia* with Schippers); but she lacked expressiveness (her last awful *Traviatas* in America whilst she was in full decline are proof enough).

Sills can be considered the heir of Lily Pons for her ease in the coloratura passages and her prodigious technique.

In the romantic, and in particular, in the Rossini repertory, the top today is represented by **June Anderson** and **Lella Cuberli** (Austin, Texas 1945): both have well educated voices, knowledgeably managed, ideal for operas such as *Semiramide* or *Turco in Italia*.

Anderson resembles Joan Sutherland in ap-

pearance and reminds us somewhat of her older colleague in her inflexions and virtuoso fantasy. Amongst her favourite roles there are Lucia, Amina and Violetta. Cuberli does not dare so much. Her repertory concentrates on some Rossini parts, baroque compositions, and an intelligent interpretation of Neapolitan comic opera, best seen at Martina Franca, where the annual festival of the Valley d'Itria is held. She is very good in Mozart and Handel.

The gifted but unlucky **Anita Cerquetti** (Montecosaro, Macerata 1931) could be called the last authentic Verdi soprano considering the beauty of her timbre, her pure emission, and her exceptional musicality. She was the ideal Amelia in *Ballo in Maschera*, Elena in *Vespri Siciliani*, and *Aida*; but she was also able to render the vocal strength of Norma and Abigaille almost perfectly.

The Callas Imitators

In the great after-wave created by Maria Callas, numerous copies of the original have emerged, more or less successful - depending on the individual. They are sure that they can repeat their idol's greatness and her ever so personal technique. Thus from 1965 until today we have had to put up with a quarter of a century of flagrant imitation. As always happens, the "copy-cats" tend to repeat the defects rather than the good qualities, accentuating the former pitifully.

We will mention a few of the most obvious cases. Let us begin with **Elena Suliotis** (Athens 1943) who managed to seem like a possible successor to "La Divina" for a few years. However, chronic hay-fever, shakey nerves, a lack of technique, over-work, and a wrong choice of repertoire made a lethal cocktail which brought her good natural talent to a very premature decline. Another who did not manage to escape from an early decline is **Teresa Stratas** (Toronto, Canada 1938), a diva at the Metropolitan and in the German theatres for many years. She is acclaimed as Violetta (which she played also in Zeffirelli's film opera of *Traviata*), Mimì, Lulu (Berg), and *Suor Angelica*. **Silvia Sass** (Budapest 1951) has been harsh in the high register and "walked before crawling" after a few successes at the beginning of her career.

Currently we have: **Lucia Aliberti** with her thickened sounds and "Callasian" movements, all of which ruin her singing; the delicate **Cecilia Gasdia** (Verona 1959), more correct and individual in her emission but with obvious technical problems; and the young **Maria Dragoni** who has caught, a rampant case of "Callasitis" which compromises her natural talent.

Some Other Famous Sopranos

After our chapter dedicated to the greatest sopranos of this century we wish to add this table in which we will include the names of other sopranos worthy of being mentioned. Beside each name we have included the main titles in her repertory and a brief note on her vocal characteristics and career.

NAME	BASIC REPERTORY	REMARKS
Ackté, Aïno (1876-1944) Dramatic.	Wagner, Strauss	A singing actress of strong temperament, a luminous and powerful voice. She wrote an opera libretto and two autobiographies (1925, 1935).
Augér, Arleen (1939) Coloratura.	Handel, Mozart, Oratorio and Cantatas.	Flexible, musical, clear and penetrating timbre.
Baillie, Dame Isobel (1895-1983) Lyric.	Oratorio, Cantatas, Lieder, and Chamber songs.	One of the most important English recital singers of the century. She wrote an autobiography in 1982.
Benackova, Gabriela (1947) *Lirico spinto.*	Smetana, Dvorak, Puccini.	Lovely vocal colour, well projectd. A sensitive interpreter of the late Romantic and Verist repertory.
Collier, Marie (1926-1971) *Lirico spinto.*	Tosca, Butterfly, Jenufa, contemporary operas.	One of the best and most moving actresses of the opera stage; she was the first Hecuba in *King Priam* by Tippett.
Cruz-Romo, Gilda (1940) *Lirico spinto.*	*Aida, Forza del Destino, Ernani, Luisa Miller, Otello.*	Good natural means, good phrasing, excellent stage presence, however with some technical difficulties and a limited extension in the high register.
Curtin, Phyllis (C. Smith, 1922) Light lyric.	Mozart, contemporary composers.	A refined and sensitive Mozart singer and of many works of this century.
Dobbs, Mattiwlda (1925) Coloratura.	Lucia, Rosina, Gilda, Olympia.	One of the first black singers to undertake a splendid international career.
Dvorakova, Ludmila (1923) *Lirico spinto.*	Wagner, Strauss, Smetana, Dvorak.	A good Wagner interpreter although more for her imposing presence on stage than for her vocal virtues.
Gayer, Catherine (1937) Coloratura.	Verdi, Donizetti, contemporary operas.	Flexible and extended voice, pleasant scenic presence; she was in the inaugural performances of *Intolleranza*, by Nono, *Ulisse*, by Dallapiccola, and several other operas of this century.
Goltz, Christel (1912) Dramatic.	Wagner, Strauss, contemporary operas.	Extraordinary power and extension, intense actress. First interpreter of *Antigonae* by Orff, and of *Penelope* by Liebermann.
Gomez, Jill (1942) Lyric.	Mozart, English and Spanish opera, contemporary works.	A well-prepared musician with a notable stage talent.
Harwood, Elizabeth (1938-1990) Light lyric.	Mozart, Musetta in *Bohème*, operetta by Lehár and Johan Strauss.	She had a brilliant start, with world-wide success and many recordings; but technical problems and too much work unfortunately cut her story short.
Hidalgo, Elvira de (1892-1980) Coloratura.	Gilda, Rosina, Lucia, Amina, Norina.	Liberty style nightingale for the first quarter of the century; she was an appreciated teacher. Her most famous student was Maria Callas.
Kniplova, Nadezda (N. Pokorna, 1932). *Lirico spinto.*	Wagner, Strauss, Smetana, Dvorak.	An intense dramatic actress, incisive voice.
Kubiak, Teresa (1937) *Lirico spinto.*	Puccini, Mussorgsky, Tchaikovsky.	One of the most interesting artists to come from Poland during this century. A voice of a lovely colour. Excellent on stage.

Kupper, Annelies (1906-1988) Lyric.	Mozart, C.M. von Weber, contemporary works.	A specialist in the role of the countess in *The Marriage of Figaro*; first interpreter in 1950 of *Die Liebe der Danae* by Richard Strauss.
Lazlo, Magda (1919) Lyric.	Kodaly, Bartok, contemporary operas.	She was the first to perform Cressida in *Troilus and Cressida* by Walton, and *Il Prigioniero* by Dallapiccola.
Lear, Evelyn (E. Schulman; 1928) *Lirico spinto*.	Mozart, Strauss, Berg, contemporary operas.	A refined and intelligent interpreter, with wide interests and catholic tastes. Wife of the baritone Thomas Stewart.
Lenya, Lotte (Karoline Whilhelmine Blamauer; 1898-1981) Light lyric.	Weill.	A singer-actress of great talent. She married Kurt Weill and became the sublime interpreter of his music. She was the first Jenny in *Die Dreigroschenoper*, and Anna in *Die Sieben Todsünden*.
Lindholm, Berit (B. Jonsson; 1934) Dramatic.	Wagner, Strauss.	One of the most important Wagner singers of the Seventies.
Lott, Felicity (1947) Lyric.	Mozart, Strauss, French operas, Lieder.	One of the most refined singers. Specialist in the role of the Mozart Countess and in *Arabella*. Excellent Lieder singer.
Martin, Janis (1939) *Lirico spinto*.	Wagner, Berg.	She started singing as a soprano in 1971 after having been a mezzo. However she always had some problems in the very high register.
Masterson, Valerie (1937) Light lyric.	Handel, Mozart, English operetta, contemporary operas.	A well prepared musician with a lovely vocal colour. Excellent in the operas of Benjamin Britten.
Mastilović, Danica (1933) Dramatic.	*Turandot*, Brünnhilde, *Elektra, Salome*.	One of the most powerful and voluminous voices ever heard in a theatre. Her intonation and expressive variety were not perfect, however.
Mesplé, Mady (1931) Light lyric.	French operas and operettas. Chamber music repertory.	A small voice with a vibrato ressembling a goat's bleat; but she was a very musical and much appreciated singer; extremely good in French operetta.
Migenes-Johnson, Julia (1945) Lyric.	American Music Halls, Concerts.	Became famous with the Rosi film of *Carmen* in 1984. Her voice is nothing special but she is a superb actress.
Nebbett, Carol (1946) *Lirico spinto*.	Contemporary opera. Puccini.	Specialist in the role of Minnie (*Girl of the Golden West*). A singer-actress of exceptional natural gifts.
Neway, Patricia (1919) *Lirico spinto*.	Contemporary operas.	A notable dramatic talent. The first interpreter of *The Consul* and of *Maria Golovin*, both by Menotti.
Pilarczyk, Helga (1925) *Lirico spinto*.	Contemporary operas.	A great interpreter of operas of this century: Berg, Schönberg, Henze, Křenek.
Robin, Mado (1918-1960) Coloratura.	Gilda, Lucia, Amina, Lakmé, Olympia, Queen of the Night.	The highest voice which has ever existed, capable of reaching high d'''' flat!
Slobodskaia, Ode (1888-1970) Lyric.	Tchaikovsky, Glinka, Mussorgsky, Stravinsky.	The first performer of *Mavra* by Stravinsky. She lived for many years in London where she was also noted as a great star of operetta.
Svobodová-Janků, Hana (1940) Dramatic.	*Turandot*, Brünnhilde, *Elektra*, Czechoslovakian operas.	A voice of steel, with a beautiful low register.
Tinsley, Pauline (1928) *Lirico spinto*.	*Macbeth, Nabucco, Turandot*.	A singer who was under-valued by the critics but who possessed a voice of power, vibrant in the high register.
Vaness, Carol (1952) Lyric.	Mozart, Gluck, Verdi.	A favourite of Riccardo Muti, she is a discreet interpreter of Donna Anna, Elettra in *Idomeneo*, but with precise limits of extension.

Varady, Julia (1941) *Lirico spinto*.	Mozart, Verdi, Strauss, contemporary operas.	An extended voice of a fine colour, used with intelligence and good taste. She married the baritone Dietrich Fischer-Dieskau.
Vaughan, Elizabeth (1936) *Lirico spinto*.	Verdi, Puccini.	An appreciated interpreter of *Madama Butterfly* in Anglo-Saxon countries.
Vyvyan, Jennifer (1925-1974) Lyric.	Handel, Britten.	Among the most refined of English singers; a favourite of Benjamin Britten.
Watson, Claire (C. Mc Lamore, 1927-1986) Lyric.	Mozart, Strauss.	A voice with lovely timbre, supported by an excellent technique, and by an intense acting skill.
Watson, Lillian Light lyric.	Mozart, English and German operettas.	A specialist in the roles of the soubrette.

John Charles Thomas *as Germont in Verdi's* La Traviata.

THE BARITONES

The Baritone Voice: Extension and Phonation

The extension of a typical baritone voice goes from G or G flat up to a′. Of course these limits can be surpassed both in the low notes and in the high notes; Benvenuto Franci, and (more recently) Sherrill Milnes, Leo Nucci, and Piero Cappuccilli are all baritones who have a high c″ in their range.

A correct baritone phonation requires extended chest resonances up to c′, then passing into head resonances: to achieve this technique a singer must in part renounce artificially darkened sound and acquire some decidedly tenorlike inflexions and colourings. It is for this reason that many baritones over the last decades have considered the old rules of phonation almost a *diminutio*, preferring to push their chest voice up to e′, for this increases vocal power and volume; but the high notes become harsher and forced, and the *mezzavoce* becomes difficult.

Baritone Categories in the Twentieth Century

Observing the wide range of characteristics in the baritone voice in this century we can make the following divisions: the Verdi baritone (both lyric and dramatic), with a clear and vibrant timbre, sufficiently extended and agile voice, soft and delicate in moments of pathos, and incisive in the dramatic passages; the baritone *vilain* — the "bad guy" of the verist repertory (Alfio, Scarpia, Tonio), who has a malevolent, menacing sound; the baritone *grand seigneur* (the German *Kavalierbariton*), noble and refined, suited to the parts of kings and emperors in Bellini, Donizetti, the early Verdi (Don Carlo in *Ernani*) and Richard Strauss (the Count in *Capriccio*); the *Heldenbariton* in Wagner's operas (Telramund in *Lohengrin*, Kurwenal in *Tristan and Isolde*, Gunther in *Götterdammerung* has a powerful and robust voice; the *Spielbariton* or the *Buffo*, is the comic element with a clear and flexible voice suited to interpret parts such as Papageno, Figaro, Dandini, and all the other comic roles in the eighteenth and nineteenth century opera which were once upon a time written for the basses or for the *concordant*.

THE VERDI BARITONES IN THE NINETEEN HUNDREDS

We open this glorious series with the great **Giuseppe Kaschmann** (Lussimpiccolo, Istria 1850 - Rome 1925) who had an extraordinarily long and much-honoured career. Thanks to a top school of singing applied to a rich, harmonic timbre (which was spoiled only by an annoying *vibrato stretto*) and to a natural musicality, he was able to sing an extremely wide repertoire: from *La Favorita* (in which he made his debut in 1876 at Turin) to *Don Carlos*, *Lucia* and *Forza del Destino*, distinguishing himself from 1892 on as a worthy Wagnerian performer. He was the only Italian to be admitted into the Bayreuth "temple".

His career ended in 1921, with Cimarosa's opera *Le Astuzie Femminili* in Rome. During the last years Kaschmann had dedicated himself to comic opera, producing a fantastic Don Bartolo (*Barbiere*) and Don Pasquale.

In Kaschmann's case, as with so many other singers from 1900 - 1920, the recordings we have contradict everything his contemporary critics claimed for him. In his recording of "Oh de' ver-d'anni miei", made when he was just over fifty,

Giuseppe Kaschmann in a photo taken on Ist July, 1892, when he interpreted Amfortas in Parsifal in Bayreuth. He was present at the opening of the Opera Theatre in Zagreb (1870, Mislav by Zajc) and the inauguration of the Metropolitan of New York (1883, Lucia). (Historic Archives of the Rome Opera Theatre).

formed many of these works with Caruso at the Met.

Titta Ruffo (whose real name was Ruffo Titta, Pisa 1877 - Florence 1953) exhibited a noteworthy vocal power, using his facial cavities to the utmost to make his high notes more penetrating. (His high g''s and a''s thundered across auditoriums, enthusing the public).

His debut took place in Rome, as the Herald in *Lohengrin*; but soon the ideal parts for this great singer became Rigoletto, Scarpia, the Conte di Luna, Figaro, Renato in *Ballo in Maschera*, Gérard, and Hamlet. It was in this last opera, by Thomas, especially in the "Toast", that he reached a perfect identification with his character. At the end of the aria, Ruffo was in the habit of adding a long *cadenza* which he would perform all in one breath. Note after note would slide across the pentagram, from low to high, with such penetrating impetus that the listener's head would spin.

In the long run, however, those unnatural nasal sounds present in every one of his performances robbed Ruffo's voice of its stylistic qualities and led to a precocious decline.

He retired in 1931, performing *Tosca* and *Hamlet* in Buenos Aires; but at this point the

the singing appears tremulous and anti-musical.

A penetrating voice and precision of phrasing were the principal features of **Pasquale Amato** (Naples 1878 - New York 1942). He was an authentic Verdi champion! He made his debut in his native city playing Germont in *Traviata* in 1900, and from then on Verdi was his favourite composer, followed by some of the most prominent Verists. His phrasing was varied and eloquent in *Rigoletto*, *Falstaff*, *Ballo in Maschera*, *Tosca*, *Gioconda*, and *Pagliacci*. In these operas he showed an almost tenor-like extension in the high notes and a soft, smooth emission worthy of the best belcanto traditions. What is more, he was a formidable actor, dominating the stage completely. About 1920 a certain tiredness could be heard in his voice, partly caused by a delicate kidney operation; but Amato continued to sing until 1933 - 34. His last performance took place at the Chicago Opera.

Antonio Scotti (Sarno, Naples 1866 - 1936) had authentic vocal and acting skills. He was active from 1889, when he made his debut in Spontini's *Vestale*, until 1933, when he sang for the last time at the Metropolitan. He was a greater actor than singer; but his technique always allowed him to respect the dynamics desired by the composers, from feather-like *pianissimi* to his fluid *legato*. Amongst his best operas there were *Ernani*, *Faust*, *Carmen*, *Falstaff*, *Aida*, *Don Giovanni*, and *Tosca*. He per-

*Very popular in the United States, **Pasquale Amato** taught from 1935 on at the University of Louisiana, gaining the esteem and affection of many students. (Historic Archives of the Rome Opera Theatre).*

140

Antonio Scotti, in Mozart's Don Giovanni. Whether in London or at New York's Metropolitan, he was the first to perform many important baritone roles, among them Scarpia and Sharpless.

terpreters of the time who was able to respect what was written by the composers without adding exaggerations; **Eugenio Giraldoni** (Marseille 1871 - Helsinki 1924), the first Scarpia at Rome and at La Scala, famous as Gérard in *Andrea Chénier*; **Enrico Nani** (Rome 1873 - 1940), an excellent Nabucco; **Mario Basiola** (Annico, Cremona 1892 - 1965), renowned as Iago and Amonasro; the great **Giuseppe Danise** (Naples 1883 - New York 1963), a voice which was robust, flexible, and expressive; **Giovanni Inghilleri** (Porto Empedocle, Sicily 1894 - Milan 1959); **Emilio Ghirardini** (1885 - Ferrara 1965); **Dinh Gilly** (Algeria 1877 - London 1940), much sought after as Amonasro; **John Charles Thomas** (Meyersdale, Virginia 1891 - Apple Valley, California 1960) who was a wonderful Germont at the Met during the thirties; **Armand Crabbe** (Brussels 1883 - 1947); **Giacomo Rimini** (Verona 1888 - Chicago 1952); **Denis Noble** (Bristol 1899 - Spain 1966); **Jean Noté** (Tournai, Belgium 1859 - Brussels 1922) — famous as Rigoletto; **Willi Domgraf-Fassbaender** (Aachen 1897 - Nuremberg 1978) an exceptional singing-actor who performed in a wide repertoire.

*An eloquent expression by **Riccardo Stracciari** in Verdi's Rigoletto. During the years from 1920 to 1940 he played Figaro more than nine hundred times, sharing public favour with Ruffo and De Lucia.*

fantastic *cadenza* could no longer be finished in only one breath.

Considering his amazing capacity and his triumphal career, we must conclude that Titta Ruffo constituted a fundamental turning point in the story of the baritone voice in this century. After the light almost tenor baritone in the nineteenth century style, we began to encounter the baritone with a wide and powerful central range, very different from any tenor model. From the twenties on no one could deny the incomparable polish of the great Titta.

Despite the fact that many turn-of-the-century baritones have not been well served by their recordings (many of which are quite colourless and show very little respect for the value of the musical notes) we would like to mention the most important among them: **Adolfo Pacini**, who studied with Cotogni; **Mathieu Ahlersmeyer** (Cologne 1896 - Garmisch 1979), a great Macbeth; **Apollo Granforte** (Legnano 1886 - Milan 1975), a thundering voice with a splendid timbre; **Mario Ancona** (Leghorn 1860 - Florence 1931), the first Silvio in *I Pagliacci*, an opera in which he would later become legendary as Tonio; **Joseph Schwarz** (Riga 1880 - Berlin 1926), a noteworthy Rigoletto, and one of the few in-

"All'idea di quel metallo", Figaro (*Barbiere*): Riccardo Stracciari

Because of his correct singing line, the weight and richness of his timbre, and his great acting skills, **Riccardo Stracciari** (Casalecchio, Bologna 1875 - Rome 1955) was one of the greatest baritones of our century: an incomparable Figaro, Rigoletto and Germont.

To demonstrate that, with a solid technique and a sense of moderation and vocal composure, one can preserve one's vocal organ for decades without wear, we need only note that the Italian baritone began to sing in 1899 and continued until 1944 when he retired with a memorable *Traviata* at the Teatro Sociale of Como. We can admire his perfect *legato* and his exemplary breath distribution in the recording of Don Carlo's aria from *Ernani* "Oh de' verd'anni miei", with a rounded and penetrating a' flat in the final.

In his loved role of Figaro (heard in the recording, of course), we can not help but be amazed at the variety of his expressions, and, above all, at the super-fast "patter" in the recitatives, which was great fun as well as being part of the art of a virtuoso. His "All'idea di quel metallo" remains famous.

One of Stracciari's students was **Alexander Svéd** (Budapest 1906 - 1979). He was one of the most correct and incisive singers of the thirties and forties, famous for the beauty of his timbre and smoothness of emission in operas such as *Rigoletto*, *Ballo in Maschera*, and *Trovatore*, but he performed in the French and Wagnerian repertory as well.

Stabile, A Legendary Falstaff

Another baritone of immense importance was **Mariano Stabile** (Palermo 1888 - Milan 1968), active for over half a century and the greatest Falstaff we have known. He sang this role about one thousand two hundred times, starting in 1921-22, when he performed it at La Scala under the baton of Toscanini, after having meticulously prepared the part with the famous conductor. Even the phrase "Due Fagiani, un'acciuga" in the first act was tried over and over again (apparently seventy times!) to obtain the right inflexion, accent, and colour.

Apart from the corpulent knight, Stabile included in his repertory a sinuous Iago, Figaro, the sheriff Rance, Gérard, Don Giovanni, Don Alfonso, and Prosdocimo in *Turco in Italia* (revived in Rome in 1950 for the first time in this century).

His success derived, above all, from his perfect acting, which was studied in the minutest detail,

like an authentic *comédien*, and from the extreme flexibility of his voice - neither beautiful nor powerful, but able to exhibit a series of nuances which was very wide indeed. By pronouncing the phrase "Vado a farmi bello" in the second act of *Falstaff* with a whisper of voice, ambiguous and enchanting, Stabile won a warm applause from the audience every time.

Another exceptional stage presence was **Lawrence Tibbett** (Bakersfield, California 1896 - New York 1960) who made his debut in 1923 at the Metropolitan, but was really launched when he performed an exceptional Ford in *Falstaff* during the 1925 season, with Scotti in the title role. The audience acclaimed the young singer at length, awarding him an unprecedented triumph.

From that moment Tibbett's career was a constant upward climb: Amonasro, Scarpia, Iago, Simon Boccanegra, Rigoletto: roles which require enormous effort were resolved with ease, good high notes, a smooth emission, and the right shadings for every phrase. He sang at the Metropolitan until 1950, idolized by the public.

Leonard Warren (New York 1911 - 1960), the heir of Tibbett, did his advanced studies in the great school of De Luca, from whom he learnt all the secrets of the classical belcanto style. In January 1935 he made his debut at the Metropolitan as Paolo in *Simon Boccanegra*, with Tibbett in the leading role. And, exactly as had occurred ten years earlier for his illustrious colleague, Warren had an enormous success. With his wide and pliant vocality, ease in the high

Mariano Stabile, *taken during the first act of* Falstaff *which opened the 1952-53 season of the Rome Opera. Stella, Elmo, Silveri, Lazzari and Neri sang with him. On the podium, Franco Capuana. Even doing his make-up, Stabile took great care, as affirmed by this photo. (Historic Archives of the Rome Opera Theatre. Photo: Savio).*

Leonard Warren in the title role of Verdi's Macbeth.

This tiring vocal indecision was made possible only by the Italian singer's hardy physique; during his best years he had a warm, robust, and slightly melancholic voice. Thus he was an excellent Conte di Luna, Simon Boccanegra, Iago, Scarpia, Gérard, Germont and Rigoletto, a singer who was able to obey all the expressive signs on the scores.

We must also mention: **Giuseppe Valdengo** (Turin 1914) who owes all his fame to the three recordings made with Toscanini in the roles of Iago, Amonasro, and Falstaff; **Enzo Mascherini** (Florence 1911 - Leghorn 1981); **Mario Zanasi** (Bologna 1927); **Mario Sereni** (Perugia 1928); and **Giorgio Zancanaro** (Verona 1939). All of these singers possessed some good qualities, but they were, on the whole, quite monotonous, lacking the essential spark that makes an artist great.

Last but not least, we come to **Robert Merrill** (Brooklyn 1917) - a valued member of the Metropolitan ensemble for many years; he had a robust and penetrating vocal instrument and was an excellent interpreter of the Verdi repertory, with a pre-disposition for the roles of the "bad guy". The colour and the power of his emission were always his special assets. However, one often noticed a certain monotony in his phrasing, and a tendency to sing everything loudly. We must note his longevity, which has allowed him to appear in public in 1991 with an almost intact vocal quality.

notes and in the *mezzevoci*, and his very long breaths, the American baritone took on key roles such as Rigoletto, Macbeth, Conte di Luna, Simone, Don Carlo in *Forza del Destino*, Tonio in *I Pagliacci*, Iago, and even *Falstaff*; the Metropolitan public acclaimed him time and again. He died on stage at the Metropolitan after having sung "Urna fatale" in *Forza del Destino*.

Another baritone who specialized in Verdi was **Aldo Protti** (Cremona 1920), an excellent Rigoletto, Iago, Amonasro and Don Alvaro but also renowned as Gérard, Tonio and Barnaba. He has been active from the fifties until today, thanks to his notable technical ability.

Both of these baritones distinguished themselves for their correct emission, robust voices and stylistic fidelity to the Verdi repertoire.

The singular artistic progress of **Paolo Silveri** (Ofena, L'Aquila 1913), a vigorous Verdi baritone from 1943 until 1959, began after he started as a bass at Rome (1939-43). In 1959 he attempted to rise to the tenor range, without great success, making a debut as Otello in Dublin. In 1960 Silveri wisely returned to singing as a baritone.

The "best-beloved" at the Metropolitan during many appearances, *Lawrence Tibbet* interpreted many first-ever "prime". He was also active as a silver screen actor. (Historic Archives of the Rome Opera Theatre).

143

The Misunderstood Baritone: Ettore Bastianini

Ettore Bastianini (Siena 1922 - Sirmione, Brescia 1967) was another baritone who began singing as a bass (as Colline in *Bohème* in Ravenna, 1945) then went on to sing as a baritone from 1952 on. A thick, rich timbre, a seductive manner, aimiable sound: these were the best vocal characteristics of this Italian artist, who died prematurely in 1967 after the first tragic signs of his malady had obliged him to abandon the stage in 1965.

The Italian critics, however, were never well-disposed towards this meritorious singer. He was always accused of singing everything at full voice (but what a voice!), of not having a correct technique over the *passaggio* from centre to high range, and of thus being stylistically inadequate in many of his roles. These claims do have some truth; but they ignore Bastianini's huge popular success in such operas as *Trovatore, Ballo in Maschera, Ernani, Don Carlos* (with von Karajan at Salzburg in 1958), *Forza del Destino, Traviata* (with Callas and Di Stefano in Visconti's legendary production at La Scala in 1955) without forgetting his important performances of *Mazepa, Eugene Onegin* in 1954, and the reproposals

*Ettore Bastianini, in dark jacket in the centre, with some friends and colleagues: from left **Renata Tebaldi**, **Giulietta Simionato** and **Franco Corelli**, all singing in* Adriana Lecouvreur. *To put together such a galaxy of stars today (and even more so for Adriana) is unthinkable: in forming a cast nowadays one aims at a good principal and a discreet partner. The lack of authentic voices just does not allow for a full cast of four "giants" like these in the photo. (Historic Archives of the San Carlo Opera of Naples).*

of *Pirata* and *Poliuto* (with Callas).

Cornell MacNeil (Minneapolis 1922) has been on stage in all the world's major theatres for over forty years, distinguishing himself not only for his admirable technique but also for his great acting skills, especially noted in the parts of Scarpia, Iago, and Germont.

During his best years, 1955-70, the American baritone exhibited a noble singing line, being easily able to sustain the long *legato* passages of the Verdi arias, diminishing and reinforcing the sounds with an authentic *mezzavoce* and tenor-like high notes (up to high b′flat in the finale of Gusman's *cabaletta* in *Alzira* in Rome in 1967). His most successful characterisations were those of Rigoletto, Don Carlo in *Ernani*, Nabucco, Amonasro, Rance, and the above mentioned Scarpia, Iago, and Germont, roles which he took on in his last years.

We must say that, right from the start, Mac-Neil's voice tended to wobble over the *passaggio*: this did not much matter in a young, fresh voice; but it proved fatal when he was older. If this problem had been resolved in time, the singer would not now have to rely solely on his acting skills; he would have been able to continue launching high notes and modulating his voice as he pleased.

The list of great contemporary American baritones must include the name of **Sherrill Milnes** (Downers Grove, Illinois 1935); he started in 1963, but was "launched" in 1965 when he sang the part of Valentin in a Met. *Faust*.

His is a well-placed voice, full of expressive nuances (*mezzevoci, smorzature*, and even trills!) with easy high notes (past high b′ and as penetrating as a tenor's); but he has difficulty with the notes immediately following a *passaggio* (f′, f′sharp, and g′); they tend to go "backwards", for he, as opposed to most baritones, passes on f′sharp, like a tenor. His excellent interpretations of *Rigoletto, Forza del Destino, Otello, Macbeth, Simon Boccanegra, Trovatore*, and *Vespri Siciliani* have always been marred by some ugly sounds.

Tall and sturdy, Milnes compensates his technical defects with dynamic acting and a realistic make-up: his Scarpia appears on stage with a black beard and hair, looking youthful and virile, with a whip in one hand. In the finale of the second act, when he is stabbed by Tosca, he rolls over and over several times, together with his armchair, making one fear for his safety.

Cappuccilli: Technique and Nature

Piero Cappuccilli (Trieste 1928) is currently the best Italian Verdi baritone. His breath control is perfect, and his superb *legato* is envied and copied by many of his famous colleagues - above

Cornell MacNeil in the role of Baron Scarpia, in a Tosca performed at the splendid Sferisterio in Macerata, 1979.

Side by side during a recording session, **Sherill Milnes** left, and the tenor **Nicolai Gedda**. Milnes is very active in the recording world. (Historic Archives of EMI. Photo: R. Wilson).

Ettore Bastianini in Lucia, in the role of Lord Ashton. Incomprehensibly, this artist from Tuscany has been severely attacked by the Italian critics, who, it seems, have forgotten the actual disastrous state of the Italian baritone school. At the time of Bastianini (and this is the truth!), there was too much competition: Bechi, Gobbi, Taddei, Silveri, Protti, MacNeil, Mascherini, Guelfi, Panerai, and many others. (Historic Archives of La Fenice Theatre, Venice).

Ettore Bastianini in the role of Count di Luna in Il Trovatore.

all by Pavarotti, who has no qualms in admitting the superiority of Cappuccilli's technique. This superiority is confirmed by the recent *Don Carlos* at Salzburg conducted by von Karajan (Easter, 1986). Rodrigo's death scene "Io morrò, ma lieto in core" was sung with very few, almost imperceptible breaths, giving the effect of a single sweep of sound - a wonderful accomplishment considering Karajan's slow tempo.

Cappuccilli now has over thirty career years behind him, having made his debut in 1956 at the Teatro Nuovo in Milan in *Pagliacci*. Initially his characterisations were impeccable but a little cold and even monotonous; then, from 1971 on, when he was the protagonist of the memorable *Simon Boccanegra* and *Macbeth* under Strehler's direction, the artist reached his vocal and scenic maturity, and began the second part of his career. For at least fifteen years he has obtained world wide triumphs as Rigoletto, Iago, Amonasro, Macbeth, Simone Boccanegra, and also in the lesser known role of *Attila*, where he was acclaimed for his tenor-like b'flats at the end of the *cabaletta* "È gettata la mia sorte", which was always encored by popular demand. (We must remember, in particular, the performances in Vienna in 1980).

*Figaro is a role not frequently sung by **Cappuccilli**, perhaps because it contains too many patter passages. In the photo the artist is very involved in singing a high note, with Rosina, the mezzo-soprano **Alicia Nafé**; during a performance in 1982. (Historic Archives of the Opera Theatre of Pretoria.*

Aida: *under the baton of von Karajan, there gathered famous names such as **Cappuccilli** (Amonasro), Freni (Aida), Horne (Amneris), Ghiaurov (Ramfis), and Carreras (Radames). (Historic Archives of the Salzburg Festival).*

Simon Boccanegra *was taken on tour to Japan by La Scala. The role of the Doge has been thoroughly studied over the years by **Cappuccilli**, supported in the photo by **Freni** and the tenor **Luchetti**. (Bunka Kaikan. Tokyo. September, 1982).*

THE *VILAIN* BARITONES IN THIS CENTURY

The more malevolent and shady the character, the more the powerful voice of **Benvenuto Franci** (Pienza, Siena 1891 - 1986) seemed to be at home. It was ideal for the "bad guy" roles, such as those of Iago, Rance, Barnaba, or Scarpia. He was in his full vocal glory during the twenties and thirties, and whilst vocalizing could easily emit high "c″'s" worthy of a tenor, maintaining a singular homogeneity between the registers.

What was amazing about **Domenico Viglione-Borghese** (Mondovì 1877 - Milan 1957) was his enormous volume and fiery accent, especially in the parts of the sheriff in *Fanciulla del West*, Barnaba, Iago, and Amonasro.

Andrea Mongelli (1901 - Milan 1970) had a less beautiful timbre; but had such a powerful high f′ that it permitted him to thunder as Rance, Gérard, Scarpia, and Amonasro.

Cesare Formichi (Rome 1883 - 1949) made his operatic debut at the Teatro Lirico of Milan in 1911, and revealed a torrential voice, ideal for the villain baritone roles: Iago, Klingsor in *Parsifal*, Barnaba.

An elegant and refined Don Carlo in Ernani *by Verdi:* **Gino Bechi**. *This singer played in many successful films, in which he was obviously exploited for the sound track. A little light song remains famous in the Bechi version: "Vieni, c'è una strada nel bosco" (Come, there's a path in the woods). (Historic Archives of the Rome Opera Theatre).*

Benvenuto Franci *in* Guglielmo Tell. *His performances in London of Scarpia, Rigoletto, and Gérand, often at the side of Jeritza, signalled an epoch. (Historic Archives of the Rome Opera Theatre).*

Another huge voice was that of **Antenore Reali** (Verona 1897 - Milan 1960) whom we can admire in his recording of *Il Tabarro* with Clara Petrella.

Gino Bechi (Florence 1913) was not a *vilain* in the strict sense of the word, having played different roles not always of the verist type.

Right from his debut (in *Traviata* at Empoli in 1936) his vocal dutility and extension were stunning, and, when necessary, he performed interminable *filature* and high notes up to a′. His physical presence completed the whole; and the baritone from Tuscany dominated the stage as Amonasro, Rigoletto, Nabucco, Figaro, Iago, and even Falstaff (under the baton of De Sabata, with the La Scala company at London in 1950).

Unfortunately he had some stylistic weaknesses (such as his tendency to hold his high notes too long, to ham parts, and to often exaggerate needlessly) and also some technical defects (an imperfect intonation and a nasal way of singing intended to make the characters sound more evil and his high notes more penetrating). And this was why the golden years of this singer lasted only from 1936 until 1950. His final withdrawal from the stage occurred in 1965. Bechi now teaches singing, with a special interest in young, talented, Chinese students.

"Three Cops and a Carriage..." (Scarpia)

Tito Gobbi (Bassano del Grappa 1913 - Rome 1984) had a huge repertoire (consisting of more than one hundred operas) and a career that outlasted that of Bechi: he made his singing debut as Count Rodolfo (*Sonnambula*) — a bass part — in Gubbio, 1936; his official debut as a baritone came in 1938 at the Teatro Adriano of Rome in *Traviata*.

During the first part of his career (1936 - 56) he displayed a voice which was not powerful, but had a lovely timbre, smooth and delicate in the *mezzavoce*, flexible in the *legato*; this talent was aided by noteworthy intelligence and stage presence. With rare style and musicality he played Figaro, Rigoletto, Wozzek, Rodrigo (*Don Carlos*), Iago, Tonio, Gianni Schicchi, Scarpia, Falstaff, Simon Boccanegra, Don Giovanni, and Michele (*Tabarro*). However he had quite serious problems in placing high notes, which were always approached without correct positioning in the facial mask and seemed closer to a scream than to a sung note. It would be too easy and, for that matter, unjust to continue harping on this point, considering that the second part of Gobbi's career (1956 - 1976) was seriously damaged by his problems in the upper register. What was exceptional about the Venetian baritone was his ability to enter into the psychology of a character, studying the era and its customs with attention to both the historic and musical background of the opera being performed. To this type of preparation Gobbi added formidable make-up and costuming and a fantastic stage presence, moving before his audience with the skill of a great actor.

No one can remember a more cynical Baron Scarpia, a falser Iago, a shrewder Schicchi, a more lurid Tonio than those offered by Gobbi for decades in theatres all over the world. His gesture as Scarpia of running his goose-feather pen down Tosca's arm just after having used it to write Cavaradossi's sentence used to make the audience shiver with disgust.

As the Doge in *Simone Boccanegra* Gobbi knew how to be noble and profoundly human, finding moving shadings and accents in the death scene. His Figaro was an aimiable rascal, his Falstaff an aristocratic rogue; his Don Giovanni was exuberant and proud. He also sang this part at Salzburg with Furtwängler.

Right up until 1976, when Gobbi sang his last

Gobbi in Pagliacci *by Leoncavallo. With a glance, a small smirk, a gesture, Gobbi succeeded in making his character come alive. (Historic Archives of the Rome Opera Theatre. Photo: O. Savio).*

The role of Renato in Ballo in Maschera, *a role* **Gobbi** *did not really like; and yet just look at the proud nobility he displays in this photo. (Historic Archive of EMI).*

148

Falstaff in Germany, he was one of the public's best loved and most acclaimed artists.

Cyclone Guelfi

Lauri Volpi calls **Giangiacomo Guelfi's** (Rome 1924) voice "a true foghorn"; and one cannot disagree, considering its power and volume. After his debut in 1950 as Rigoletto, he won the Spoleto Experimental Theatre competition, and then his career took off in some well defined roles: Ezio in *Attila*, Rance in *Girl of the Golden West*, Macbeth, Gianciotto in *Francesca da Rimini*, Amonasro in *Aida*, Telramondo in *Lohengrin*, and Scarpia in *Tosca*.

However we must not think of Guelfi's vocal instrument as a sort of hurricane or as a machine for huge sounds. His memorable interpretation of the Doge Foscari in the reprisal of Verdi's opera in 1957 under the baton of Tullio Serafin (La Fenice Theatre, Venice) demonstrated that

*And here is that friendly rogue, Gianni Schicchi, to whom **Gobbi** gave a special voice - "yellow", the baritone described it. (Historic Archives of the Rome Opera Theatre. Photo: O. Savio).*

*26th December, 1960. **Mario Del Monaco** and **Tito Gobbi** in Verdi's Otello, conducted in Rome by Franco Capuano. The darts of the Italian voice critics were aimed at Gobbi, just as at Bastianini - a criticism that can never darken the memories left by these two truly great artists. (Historic Archives of the Rome Opera Theatre. Photo: O. Savio).*

*In the gallery of characters made forever memorable by **Tito Gobbi** we must justly insert his cruel and introspective Michele of Il Tabarro. (Historic Archives of the Rome Opera Theatre. Photo: O. Savio).*

Guelfi strikes the poor Corelli without pity, in the opera Romulus by Allegra. Whether for their voices or for their physique both singers, were perfectly suited to the roles of mythical heros. (Historic Archives of the Rome Opera Theatre. Photo: O. Savio).

he has a more than correct *mezzavoce* and use of soft singing: bending his voice to the dictates of the score, his rich timbre assumed melancholy inflections that were very moving.

Obviously the weight of his voice and his incisive accent made him ideal for the *vilain* roles, first amongst them Puccini's sheriff. It is also true that his premature vocal fatigue has been due to his excessive use of bombastic resonances and of sounds which were forcibly widened without ever lightening his voice as is technically necessary.

Other names amongst the current *vilain* baritones: **Matteo Manuguerra** (Tunis 1924) who has good qualities but is too nasal; **Louis Quilico** (Montreal 1930) has a rich vocal consistency but is stylistically lacking and monotonous in his phrasing; **Ingvar Wixell** (Lulea, Sweden 1931) has neither a powerful nor extended vocality, but he is correct and controlled, even too much so in parts like Nabucco or Scarpia.

We must also list the Frenchman **Alain Fondary** and the Italian **Silvano Carroli**, who are both quite enthralled with the idea of being able to make the columns of the Orange Ampitheatre or the Terme of Caracalla crumble under the power of their voices, so emphatically projected in operas such as *Nabucco, Tosca, Otello,* and *Aida*. It's a pity that they do not put as much effort and good will towards an adequate style.

*A memorable performance of I Due Foscari (Verdi) given at La Fenice Theatre of Venice on December 26th, 1957. The leading performers were **Giangiacomo Guelfi** (Doge), left in the photo; at the centre is Maestro Serafin, and to the right **Leyla Gencer** (Lucrezia) and **Mirto Picchi** (Jacopo Foscari). The evening was a triumph, thanks to vibrant performances. (Historic Archives of La Fenice Theatre of Venice. Photo: Giacomelli).*

THE GRAND SEIGNEUR BARITONES

Three Aces:
De Luca, Galeffi, Tagliabue

Giuseppe De Luca (Rome 1878 - New York 1950) made his stage debut in 1897 at Piacenza, singing Valentine in *Faust*. His beginning in provincial theatres saw him performing, above all, comic parts, and secondary ones at that: Lescaut, Silvio (*Pagliacci*), Marcello (*Bohème*); and then he took part in the first performance of *Adriana Lecouvreur* (Milan 1902), creating a magnificent Michonnet. It was the big turning point in his career. He was signed up by all the major theatres year after year in a wide selection of operas (*Favorita, Puritani, Rigoletto, Traviata, Barbiere, Don Pasquale, Tosca, Aida, Mastersingers of Nuremberg, Butterfly*) - always with great success.

He was impeccable in style, refined in phrasing, and possessed a controlled and fluid emission which he put to the service of a clear tenor-like timbre. De Luca can be considered the first *grand seigneur* baritone of this century. Due to the quality of his technique and to his aristocrat-

*An elderly but always formidable **De Luca** performs with **Martinelli** and the blond **Maria Jeritza**; accompanied at the piano by Arturo Toscanini. A memorable concert!*

*A fine photo of **Carlo Galeffi**, Rigoletto of outstanding talent. (Historic Archives of the Rome Opera Theatre).*

ic acting, he managed to confer nobility even to more violent parts such as Amonasro, Barnaba, Scarpia, or Beckmesser in *Mastersingers*. He also demonstrated a great variety of nuances in his favourite characters: Rigoletto, Figaro, Germont, Rodrigo, and Malatesta (*Don Pasquale*).

After having sung over one hundred different opera roles, and having conceded himself the luxury of performing *Rigoletto* when he was over seventy, he celebrated his golden jubilee in 1947 with a legendary concert at the Town Hall of New York. His recording of the Figaro-Rosina duet, together with Lily Pons, made in 1940, continues to amaze us because of his intact vocal means.

De Luca never had a very powerful voice, quite otherwise, — he was often obliged to avoid the extreme high notes with clever tricks. Notwith-standing this, he was a great singer and a good teacher, always full of advice for young singers.

Whilst a vocal lyric tendency was immediately apparent in De Luca's singing, that was not true for **Carlo Galeffi** (Malamocco, Venice 1884 - Rome 1961), who exhibited a great vocal volume and a certain arrogance in the first part of his career, especially when he sang Amonasro, Scarpia, Escamillo and Tonio.

He made his debut in 1889 in a minor part in *Forza del Destino*, and this was followed by sporadic performances of *Lucia*, *Pagliacci*, and *Rigoletto* in Rome. His excellent vocal placement, his musicality and his sensitivity as an artist led him to a constant growth process which allowed him to acquire greater softness and poise in his singing, until he reached a truly stylised and noble singing line.

He was the first to perform some of Mascagni's compositions (*Amica*, *Parisina*, *Isabeau*), the role of Fanuel in Boito's *Nerone*, Manfredo in *L'Amore di Tre Re* by Montemezzi; and he also gave the first performance of Amfortas in Italy and the first Schicchi in Europe. However his great roles, between 1910 and the mid-fifties, were *Rigoletto*, *Nabucco*, *Guglielmo Tell*, *Ballo in Maschera*, *Simone Boccanegra*, and especially the aristocratic roles of Rodrigo and Carlo V (*Ernani*), without forgetting his woeful *Boris Godunov*, sung under the guidance of Arturo Toscanini.

Carlo Tagliabue (Mariano Comense, 1898 - Monza 1978) took on De Luca's and Galeffi's inheritance, demonstrating that class and a refined technique can allow one to remain on stage for decades without feeling the weight of a wide repertoire or the passing of the years. The Italian baritone, in fact, sang from 1922 (when he debuted in *Loreley* at Lodi) until 1958, when he decided to retire whilst still in full possession of his vocal means.

With his heavy, rich, but flexible and smooth voice, Tagliabue was an excellent King Alfonso in *La Favorita*, Don Carlos in *Forza del Destino*, Germont, Rigoletto, Conte di Luna, Riccardo in *Puritani*, Gérard, Scarpia, and Enrico in *Lucia*, allowing us to admire the beauty of his authentic *legato*, his full *mezzavoce* which was never falsetto, and his class.

Good Old Sir John

For various reasons the artistic activity of **Giuseppe Taddei** (Genoa 1916) has something of the miraculous: half a century of career, from 1936 (debut at Rome as the Herald in *Lohengrin*) until today, notwithstanding the tragic period he spent in a German concentration camp during the Second World War, which could have seriously damaged his voice and health. In 1946, thanks to the decisive action of the American troops, the young baritone was able to trod the Austrian stages and was immediately signed up by the Vienna Staatsoper. From then on his realtionship with this theatre is one of the most profound devotion, a sentiment returned in full by the incredible affection the Austrian public has for him.

His voice has a rare timbric beauty and has been often, without any exaggeration, compared

Carlo Tagliabue (Rigoletto) with the soprano Dolores Wilson (Gilda) in a performance during the 1950-51 season at La Fenice, Venice. (Historic Archives of La Fenice, Venice. Photo: Giacomelli).

to the smooth and velvety *cavata* of a cello - a "fat" blend of sound, emitted with technical expertise. Taddei also possesses an innate taste and interpretive imagination, succeeding in finding the right vocal expression (accents, colouring and inflexions), the right make-up, stage movements and characterisation for each role.

It is obvious that with all these gifts his repertoire could be nothing but wide and varied, with over fifty parts: from his splendid Mozart (Figaro, Leporello, Papageno, and Guglielmo in *Così fan Tutte*) to his unabashed Falstaff, the role with which he celebrated his golden jubilee at the Metropolitan, with James Levine conducting, under the direction of Franco Zeffirelli; from his mature Verdi (*Macbeth*, *Rigoletto*, *Traviata*, *Vespri Siciliani*, *Simon Boccanegra*, *Otello*) to the most important Verist roles, amongst which we mention at least Scarpia, Tonio, Schicchi, and Gérard. His performances are almost always resolved with incisive phrasing and a variety of shadings.

But we must not forget some other roles which have played an important part over the span of Taddei's long career: his poetical and lovable Hans Sachs in *The Mastersingers*, his shady and sombre *Flying Dutchman*, his Prince Igor, and his unforgettable *Eugene Onegin*.

Even nowadays he dominates the stage like a proud lion, entering on Dulcamara's cart at the Vienna State Opera, selling his elixir of love to the public: a magical potion of which few have

Giuseppe Taddei, *Dulcamara in Elisir d'Amore staged in Florence in 1984. To the right we can recognise **Luciana Serra** and **Alfredo Kraus**. At over seventy years of age Taddei is still in excellent vocal form. (Historic Archives of the Theatro Comunale of Florence. Photo: Marchiori).*

***Taddei**-Dulcamara triumphantly demonstrates his miraculous elixir — does the secret of his extraordinary artistic longevity lie in that magic bottle? (Historic Archives of the Rome Opera Theatre. Photo: Reale).*

*Falstaff, 1982: for his new Salzburg production von Karajan called on **Giuseppe Taddei, Rolando Panerai, Raina Kabaivanska, Francesco Araiza** and **Christa Ludwig**. It was an enormous success, captured on disc by Deutsche Grammophon. (Historic Archives of the Salzburg Festival. Photo: Weber).*

153

*A fine portrait of **Giuseppe Taddei** as Germont.*

Vienna in 1989 with Claudio Abbado, also his *Rigoletto* the same year, and his incredible Falstaff at Stuttgart in 1990. These are all proof of a vocality, a class, and a love for profession which has few equals in our century.

A Classy Bruson

Renato Bruson (Ganze, Padua 1936) has partially inherited Taddei's noble phrasing and rich timbre, even if he lacks fantasy compared to his illustrious colleague. Yet thanks to his assiduous studies with his teacher Fava Ceriati, and to his long apprenticeship in Donizetti and Verdi's early works, the Venetian singer is able to modulate his voice very well, obtaining *smorzature* and an extremely sweet *legato*. From 1975 until today (following an initial dedication to memorable rediscoveries of proto-romantic operas suchas *Maria di Rohan*, *Il Pirata*, *Masnadieri*, *Linda di Chamounix*, *Caterina Cornaro*), Bruson has showed a strange lack of imagination when affronting characters like Don Carlo (*Forza del Destino*), Rigoletto, Germont, or Miller (*Luisa Miller*), as if he were afraid of seeming vocally weak had he used his *mezzevoci* profusely. This is apparent above all in his studio recordings. The artist is far superior "live". As the Marquis of Posa in *Don Carlos* he succeeds in finding delicate *pianissimi* in phrases such as "Ei fu Neron!" or the repeat of "Io morrò", which is splendidly *legato*. His vocal means are also very suited to the roles of Carlo V in *Ernani* and King Alfons in *Favorita*, in which he demon-

understood the formula. Amongst the recent appearances of the Italian baritone we must remember his *Don Pasquale* at Rome with his wonderful patter in the "Vedrai se giovano" duo with Dr. Malatesta, presenting us with an artistry which is almost lost nowadays. Neither must we forget his extraordinary *Simon Boccanegra* in

Renato Bruson in I Masnadieri *by Verdi, presented in Rome on 25 November, 1972. For at least a decade during the sixties, although taking part in many important productions, Bruson was almost ignored by the critics and the recording industry. (Historic Archives of the Rome Opera).*

*The combination of two great singing actors, **Renato Bruson** (Germont) and **Raina Kabaivanska** (Violetta) in the second act of* Traviata, Macerata, 1984. *(Photo: A. Tabocchini).*

strates a total adherence to the authentic bel-canto style. His Iago is subtle and measured, finally the false priest which Verdi wanted, not a common little villain. We are not able, however, to put Bruson's Falstaff amongst his best performances. He sang it at Los Angeles and at Florence in 1984, under Giulini's baton. He was perhaps too much a knight and too little a rogue, not at all amused or amusing. We prefer his Macbeth and Simon Boccanegra which are controlled in their precise vocal and scenic definition.

In the meanwhile several young talents have emerged, whom we shall briefly mention: the Canadian **Gino Quilico**, son of the famous Luis, whose voice is smooth and flexible, and who is active in the French and comic Italian repertory; the Italian **Paolo Coni**, who is excellent in the Bellini-Donizetti repertoire, but not yet ready for Verdi (Posa, Germont, Renato) in which he is not at all convincing. There is also **Roberto Frontali**, from Rome, who has all the possibilities of emerging as a *grand seigneur*, on condition that he chooses his repertoire carefully!

Heldenbariton: The Wagnerian Baritones of the Twentieth Century

Among the best performers of the difficult Wagnerian baritone parts in our century we must first list **Anton van Rooy** (Rotterdam 1870 - Munich, Bavaria 1932), a most profound and vocally gifted Wotan, Sachs and Kurwenald in the years between 1897 and 1914. For having sung Amfortas in the *prima assoluta* of *Parsifal* at New York in 1903, violating the Wagnerian dictate that forbade the opera being performed out of Bayreuth, he was banned from the "sacred city" until 1913.

Friedrich Schorr (Nagyvàrad 1888 - Farmington, Connecticut 1953) can be considered the heir of van Rooy, for he was the greatest Wotan, Sachs and *Flying Dutchman* from 1920 until 1940. His recordings reveal a rich, warm timbre, a particularly incisive voice in the dramatic passages and caressing *mezzevoci*.

Rudolf Bockelmann (Luneburg 1892 - Dresden 1958) also proved exceptional in the most perilous Wagnerian parts, singing between 1923 and 1945 and rivaling Schorr. Because of his Nazi tendencies he had to interrupt his career in the immediate post-war period, dedicating his time to teaching singing.

A group of eminent performers populate the beginning of our century; **Leopold Demuth** (Brünn 1861 - Czernowitz 1910); **Friedrich Weidemann** (Ratzeburg in Holstein 1871 - Vienna 1919), who performed in many first performances at Vienna (*Elektra* in 1909, *Pélleas* in 1910, *Der Rosenkavalier* in 1911) and was also a Mozart specialist; **Martial Singher** (Oloron, Pyrénées 1904 - 1990) was an excellent Amfortas; **José Beckmans** (Belgium 1897), whose repertoire was limitless (more than 300 operas!) was most applauded as Kurwenald (*Tristan*) and Wotan, especially in his performances at the Opera Theatre of Monte Carlo.

Emil Schipper (Vienna 1882 - 1957) first Barak in *Die Frau ohne Schatten* in 1919, was an acclaimed Wagnerian baritone until 1938.

Herbert Janssen (Cologne 1895 - New York 1965) had a smooth and well modulated voice. It was particularly suited to noble and melancholy characters like Wolfram (*Tannhäuser*) and Amfortas (*Parsifal*). He sang from 1924 until 1951 in Germany, America and England, specializing above all in one role: that of Kothner in *The Mastersingers*.

About **Heinrich Schlusnus** (Braubach 1888 - Frankfurt 1952) and his follower, **Josef Metternich** (Hermülheim, Cologne 1915), what is most remembered is their important work in popularising Verdi in Germany (the Verdi revival began in Germany in 1930); but their important Wagnerian activity must not be forgotten either. Metternich, in particular, revealed himself as a truly diabolical Telramond.

Paul Schöffler (Dresden 1897 - Amersham, Buckinghamshire 1977) was one of the most complete baritones in every sense singing between 1926 and 1965: he had a rich, well emitted voice which extended from a warm, low register to easy, penetrating high notes. He was very musical and very precise regardings every expressive sign left by the composer, be it Mozart, Wagner, or Richard Strauss. Schöffler rendered famous interpretations of Sachs, the Flying Dutchman, Jochanaan (*Salome*), Don Pizzarro (*Fidelio*), Figaro and the Count in *The Marriage of Figaro*, and Don Giovanni.

One of the greatest German singing actors ever is **Erich Kunz** (Vienna 1909). The Vienna State Opera audience was able to continue applauding him into the eighties, when the elderly singer would still perform small parts, always demonstrating his extraordinary acting gifts and his mastery of "singing-speaking".

He made his debut many years ago in 1933 as Osmino (a bass-profondo part) but the roles which were most suited to his flexible and aimiable voice were Papageno, the sarcastic Beckmesser, and the extravert Leporello, roles which he frequently sang at Salzburg, Vienna, New York, London, and in Italy.

Amongst the most aristocratic singers belonging to the generation following Schöffler, we remember **Eberhard Wächter** (Vienna 1929-1992) still active at the beginning of the 1980's even though in full decline.

In the period from 1950 until 1960 he was one of the most acclaimed Amfortas, and, in the Verdi repertory, Renato and Rodrigo. Under the guidance of the greatest conductors he was also

*The historic and insuperable Papageno of **Erich Kunz**, a master of "Sprechgesang"; a likeable and dynamic actor; a much loved favourite at the Vienna Staatsoper. (Historic Archives of the Rome Opera Theatre).*

a Count Almaviva and a Don Giovanni of rare scenic and vocal completeness.

King Dietrich I

The uncontested king of the Germanic baritones remains **Dietrich Fischer-Dieskau** (Berlin 1925), even after more than forty years of career. He made his debut in 1947 at Fribourg as a solist in Brahms' *German Requiem*. He does not have a particularly wide or powerful voice; but it is exceptionally flexible and well extended (from low E to high b'), capable of penetrating the profoundest meaning of a score, be it Bach, Handel, Mozart, Verdi, Wagner, Strauss, or the entire Lieder repertory, which he performs with particular interpretative intelligence and musicality.

Thanks to his perfect Italian pronunciation, which is more clearly understandable than that sung by many Italians, Fischer-Dieskau has been able to include Falstaff, Rigoletto, Iago, Rodrigo, Renato, Sharpless, Scarpia, Germont, and Guglielmo Tell in his repertoire, finding for each opera the right inflexion, colouring and dramatic definition.

Amongst his best characterizations we must mention his elegant Mandryka in *Arabella*, his noble Wolfram in *Tannhäuser*, his sorrowful Amfortas in *Parsifal*, his poetic Sachs in *The Mastersingers*, and his Count in the *Marriage of Figaro*, an unsurpassable performance.

The extraordinary artistic story of Fischer-Dieskau, apart from his vocal contribution to the history of interpretation (which is often easily overlooked), is summed up in his decisive presence as a singing "musician", that is, in his capacity to follow the directions given by the composer without ever exceeding and always respecting what is written on the score.

We must, finally, consider some noteworthy singers who are active in the most important theatres the world over, like **Hermann Prey** (Berlin 1929), an exceptional Beckmesser, an acclaimed Figaro (both in Mozart and in Rossini), and a much appreciated Lieder singer, even though his precise vocal limitations prevent him from including Verdi and the Italian romantics in his repertoire. **Walter Berry** (Vienna 1929) is excellent in the Mozart roles of Leporello, Don Alfonso, Papageno, Guglielmo and Figaro, and the Wagnerian parts of Klingsor, Wotan and Telramond, executing all these roles with great scenic ability and vocal security. One of his best portrayals over the last few years is that of Barak in *Die Frau ohne Schatten* by Richard Strauss. The Englishman **Norman Bailey** (Birmingham 1933) has been a Wotan par excellence at the Sadler Wells company of London; but he is also much acclaimed in the roles of Pizzaro, Gunter, Hans Sachs, and Kutuzov in *War and Peace*. **Donald McIntyre** (Auckland, New Zealand 1934) is active as a Wagnerian baritone (Wotan, Kingsor, Amfortas) at Covent Garden. **Thomas Stewart** (Texas 1928) is a stable member of the Deutsche Oper of Berlin and also performs at Bayreuth in the parts of Wotan, the Flying Dutchman, and Amfortas. His voice is smooth and well projected and he is equally good as an actor.

Reinforcing the ranks of contemporary German repertory baritones we have the solid and flexible voices of **Bernd Weikl** (Vienna 1942) and **Wolfgang Brendel** (Munich of Bavaria 1947), both of whom are excellent singers and gifted actors. Brendel reaches high b′ without effort in chest voice (*Carmina Burana*) with a beautiful timbre. He performs Papageno, Wolfram, Figaro, Renato, and Silvio in *Pagliacci*, principally in Monaco: at the worst, one can accuse him of being a little indifferent. With a touch more imagination and psychological depth he could aspire, and justly so, to being the successor of Fischer-Dieskau.

For his part Weikl is more dynamic and brilliant: his Doctor Falke in *Die Fledermaus* by Johann Strauss is great fun, and punctually repeat-

Dietrich Fischer-Dieskau.

ed each New Year at Vienna; another of his oft repeated roles is that of Belcore in *L'Elisir d'Amore*. Strangely enough, even if he has a voice with a beautiful timbre and a good extension at his disposition, Weikl does not succeed in being believable as Germont or Figaro (Rossini). He exaggerates too much, and abuses the high notes. On the other hand, his performances in *Eugene Onegin*, *The Mastersingers* (Hans Sachs) and *Parsifal* (Amfortas) are excellent, and in them he demonstrates a noble phrasing and stylistic fidelity.

To cite another excellent northern talent: **John Bröcheler** (Vaals, Holland 1945), who did his master studies in Paris under Pierre Bernac. Singing mainly in United States and German opera houses, he is best known for his participations in *Don Giovanni*, *Arabella*, *Parsifal*, and *Elektra*. He is justly acclaimed for a voice characterised by its magnificent polish and powerful sound.

In the young generation **Olaf Bär** is a new shining light. He is a singer with good vocal means and intelligence, who is mainly tied to Mozart and Strauss.

THE COMIC BARITONE
IN ITALIAN COMIC OPERA AND IN MOZART

In the difficult art of the farce one must be able to unite vocal gifts (agility, extension, and speedy patter) with scenic qualities: the artist needs to be having good fun himself, first of all, to be able to make us have fun. Apart from the great Taddei, already included in the list of *grand seigneur* baritones, we must discuss **Sesto Bruscantini** (Porto Civitanova, Macerata 1919) who is a master of the comic genre, but also an interpreter of many roles from all the baritone repertory: Riccardo (*Puritani*), Rodrigo (*Don Carlos*), Simon Boccanegra, Germont, Scarpia, Falstaff, Rigoletto and Atanaele (*Thaïs*). In these operas the intelligent Italian singer has been able to substitute the arrogance and exaggeration of many bad performers with a knowing use of *mezzevoci*, varied accents, and imaginative and stylised phrasing of great class.

Certainly Bruscantini's voice found fertile ground in the comic repertory right from his start in 1949 (Don Geronimo in *Matrimonio Segreto* at La Scala). He never hammed his acting by inserting jokes of dubious or bad taste. Instead he followed a moderate line founded on the correct use of recitative and authentic virtuosity. Sesto Bruscantini has recently triumphed as Dulcamara, Don Pasquale, Don Bartolo in *Barbiere*, and Don Alfonso in *Così fan Tutte*, giving genuine singing lessons to many of his younger colleagues.

Among the turn-of-the-century comic baritones we must at least mention: **Jean Périer** (Paris 1869 - Nevilly 1954) was active in the French and Mozart repertoire; **André Pernet** (Rambersville 1894 - Paris 1966) was an acclaimed Don Giovanni; **Francisco d'Andrade** (Lisbon 1859 - Berlin 1921) performed a legendary Don Giovanni until 1919; **Alfred Jerger** (Brünn 1889 - Vienna 1976), a perfect Mozart singer mainly active at Salzburg; **John Forsell** (Stockholm 1868 - 1941), who taught Jussi Björling and Set Svanholm; **Gerhard Hüsch** (Hanover 1901 - Monaco 1984), an excellent Papageno; **John Brownlee** (Geelong, Australia 1900 - New York 1959) a grand Don Giovanni and Guglielmo in the *Così fan Tutte* conducted by Busch; **Lucien Fugère** (Paris 1848 - 1935) was a legendary interpreter of the now little performed French *comique* repertoire, as was **Maurice Renaud** (Bordeaux 1861 - Paris 1933), one of the most extraordinary personalities of the French school, as luckily we can hear from his recordings.

Lucien Fugère performed from 1870 to 1933,

*Rightly famous, the Figaro of **Bruscantini**, here photographed during a performance at Parma for the 1966-67 season. (Historic Archives of the Teatro Regio of Parma. Photo: Montacchini).*

when he once again sang as Bartolo in *Barbiere* at the Trianon-Lyrique in Paris. He has remained one of the mythical interpreters of the French lyric and comic repertory, especially known for his performances as the Duc de Longueville in Messager's *La basoche*. Further accolades arrived for his highly entertaining interpretations of Leporello, Falstaff and Papageno.

Maurice Renaud started his career in Brussels in 1884. After his acclaimed performances in Paris, London and Berlin and at The Scala and the Met, he was nick-named "the French Battistini". As a singing-actor his niche in history is secure, and he is still remembered for his crystal clear diction and his interpretative creativity, particularly when he played Mefistofele in *La damnation de Faust*, a role he also sang in a noteworthy 1902 production at The Scala, with Toscanini conducting. His was a wide-ranging repertory, including Iago, Don Alfonso, Don Giovanni, Scarpia, Rigoletto, Figaro and Germont. His final performance was in Offenbach's *Monsieur Choufleuri* in a Paris production.

At a somewhat later date **Michel Dens** and **Renato Capecchi** came to international attention. Dens (Roubaix 1914) specialised in the role of Figaro in *Barbiere*. But he had a wide repertory and a long career, singing until the end of the 1980's. Capecchi (Cairo 1923) made his debut in Reggio Emilia in 1949 and his career is still in full force in 1992, although nowadays he performs almost exclusively in the United States. An excellent singing-actor, he can range from the dramatic parts of Iago, Ashton (*Lucia di Lammermoor*) or Amonasro to a wide variety of comic and brilliant roles, such as Figaro, Leporello, Dr. Bartolo, Falstaff and Dulcamara, and all this without neglecting the contemporary repertory. Among his most famous characterisations: Ford and Fra Melitone (*Forza del Destino*).

In our historic overview, we can not skip names such as **Alberto Rinaldi** (Rome 1939) and **Richard Stilwell** (St. Louis 1947). Rinaldi has been best known in Germany, Austria and England, and is especially noted for his performances as Dandini, Ford, Figaro and Malatesta. Stilwell boasts a wide repertory, ranging from Monteverdi to Britten. He is renowned as Pelléas and the Count (*The Marriage of Figaro*).

We should like to briefly highlight the career of **Gabriel Bacquier** (Beziers 1924). He has been active since 1949, offering a repertory that includes operettas as well as opera. Gifted with a full yet pliant voice, he began his career alternating between a series of Mozart roles (The Count of Almaviva, Don Alfonso, Leporello, Don Giovanni) and the more dramatic parts of Iago, Scarpia and Marcello (*Bohème*). In this past decade he has devoted his talent to comic roles, from Don Pasquale to Gianni Schicchi and from Sancho Panza (Massenet's *Don Quixote*) to Falstaff, performing with exuberant verve and demonstrating that he is still in full command of his vocal power.

English-speaking countries have been the main province of **Sir Geraint Evans** (Pontypridd, Wales 1922). He was a standby at Covent Garden from 1948 to 1984 when he bid farewell to the stage in his final Dulcamara (*Elisir d'Amore*). The characters best suited to his intelligent interpretations were Beckmesser (*The Mastersingers*), Papageno, Leporello, Mr. Flint (*Billy Budd* by Benjamin Britten), Falstaff and Figaro (Mozart). After his retirement he became active in stage direction, working in various American theatres and with the Welsh National Opera.

There is no disputing the fact that **Thomas Allen** (Seaham, Durham 1944) is in the first rank of today's international stars. Starting out in London in 1969 as Figaro in *Barbiere*, he has

Francisco d'Andrade is Don Giovanni beside the legendary **Lilli Lehmann's** Donna Anna.

Gabriel Bacquier as Coppelius in Offenbach's Les Contes d'Hoffmann. He became internationally known in a variety of roles, including those of Scarpia (Tosca) and Boris Godunov.

159

Rolando Panerai in Gianni Schicchi, *singing with* **Cecilia Gasdia** *(Lauretta) and* **Alberto Cupido** *(Rinuccio). The spoken final of Schicchi "Ditemi voi signori" aroused an enormous response from the Florentine audience when Panerai declaimed it with a genuine Tuscan accent. (Historic Archives of the Teatro Comunale of Florence. Photo: Marchiori).*

developed an extensive and eccletic repertory. His well-positioned voice is very smooth, with a good extension and beautiful colour. And his acting talents contribute to his success, particularly in the noble roles of Eugene Onegin, Pelléas, the Count in *The Marriage of Figaro*, Valentin in *Faust* and Don Giovanni (La Scala production, 1987). Since 1973 he has regularly taken part in the annual Glyndebourne Festival where he has sung almost all his favourite roles. **Derek Hammond-Strand** (London 1929) studied with Hüsch and is noteworthy in roles like Melitone, Bartolo, the sacristan in *Tosca*, but is also a success in the roles of Alberich and Beckmesser. **Zoltán Kélémen** (Budapest 1933 - Zurich 1979) was a specialist in the part of Alberich, singing at Bayreuth, Salzburg and the Metropolitan. The English **John Shirley Quirk** (Liverpool 1931) was an excellent and refined performer in a wide repertoire ranging from Purcell to Mozart but also including the contempory English composers, and oratorio. The Swedish **Hakan Hagegard** (1945) was Papageno in Ingmar Bergman's film *The Magic Flute*. **Benjamin Luxon** (Redruth 1937), active since 1972 at Covent Garden and applauded as the Conte d'Almaviva, Don Giovanni, Eisenstein in *Die Fledermaus*, and in *Eugene Onegin*. **Giorgio Gatti**

(Poggio a Caiano 1949) is active in the late renaissance and Monteverdi repertoire, but makes agreeable excursions into Rossini and Donizetti.

Unbeatable Rolando

Rolando Panerai (Campi Bisenzio, Florence 1924) is another illustrious veteran still in remarkable vocal form, especially if you consider his long career (he made his debut in *Werther*, in Florence, 1947) and his wide, demanding repertoire. Showing an uncommon vocal dexterity and resistance, he has been able to sing *Trovatore*, *Favorita*, *Puritani*, *Rigoletto* and *Bohème* and also *Don Pasquale*, *Mosè*, *Barbiere*, *Cenerentola*, *Così fan Tutte* (both as Guglielmo and Alfonso) and many twentieh century operas (Hindemith, Prokofiev and Turchi). The results have not always been positive: there are occasional slips of intonation, and an abusive use of added high notes. This is especially true of his performances in Verdi or in the romantic operas on the whole, whilst where comic opera is concerned Panerai has always communicated high spirits, amiability and good taste, being perfectly at his ease as Dulcamara, Malatesta, Don Alfonso, Leporello,

Taddeo (*Italiana in Algeri*), and Figaro. He has totally identified himself with one role: that of Ford in *Falstaff*, of which he was Karajan's favourite interpreter for over thirty years.

The latest comic baritones to have arrived on the scene are **Leo Nucci** (Castiglion de' Pepoli, Bologna 1942) and **Alessandro Corbelli**. The first is very active in the Verdi repertoire (*Rigoletto, Trovatore, Ballo in Maschera, Luisa Miller, Traviata*) whilst the second has tended to follow Bruscantini's example in the comic parts - from the eighteenth century comic Neapolitan operas to Donizetti.

Nucci distinguishes himself for his lovely voice timbre, his secure agility (performed however with the use of aspired notes), and his extended high notes (up to a shining b' flat). He is currently much in demand as Figaro, Ford, Malatesta, Belcore, and in the above mentioned Verdi operas, which have lately become more frequent among his performances. He has to his credit many recordings made with the best of today's ensembles.

Corbelli has a less extended voice and a somewhat less lovely timbre than his colleague; but he is fluid in the vocalised passages and is well suited to many Rossini and Donizetti roles.

We must not leave out the promising **Lucio Gallo**, an applauded Mozart baritone (his *Così fan Tutte* at Vienna with Harnoncourt conducting, and his Leporello with Abbado at Vienna in 1990 have been among his first international successes).

*Due to his secure vocal technique and his interpretive intelligence, **Leo Nucci** succeeded in handling the difficult role of Simon Boccanegra in Bologna in 1984. Here he is during the prologue of the opera, with the bass **Bonaldo Giaiotti**, an excellent Fiesco. (Historic Archives of the Teatro Comunale of Bologna. Photo: Magic Vision Gnani).*

*Figaro is **Leo Nucci**'s favourite role. La Scala, on tour in Japan, took Nucci as their likeable and vigorous barber; **Valentini-Terrani** (Rosina), **Francisco Araiza** (Almaviva) and **Enzo Dara** (Bartolo). On the podium, Claudio Abbado. (Bunka Kaikan. Tokyo. September, 1981).*

Some Other Famous Baritones

After our chapter dedicated to the best baritones of this century, we wish to add this table in which we will include other artists not less worthy of being mentioned. Beside each name we have listed the principal titles in his repertoire and a brief note on his vocal characteristics and on his career.

NAME	BASIC REPERTORY	REMARKS
Blanc, Ernest (1923) Baritone *Grand Seigneur*.	French repertory. (Massenet, Bizet, Saint-Saëns).	An intense vocality of beautiful colour, smooth emission.
Bösch, Christian (1941) *Spiel Bariton*.	Mozart, J. Strauss, Lehár, Offenbach.	An agile and self-possessed actor. His voice was not particularly powerful or extended. An excellent Papageno.
Glossop, Peter (1928) Verdi Baritone.	*Otello, Ernani, Forza del Destino, Ballo in Maschera, Traviata, Rigoletto*.	An appreciated interpreter in the Verdi roles, especially in England. His vocality was a little harsh but he had good scenic gifts.
Gramm, Donald (D. Gramsch; 1927-1983) Bass-Baritone.	Mozart, Rossini, contemporary operas.	First rate quality as a singer-actor, with scenic verve and discreet vocal gifts.
Hemsley, Thomas (1927) Baritone *brillant*.	Wagner, Britten, contemporary operas.	Specialist in the role of Beckmesser; first interpreter of Demetrius in *A Midsummer Night's Dream*.
Herinex, Raimund (1927) Bass Baritone.	Wagner, Verdi, Puccini, Massenet, contemporary operas.	A wide and diverse repertory. The first performer of works by Maxwell Davies, Williamson, Henze, Tippett.
Hvorostovsky, Dmitri (1962) Verdi Baritone.	*Don Carlos, Ernani, Puritani*, and *Eugene Onegin*.	He's the young hope among the Verdi Baritones. Voice of a fine colour, smooth, well projected.
Hynninen, Jorma (1941) Baritone *brillant*.	Mozart, Verdi, contemporary Finnish operas.	A refined and intelligent artist with a vast repertoire. Since 1984 he has been artistic director of the Finnish National Opera.
Kraus, Otakar (1909-1980) Bass Baritone.	Wagner, Stravinsky, Britten, Walton.	Specialised in the role of Alberich; bound for many seasons to Covent Garden; singer in many first-ever performances. An esteemed teacher: among his students Robert Lloyd, Gwynne Howell, Elizabeth Connell.
Kusche, Benno (1916) Baritone *brillant*.	Wagner, Strauss, operetta.	A character actor of good quality in opera and German operetta. The first interpreter of *Antigonae* by Orff.
Leiferkus, Sergei (1946) Baritone *Grand Seigneur*.	Verdi, Tchaikovsky, Mussorssky, Rimsky-Korsakov.	One of the best Russian artists of recent generations. A complete artist, possessing a rich voice, well placed.
Lisitsian, Pavel (1911) Verdi Baritone.	Verdi, Russian repertory.	The first Russian artist invited to the Metropolitan of New York in 1960. Great natural means and scenic talent.
Massard, Robert (1925) Baritone *Grand Seigneur*.	French operas.	Excellent singer-actor. Specialist in the role of Escamillo and of Valentino (*Faust*).
Mazurok, Juri (1931) Verdi Baritone.	Verdi, Tchaikovsky, Rimsky-Korsakov, Russian repertory.	A voice of a lovely colour emitted with a skillful technique; however he is rather static on stage and monotonous in his phrasing.
Nimsgern, Siegmund (1940) Baritone *Vilain*.	Verdi, Wagner, Strauss, contemporary repertory.	A singer-actor of note, much appreciated by directors and famous orchestra conductors. His voice presents some technical blanks.

Nissen, Hans Hermann (1893-1980) Bass Baritone.

Wagner, Strauss.

Specialist in the roles of Wotan and Hans Sachs in the period between the two world wars. His voice was velvety and technically perfect.

Paskalis, Kostas (1929) Verdi Baritone.

Verdi, contemporary operas.

A grand actor and sensitive interpreter, specialising in the roles of Macbeth and Rigoletto despite a defective intonation sometimes in evidence.

Reardon, John (1930-1988) Baritone *brillant*.

Opera and operetta (English), contemporary repertory.

An American artist with a very wide repertory. Often asked to work in films and on television.

Roich, Günther (1921-1988) Baritone *brillant*.

Contemporary operas.

Famous in the part of Dr. Schön (*Lulu* by Schönberg) and in many other contemporary roles.

Rothmüller, Marko (1908) Verdi Baritone.

Verdi, contemporary operas.

Much appreciated in *Wozzek* by Berg and for other operas of rare execution. Noted for his considerable scenic ability and the lovely colour of his voice.

Souzay, Gérard (G. Tisserand, 1920) Baritone *Grand Seigneur*.

French repertory, Lieder and Chamber songs.

A fine and intelligent performer of the Chamber Music repertory.

Uppmann, Theodore (1920) Baritone *brillant*.

Mozart, contemporary English and American operas.

Much applauded in America as Papageno and as Pelléas. The first interpreter in America of *Billy Budd* (Britten) and of *A Quiet Place* by Bernstein.

Marian Anderson, *one of the first black solo artists to establish herself on the concert platform.*

THE MEZZO-SOPRANOS

The Mezzo-Soprano Voice: Extension and Phonation

The mezzo-soprano voice lies between that of the contralto and the soprano. The extension goes from a to a″ but can be stretched from g to b″ or even high c‴. The same is true of the contralto, the lowest female voice, which is characterised by a greater volume and a darker timbre.

Up until the middle of the nineteenth century the term "mezzo-soprano" was not used, as only the contralto existed, in various types. With the advent of the Romantic School and the consequent extension of the tessitura, there arose a need for *mezzo-soprani*: from the classic role of the soprano's rival (Amneris in *Aida*), to the principal role (Leonora in *Favorita*), from the dreamy Mignon to the sensual Carmen, from the high singing Valentine in *Les Huguenots* to the deep, low La Cieca in *La Gioconda*. In Ger-many there exists a traditional division between the *dramatischer Alt*, or dramatic mezzo-soprano, with a solid and incisive vocality (Erda in the *Ring*), and the *komischer Alt*, the comic mezzo-soprano, whose voice is more extended and agile (Frau Reich in *The Merry Wives of Windsor*, by Nicolai).

The sub-division of the mezzo-soprano and contralto voices in our century can only be based on each individual singer's repertoire, as the many definitions that exist for the tenor and soprano voice (light, lyric, dramatic, etc.) do not exist in this category.

However the mezzo-soprano repertory can be divided like this: the Romantic Italian and French works (Donizetti, Verdi, Thomas, Masse-net); the Verist repertory (the Italian Young School and French Naturalism); the German repertory (Wagner, Richard Strauss) and the Russian repertoire (the Group of Five, Tchaikovsky, Shostakovich).

THE ITALIAN AND FRENCH ROMANTIC REPERTOIRE

Our roster starts with **Margarete Matzenauer** (Temesvàr 1881-Van Nuys, California 1963), described by Lauri-Volpi as "a bewitching voice". Her debut was made in 1901, as Puck in Weber's *Oberon*; but it was not long before the public could applaud her vibrant interpretations of Azucena, Amneris, Laura (*Gioconda*), *Orfeo* (Gluck), Delilah, Fidès (*Le Prophète*), and her wonderful Wagnerian performances, even those as a soprano (Isolde, Kundry, Ortrude, Brünn-hilde).

From Monaco to New York, from London to Paris, from Bayreuth to Buenos Aires, Matzenauer was acclaimed for her absolutely exceptional voice: her rich timbre, a perfect polish, a rare extension, equality in all the registers, pow-er and penetration. These gifts were sustained by a fluid and smooth technique of vocal projection, worthy of a great singer.

Strangely, her recordings seem to demonstrate the opposite.

After 1914 she sang chiefly in contralto roles, including Kostelnička in the American première of *Jenufa*, and Eboli in the first Met perfor-mance.

Her farewell to the stage took place in 1934, at the Lewisohn Stadium in New York, with a last performance of *Samson and Delilah*.

Fanny Anitùa (Durango 1887 - Mexico City 1969) studied in her homeland but did advanced studies in Rome, and made her debut at the Teatro Nazionale (Gluck's *Orfeo*) in 1910. The statuesque Mexican must have made quite an impression when she entered on stage with her imposing physique and voice. From 1910 until 1939 she sang regularly in Italy, America, and in the Latin-American theatres, keeping *Trovatore, Ballo in Maschera* (Ulrica), *Orfeo, Aida, Samson*

and Delilah in her repertoire, and singing the role of Etra in the first-ever performance of *Fedra* by Pizzetti. Her voice was known for its extension, vigor — both in the high and low notes — and discreet agility.

Two authentic, wonderful Verdi contraltos were **Elvira Casazza** (Ferrara 1884 - Milan 1965) and **Cloe Elmo** (Lecce 1910 - Ankara 1962). Casazza created the role of Jaele in Pizzetti's opera *Debora and Jaele* (La Scala, 1922), and had low notes which sounded like those of a baritone. Cloe Elmo was an unforgettable Azucena, Quickly, and Ulrica, equal and brilliant over her entire wide range.

And we musn't omit the gifted but unfortunate **Kathleen Ferrier** (Higher Walton, Lancashire 1912 - London 1953) who died of cancer at the height of a great career. The terrain favoured by her warm, velvety, smooth and precious voice was not that of opera (even if she often sang Gluck's *Orfeo*, and a single *Carmen*) but Lied and oratorio, with a special preference for Mahler. Her version of the *Lied von der Erde* and the *Kindertotenlieder*, under the baton of the great Bruno Walter, is an example of a refined and sensitive art. She was unique for the depth

of her interpretations and the pure beauty of her vocal timbre. The cancer of which she died prevented her from completing her series of Covent Garden performance, as Gluck's Orpheus, 1953.

When she had just finished her studies **Gabriella Besanzoni** (Rome 1890-1962) seemed destined for a brilliant career as a coloratura soprano; but she soon realised that she was more suited to the dramatic soprano and mezzo-soprano *tessitura*. This drastic change did not damage her general voice placement thus proving the fantastic resistance of this singer from Rome. Her low notes were solid and generous; her high notes were luminous and penetrating; her character was fiery. With such means Besanzoni could be nothing less than a magnificent Amneris, Orfeo, Carmen, Isabella (*Italiana in Algeri*) and Cenerentola, revealing tremendous versatility. She was adored by the Latin-American public, especially in Argentina; but she also gained extraordinary success in Italy and New York, often performing together with Caruso.

Rarely in our century have we had the opportunity of hearing a more powerful or extended voice than that of **Sigrid Onegin** (Elisabeth Elfriede Emilie Hoffmann; Stockholm 1889 - Magliaso, Lugano 1943), who was always correct in the vocal line she chose for various operas.

During the period from 1912 (when she made her debut in *Carmen* at Stuttgart) until 1934, she performed in Germany, London and New York over a wide repertoire: *Orfeo*, *Le Prophète*, *Don Carlos*, Eboli, *Macbeth*, *the Ring*, the role of Brangäne in *Tristan*, and Driade in the first performance of Strauss's *Ariadne auf Naxos*.

Perhaps the recordings of the time do not do justice to her (and to most of her fellow singers); however her interpretive taste in Eboli's "Canzone del Velo" and in the aria from *La Favorita* seem quite questionable.

Marian Anderson (Philadelphia 1902) is worthy of a special mention. Despite the problems caused by racial discrimination in the United

Gabriella Besanzoni as Carmen. After her beginning as a coloratura soprano, she starred in Viterbo in 1911 as Adalgisa in Norma. (Historic Archives of the Rome Opera Theatre).

Here is **Elvira Casazza** in an heroic pose, interpreting the role she made famous - Debora in Debora and Jaele, an opera by Pizzetti. In the part of Jaéle the magnificent soprano Giulia Tess; Arturo Toscanini conducted.

States, she managed to triumph at the Metropolitan in 1955 as Ulrica in *Un Ballo in Maschera*. Anderson was famous for the incredible equality and darkness of her vocal colour. She was excellent in Lieder, and specialised in Spirituals.

Though she held her first concert in 1925, her career moved slowly and against many and great difficulties; and it was only in the following decade that she gained recognition in Europe and Australia. Miss Anderson later gave an historic concert at the Lincoln Memorial in Washington, D.C. before 75,000 people; President Franklin Delano Roosevelt was a great friend and admirer of Marian Anderson and was among the appreciative spectators at the event.

After her memorable Ulrica at the Met, she performed frequently in important theatres, exhibiting her splendid talent. In 1965 she retired after an extraordinarily successful worldwide tour.

Here are some other historical names which emerge from among the *mezzo-soprani* active in the Italian repertory at the turn of the century: **Louise Kirkby-Lunn** (Manchester 1873 - St.

and Adalgisa; **Louise Homer** (Pittsburgh 1871 - Winter Park, Florida 1947) a famous Amneris, Orfeo, Adalgisa, and Laura in *Gioconda*; **Florica Cristoforeanu** (Rimnin-Sarat, Romania 1887 - Rio de Janeiro 1960); **Aurora Buades** (Valencia 1897 - Florence 1965) a diva of the Latin-American theatres; **Maria Capuana** (Fano, Pesaro 1891 - Cagliari 1955), very involved in the Wagnerian repertory but famous also as Amneris; **Marie Delna** (Meudon 1875 - Paris 1932); **Maria Gay** (Barcelona 1879 - New York 1943) who was the wife of the tenor Zenatello, with whom she formed a historic couple in *Carmen* and *Aida*; **Marthe Chenal** (S. Maurice, Paris 1881 - 1947); **Gladys Swarthout** (Deepwater, Missouri 1904 - Florence 1969) starred in many films; **Edith Coates** (Lincoln 1908 - 1983) who worked constantly in the London theatres from 1931 until 1963, and was famous as Auntie in *Peter Grimes*; **Pia Tassinari** (Faenza 1909) was at first a lyric soprano, then from the forties on she became a sensitive and refined performer in the mezzo-soprano roles (Carmen, Charlotte); **Eugenia Zareska** (Rava Ruska 1910) active in the

Ebe Stignani in Orfeo *by Gluck, a role which she affronted with a large and powerful voice and, above all, her refined stylistic gifts. (Historic Archives of the Rome Opera Theatre. Photo: Camuzzi).*

Risë Stevens, a Met star from 1938 on, especially cherished as Carmen. She also acted in films (including Going My Way *with Bing Crosby, 1944).*

John's Wood 1930), active at the Metropolitan and Covent Garden, sounding mostly like a train whistle; **Dame Clara Butt** (Southwick, Sussex 1873 - North Stoke 1936) famed for her cavernous low notes; **Margarethe Arndt-Ober** (Berlin 1885 - Bad Sachsa 1971) famous as Eboli, Amneris, and Azucena despite her definite vocal limits in the high register; **Irene Minghini-Cattaneo** (Lugo di Romagna 1892 - Rimini 1944) whose voice was well coloured and equal, and whose temperament was formidable; the contralto **Luisa Bertana** (Quilmes, Buenos Aires 1888 - 1933) chosen by Toscanini as Preziosilla

Mozart repertory and a famed Carmen at Covent Garden; **Rosette Anday** (Budapest 1903 - Vienna 1977); **Blanche Deschamps-Jehin** (Lyon 1857 - Paris 1923) an exceptional performer in the French repertory with many premiere performances to her credit (Lalo's *Le Roi d'Ys*, Charpentier's *Louise*, and the first performance of Saint-Saens' *Samson et Dalila* in Paris).

The following generation saw these names emerging: **Irene Dalis** (San José, California 1925) was able to perform in a wide-reaching repertoire; **Grace Hoffmann** (Goldie Hoffmann; Cleveland 1925), famous as Eboli, Brangäne and Kundry in the American and German theatres; **Kerstin Meyer** (Stockholm 1928) a singing actress of worth and sensitivity who performed in many contempory operas; **Anna Pollak** (Manchester 1912) studied with Joan Cross; **Monica Sinclair** (Somerset 1926), active in the Handel repertory, often in the company of Joan Sutherland, despite her precise vocal and stylistic limits; **Rosalind Elias** (Lowell, Massachusetts 1929), very active at the Metropolitan, as were **Mignon Dunn** (Memphis, Tennessee 1932); **Viorica Cortez** (Bucium, Rumania 1935); **Rita Gorr** (Ghent, Belgium 1926), with a wide and demanding repertoire; **Risë Stevens** (New York 1913) active between 1936 and 1964 in a large number of roles, but particularly favouring those of Carmen and Orfeo. We must not leave out **Nan Merriman** (Pittsburgh 1920); **Miriam Pirazzini** (Vicenza 1918) a famous Azucena, Laura and Preziosilla; **Alicia Nafé** (Buenos Aires 1948); **Josephine Veasey** (London 1930); **Oralia Dominguez** (San Luis Potosì, Mexico 1927); **Jean Madeira** (Centralia, Illinois 1918 - Providence, New York 1972) — a splendid Dalila, Carmen, and Ulrica; and finally **Nadine Denize** (Rouen 1943).

Ebe Stignani: Her Voice Had the Sound of a Stradivarius

Among the greatest Italian singers ever, we must include **Ebe Stignani** (Naples 1904 - Imola 1974), the Verdi mezzo-soprano par excellence. After her debut at the San Carlo Theatre of Naples in 1925 (as Amneris in *Aida*) she frequently sang the roles of Amneris, Adalgisa (*Norma*),

Fedora Barbieri, a Carmen of great beauty and explosive vitality.

Eboli, Laura (*Gioconda*), Leonora (*Favorita*), Azucena, Ulrica, and Santuzza, giving to these characters a vocal polish and luminosity of unsurpassable beauty.

Her timbre was rich and limpid, completely controlled by her breathing-the technique of an authentic belcanto diva, which assured her rounded and homogeneous sounds, an impeccable legato, and cutting high notes that reached up to high c ′′′ (as witnessed by her performances of *L'Italiana in Algeri*, *Cenerentola*, *Mosè*, and even by her *Semiramide* at Florence). Her generous and monumental phrasing, supported by her clear enunciation, could be fully appreciated in Gluck's *Orfeo*, where Stignani's voice was at its natural best. She retired from the stage in 1958, still in excellent vocal form, following her last triumphal performances of *Ballo in Maschera*, *Trovatore*, and *Aida*. Farewell appearance, Azucena, London, Drury Lane, 1958.

Happily Ever After.......

A long period of apprenticeship preceded the brilliant international success of **Giulietta Simionato** (Forlì 1910). She first sang in Pizzetti's *Orseolo* at twenty-five years of age; but her big break came only in 1947, after several acclaimed performances of *Così fan Tutte* (Dorabella) and *Mignon*. It had been a long but useful training, as it had helped the singer refine not only her vocal art but also her scenic style and acting skills without fatiguing her precious voice with overwork, which leads to premature wear.

In many respects Simionato preceded the advent of the Rossini *contralto d'agilità*, like Horne, singing in some important revivals (*Semiramide* with Joan Sutherland, 1961, at La Scala, *Tancredi*, *Barbiere*, *Cenerentola*, *Italiana in Algeri*). In these performances she demonstrated an excellent use of florid singing, fluid vocalising, precise trilling and tasteful variations. These gifts were rare indeed amongst *mezzo-soprani* who were active in the pioneering years of the Rossini renaissance.

Her warm and flexible voice, governed by a refined technique and style, permitted Simionato to perform in many operas: from the legendary *Anna Bolena* (La Scala 1957) with Maria Callas, to *Norma* and *Favorita*; from *Aida* to *Trovatore*; from *Carmen* to *Don Carlos*; from Handel's *Julius Caesar* to *Les Huguenots* (as Valentina). In this last opera her death scene was simply amazing. More than for just her vocal power, one admired Simionato for her sense of moderation and vocal adaptability in every kind of opera, be it belcanto or verismo. Her discipline and technical security allowed her to sing magnificently for over thirty years. Farewell performance, Piccola Scala, Servilia in *La Clemenza di Tito*, 1966.

Regina Resnik as Clytemnestra in Elektra. *She was the Baroness in the première of Barber's* Vanessa, *1958, and Claire in the first U.S. performance of Einem's* Der Besuch der alten Dame, *1972.*

The voice of **Fedora Barbieri** (Trieste 1920) was greater in volume and power, but less stylised than that of Simionato. Fedora is unforgettable as Quickly in Verdi's *Falstaff*. It will be difficult to hear such full and resonant low g's again: the fact is that the many "Reverenza" and "Silenzio, silenzio" produced by this Italian mezzo were so powerful because they rested on the *poitrinés* — that is, on an artificially enlarged sound which in the long run is harmful to the equality of the registers. However, from the end of the fifties, after two decades of glorious career (she made her debut in 1940 at Florence singing Fidalma in *Matrimonio Segreto* one day and Azucena in *Trovatore* the next), there began to appear noticeable inequalities and harsh sounds in her voice, due to vocal stress and her inability to produce a light projection.

The beauty of her timbre and her acting ability have made Barbieri one of the most important interpreters of the roles of Azucena, Ulrica, Dalila, Amneris, Carmen, Orfeo, and the Leonora of Gusman; but she has also performed as Isabella in *Italiana in Algeri* and Cenerentola (even if with precise stylistic limits). Her amiable Quickly (which she continued to sing throughout the seventies) has become legendary, for her temperament in this part will be difficult to equal. However we must also mention her splendid Madelon in *Andrea Chénier* at Vienna in the 1982 season, where you could still hear some of her old talent. She sang at Buenos Aires, Colón, 1947; Covent Garden, 1950, 1957-8 as Azucena, Eboli and Amneris; New York, Met, 1950-4, 1956-7, 1967-8, making her début on opening night of Bing's régime as Eboli.

After having begun her career as a soprano in New York in 1942 singing Lady Macbeth, **Regina Resnik** (New York 1922) decided to change range towards the second half of the fifties, when she began to have serious difficulties in performing dramatic soprano roles. She studied the part of Amneris for a whole year, then made her debut as a mezzo-soprano at the Metropolitan, singing Marina in *Boris*. With time there followed Azucena, Carmen, Ulrica, Quickly, Clytemnestra and roles from a considerable number of contemporary works, all distinguished by her inborn stage presence and her warm, solid vocality. Notwithstanding her severe decline and damaged vocal means Resnik continued on American stages for a long time (in 1982 she was much applauded as the Countess in Tchaikovsky's *Queen of Spades*); she has always been affectionately received by her public.

The Voice-Instrument of Fiorenza Cossotto

Ebe Stignani's heir was **Fiorenza Cossotto** (Crescentino, Vercelli 1935) who possesses a voice-instrument with a precious sound polish — vibrant and incisive in the high register, delicate in the mezzavoce, passionate in her phrasing and acting. She made her debut in Milan in 1957, as Matilde in *Dialogues des Carmelites* by Poulenc: Cossotto performed with the typical characteristics of the *mezzo-soprano acuto* and with a perfect vocal placement, formed in the school of Ettore Campogalliani. In 1962 she played the difficult part of Urbano in *Les Huguenots* at La Scala, revealing a noteworthy virtuosity and a unique extension. These gifts would later allow her to sing Rossini, Handel, Bellini and Donizetti.

Quite soon Cossotto began to appear in the heavier mezzo-soprano roles, triumphing as Amneris, Eboli, Santuzza, Azucena, Leonora, and as the Princess de Bouillon in *Adriana Lecouvreur*, which is her very best interpretation.

Many of us regret her too many performances of *Aida* and *Adriana* at the expense of a more constant dedication to the belcanto repertoire;

Fiorenza Cossotto *in her phenomenal interpretation of Eboli. We especially remember the exceptional evening in Rome at the RAI at the beginning of the sixties: on the podium, Schippers; Ghiaurov (Filippo II), Cappuccilli (Rodrigo), Prevedi (Don Carlos), Zylis-Gara (Elisabetta) and a Cossotto unforgettable in the aria "O don fatale", long applauded by the audience. (Historic Archives of the Salzburg Festival. Photo: Rabanus).*

but it is also true that Cossotto's vigorous performances of "Anatema su voi!" and "Acerba voluttà" will be remembered for a long time by her audience.

The demanding repertory which she has performed for over thiry years (and an endless number of open-air performances — so damaging to the vocal chords) has had its effect on her voice today. However the intact vigour of her first high notes and the beauty of her middle range do much to compensate; and she remains the last of the real *mezzo-soprani*.

Two Shining Rivals

It is difficult to classify the ambiguous voices of **Shirley Verrett** (New Orleans 1931) and **Grace Bumbry** (Saint Louis, Missouri 1937) who are both undecided as to whether they are mezzo-sopranos or dramatic sopranos. With unhappy results, Bumbry sang as a dramatic soprano (Tosca, Agibaile, Gioconda, Aida), as did Verrett (Norma, Amelia in *Ballo in Maschera*). And it is probably better to consider these two excellent artists as *mezzo-soprani*, whose natural extension in the high register (both reach high c‴ sharp, and Verrett even goes as far as d‴) does not mean that they can resist the damage caused by a constant, fatiguing change of *tessitura*, especially difficult in the delicate *passaggio* area.

Compared to her rival, Shirley Verrett is more charming and aristocratic with a greater ease in florid singing, to the point that she can overcome the difficult Rossini parts (*Mosè, Assedio di Corinto*, and Rosina's aria, which she often sings in recital) and chooses for her favourite encore the difficult "Alleluja" from Mozart's motet "Exultate, Jubilate". Amongst the best renderings of this American artist are Carmen, Lady Macbeth, Elisabetta in *Maria Stuarda*, Dalila, and Dido in Berlioz' *Les Troyens*; she also has a noteworthy Lieder activity. Lately, however, her performances of *Cavalleria Rusticana* and Dalila, and even her concert performances, have shown clear signs of an irreversible vocal decline.

Grace Bumbry has a more fiery temperament and incisive phrasing worthy of a real "tigress". Thus her Carmen or her sensual Eboli become somewhat wild characters, who are, however, capable of languid sweetness in the more relaxed, melodic moments. Among Bumbry's best characterisations we must list Salome and Amneris, in which she also puts on show a rather attractive figure.

We must not forget that these two illustrious rivals faced each other at close range in a concert organized in America in 1984, which was later repeated, when the two singers alternated soprano and mezzo-soprano arias, concluding

The splendid **Shirley Verrett** *photographed during a memorable recital held at the Rome Opera in April, 1986. Right from the beginning of her career, Verrett has dedicated a large part of her activity to the concert platform, realising a series of uncontested successes. (Photo: Annamaria Bernardini).*

Dressed like this, **Grace Bumbry** *doesn't have much difficulty in putting on show her curvaceous figure. She is Carmen in Rome in March 1970: directed by Bolchi with scenes by Guttuso. (Historic Archives of the Rome Opera Theatre).*

172

*Recording Verdi's Don Carlos for EMI: chatting are **Shirley Verrett**, left, and **Montserrat Caballé**; respectively Eboli and Elisabetta di Valois. Verrett has a voice of large extension and agility, enabling her to dominate with confidence a very wide repertory. (Giandonato Crico Collection).*

with the duets from *Norma, Anna Bolena*, and *Gioconda*, and, in closing, the duet between Norma and Adalgisa "Sì, fino all'ore estreme".

Both born in the same year, **Tatiana Troyanos** (New York 1938) and **Yvonne Minton** (Sydney 1938) have a good reputation in many international theatres. Troyanos alternates belcanto roles (Ariodante, Adalgisa, Julius Ceasar, Seymour in *Anna Bolena*, Sesto in *Clemenza di Tito*), which she tackles with a little too much zeal, and romantic roles (Charlotte, Amneris, Carmen, Preziosilla, and Marina in *Boris*), verist parts (Santuzza), Wagnerian roles (Kundry, Venus in *Tannhäuser*), Strauss works (Octavian in *Der Rosenkavalier*, the Composer in *Ariadne auf Naxos*), and even modern pieces (she was the first to sing in the killing opera of Penderecki, *The Devils of Loudon* at Hamburg in 1969). Her voice is full and powerful, extended up to c‴, and agile, even if she needs to be strictly controlled considering her tendency to exaggerate.

Yvonne Minton is more moderate and careful of the expressive possibilities of her role. She is well known as Brangania, Orfeo, Octavian, Dorabella, and is also a worthy performer of Lieder.

A singer who has had great success over the last few years is the Greek **Agnes Baltsa** (Lefkas 1944). She is active in a repertory which ranges from Mozart (Cherubino, Dorabella) and Gluck (Orfeo) to Rossini (Rosina, Cenerentola, Isabella), Bellini (Romeo), Donizetti (Elisabetta in *Maria Stuarda*), Verdi (Eboli and Amneris), Bizet (Carmen), Massenet (Thérèse, Hérodiade) and Strauss (the Composer in *Ariadne auf Naxos*, Octavian in *Der Rosenkavalier*). Baltsa brings to these roles a well timbred voice, sweet and

velvety, a considerable agility and extension (she has easy, penetrating high notes), a perfect breath control and an elegant stage presence. She was one of von Karajan's favourite singers,

*Radiant and beautiful **Shirley Verrett** as Carmen, in the early Sixties (Giandonato Crico Collection).*

and he often invited her to sing at the Salzburg Festival, and included her in all his major recordings. In addition to her operatic activity, the Greek artist (who was already a gifted pianist at the age of seven) often performs in Lieder and concert recitals.

Personally we do not appreciate certain vulgar exaggerations which Baltsa has recently displayed in operas like *Carmen* and *Don Carlos*; but we also disapprove of the over-harsh attack on her by some critics. Agnes Baltsa remains an excellent performer who is backed by a good voice and a fine musical preparation.

The Verist Mezzo-Soprano

Given the prevalence of the Verist style during the first fifty years of this century, we should probably feel obliged to include many singers who are not truly verist (in voice type or in repertoire) but who were dragged along by the fashion of the time. However we prefer to cite

19th January, 1953. **Gianna Pederzini** and **Nicola Rossi-Lemeni** in the Macbeth *composed by Bloch; an absolute innovation for Rome. (Historic Archives of the Rome Opera Theatre. Photo: O. Savio).*

the greatest mezzo-soprano in the verist repertory and the French *Lyrique*: **Gianna Pederzini** (Vò di Avio, Trento 1900 - Rome 1988). She studied with De Lucia in Naples, and made her debut in Messina in 1923 as Preziosilla in *Forza del Destino*.

Right at the start Pederzini demonstrated a fine virtuoso talent, distinguishing herself in operas by Rossini (*Conte Ory*, *Barbiere*, *Italiana in Algeri*), Flotow (*Martha*), Bellini (*Norma*), Meyerbeer (*Les Huguenots* as the Page), accompanying her vocal arabesques with spicy acting skills. Thanks to her uncommon vocal gifts and her innate dramatic nature she was soon able to include *Aida*, *Adriana Lecouvreur*, *Carmen*, *Fedora*, *Cavalleria*, *Werther* and *Mignon*, in her repertoire, and create potent characterisations in *The Queen of Spades*, Menotti's *The Medium*, Bloch's *Macbeth*; and she took part in the premiere performance of Poulenc's *Dialogues des Carmelites* at La Scala in 1957.

Milan, Rome, London, Buenos Aires, Paris, Berlin, Barcelona are all cities in which, between 1923 and the end of the Fifties, Gianna Pederzini triumphed, dominating the stage with a rare artistic intelligence and personal charm.

Gianna Pederzini in Carmen, one of her favourite roles. (Historic Archives of La Fenice Theatre, Venice. Photo: Giacomelli).

The Belcanto Mezzo-Soprano and The *Contralto d'Agilità*

Conchita Supervia (Barcelona 1895 - London 1936) was the forerunner of the great *mezzo-soprani d'agilità* who are so fashionable today. She made her debut at Buenos Aires in 1910 (*Los Amantes de Teruel* by Bréton), and in 1914 she was already able to perform the parts of Rosina, Isabella, and Cenerentola with correct vocal style and virtuosity. In 1925 she had an extraordinary success in *L'Italiana in Algeri* at Turin conducted by Vittorio Gui; but most of the world's great theatres had the opportunity of applauding Supervia in her Rossini performances.

Nor did this singer limit her career to the composer who came from Pesaro. She was also an excellent *Carmen*, Octavian in Der *Rosenkavalier*, and Cherubino, uniting vocal talent and a bright and entertaining stage presence.

An additional name: **Jennie Tourel** (Montreal 1899 - New York 1973) who was the first mezzo-soprano to sing Rosina at the Met in 1945. She included Cenerentola, Adalgisa, Mignon and Carmen in her repertoire. Tourel was much respected by great conductors like Toscanini

and Bernstein for her musicality and style, even if her voice was not extraordinarily gifted. In 1973, not long before dying, she sang the Marquise in the *Fille du Régiment* in Chicago.

A Lady-like Carmen

After the decisive "lessons" given to mezzo-sopranos by Simionato in Rossini and by Callas to sopranos, **Teresa Berganza** (Madrid 1934) then carried on the "good work" in Mozart and Rossini, highlighting correct technique and style. Her voice has never been powerful, nor particularly extended, but her timbre is beautiful, and equal in all the registers; she is fluid in vocalisation, smooth in legato, able and imaginative in her use of shading. She made her debut some years ago in 1955, with a concert at the Ateneo of Madrid; but her career really took off after her performances at the Festival at Aix-en-Provence in 1957, when she sang Dorabella in *Così fan Tutte*. Teresa Berganza immediately displayed her skill as an extraordinarily refined stylist, and went on to perform many of the most important parts in eighteenth and nineteenth

*Poor Cinderella (**Teresa Berganza**) is pulled away by Don Magnifico (**Paolo Montarsolo**) under the gaze of Dandini (**Renato Capecchi**). (Historic Archives of the Teatro Comunale of Florence. Photo: Marchiori).*

An unequalled star of many productions of Cenerentola *and* Il Barbiere di Siviglia, **Teresa Berganza** *has even brought her Rosina to the screen.*

century opera repertory: Isabella, Rosina, Isolier in *Le Comte Ory*, Cenerentola, Zerlina, Cherubino, Dorabella; and she has even managed to restore the difficult role of Carmen to its *opera-comique* origins, ridding it of useless exaggerations and respecting Bizet's music in every detail.

The Spanish mezzo still gives concerts, which always turn into enjoyable evenings where everybody applauds her good taste, her elegant verve, and her perfect singing technique — applied to Spanish folk music, seventeenth and eighteenth century chamber arias, and to her favourite operatic arias.

We can not forget, either, the wonderful recital she gave at the Gasteig in Munich in 1986, performing with Domingo: faultlessly singing arias from *Carmen*, *Mignon*, *Don Giovanni*, and from various *Zarzuelas*, Berganza outclassed her famous colleague.

Belcanto Marilyn

Marilyn Horne (Bradford, Pennsylvania 1928 or 1934?) has appeared on the scene as the only the true *contralto d'agilità* in our century. She is able to make the lower female voice obey bel-

*After the lesson scene, **Marilyn Horne** receives the warm applause of the audience at Macerata during a performance in 1980. In place of the* rondò *written by Rossini, she revived a custom of many prima-donnas of the past, and inserted a scene taken from another Rossini opera (in this case, Tancredi) and, on the request of the public, she gave, without accompaniment, an encore of an American song by Stephen Foster.*

canto requirements in Handel and Rossini, to push it up *into* perilous *tessiture* and into impossible acrobatics. She makes her voice instrumental, and the instrument is an instrument of pathos.

This exceptional voice did not develop because of any particularly famous teacher, but grew out of her father's encouragement and her own strict self-discipline. Initially Horne alternated performances as a soprano (Maria in *Wozzek*, San Francisco, 1960, Marie in *Fille du Régiment*, San Francisco, 1962, and even Minnie in *The Girl of the Golden West*) to those as a mezzosoprano (*Cenerentola*, Los Angeles, 1956; *Carmen*, San Francisco, 1961; Arsace in *Semiramide*, New York, 1964), where she demonstrated her extremely fluid projection and her gifts as a virtuoso.

She began singing the Rossini repertory more frequently, with enormous success (*Barbiere* at Florence, 1967; *Italiana in Algeri* at the RAI in Turin in 1968; Neocle in *Assedio di Corinto* at La Scala in 1969) putting her best qualities on show. Hers is a velvety timbre (obtained by an able use of *poitrinée* technique which has not harmed the equality of her registers), and an amazing ability in all the belcanto requisites (tight trills, fast vocalisation, *roulades*, *messe di voce*, and *canto di sbalzo*): these qualities developed thanks to a unique way of singing in the throat in the centre register and a perfect use of breath on every note.

Horne is also able to display a great exuberance and incisiveness in the long recitatives in *travesti* (pants) roles (Arsace, Calbo, Malcolm, Falliero, Neocle, Tancredi, Orlando — both by Vivaldi and Handel — and Handel's Rinaldo) that often recalls the incredible *castrati* of past centuries (as far as we can judge by the praise which was written about them in their time).

Amongst her most memorable performances, we must remember her historical *Semiramide* in duo with Joan Sutherland, Handel's *Rinaldo* at Houston in 1975 (with the acrobatic aria ''Or la tromba in suon festante'' where she competed with a solo trumpet — a feat worthy of Farinelli!), and Handel's *Orlando* in Venice in 1985.

However her performances out of the belcanto repertory are not so successful, as is proved by her tired Amneris at Salzburg, where she was almost always covered by von Karajan's powerful sonority; or by her exaggerated *Carmen* in Macerata (1982), which was blatantly vulgar by the end of the opera, ruining even her fascinating renderings of the solo arias (''Habanera'', ''Seguedilla'' and ''Chanson bohème'').

''Di tanti palpiti...'' (So Many Heart-Beats): Tancredi

The *contralto d'agilità* most active in Italy is **Lucia Valentini-Terrani** (Padua 1946). She studied with Iris Adami-Corradetti, and won the Rossini competition held by the RAI at the beginning of the Seventies.

She made her debut as *Cenerentola* during the 1968-69 season at Brescia. The role has remained dear to this artist, and in it she can put on show her warm, burnished timbre, together with her exceptional technical gifts.

As prescribed by the best manuals, Valentini's agility flows rapidly on the breath and she is quite equal over all the registers, from the low to the high, thanks to her good vocal placement. She has a few problems: in the passage between her middle and lower register she gives a slightly ''out-of-focus'' result, and she does not attack the high notes forcefully. Despite this, however, we find ourselves in the presence of a vocalist of rare quality — ideal interpreter of Isabella, Malcolm (*Donna del Lago*), Cenerentola, Arsace, and Tancredi — roles which Valentini-Terrani renders without Horne's absolute security, perhaps, but with the audacious style of a real *Diva*.

Thanks to her smooth emission, her pure timbre, and her variety of vocal shadings, Valentini-Terrani has been able to include some French *lyrique* roles in her repertoire: Charlotte in *Werther*, Mignon, Dulcinea in *Don Quichotte*, and Carmen (which she sang for the first time in Bonn in 1986) with note-worthy results. She has rendered the part of Marina in *Boris Godunov* surprisingly well. The Italian mezzo is also very active in Lieder and concert repertory, having often sung Verdi's *Requiem*, Beethoven's *Ninth Symphony*, Mahler's symphonics and Lieder, and Brahms' *German Requiem*.

Recently the Venetian singer has shown a certain vocal fatigue, which has been harmful to the equality of her registers and has made her voice opaque. In summing up, however, because of her interest and extreme care and study in preparing a role Valentini-Terrani belongs to the restricted number of singers who are also ''musicians''.

Dame Janet Baker (York 1932) gave her farewell to the stage in 1982 after a final series of performances of those works which made her world famous: *Alceste* by Gluck, *Maria Stuarda* by Donizetti, and *Orfeo* by Gluck, roles which she performed at Covent Garden, the English National Opera, and the Glyndebourne Festival — the theatres most familiar to her.

Baker made her debut at Edinburgh in 1960, and soon after specialised in Handel's operas and oratorio. As time went on her repertory be-

177

came wider and included Purcell, Britten, Lully, Haydn, Mozart, Gluck, Berlioz, Monteverdi, Richard Strauss (Octavian in *Der Rosenkavalier*), Bellini (Romeo in *Capuleti e Montecchi*) and Donizetti (Maria in *Maria Stuarda*, in which she lowered the tone). All these different roles and styles were approached with great musicality and intelligence, making use of a well-educated, smooth and flexible voice. We notice a certain frigidity and lack of imagination in the Handel belcanto repertory, where, perhaps with the guidance of competent conductors, she could have added tasteful variations in the *da capo*, and thus made her characterisations more vibrant and more philologically correct.

A brief mention of the English mezzo-soprano **Carolyn Watkinson** (Preston 1949), who specialized in the Baroque repertory (Rameau's *Hippolyte et Aricie*; *Ariodante*; *Incoronazione di Poppea*), often working with prestigious companies such as La Grande Écurie et la Chambre du Roi of Jean-Claude Malgloire.

Of minor importance; but still quite interesting, are the Rossini interpretations of the American **Frederica von Stade** (Sommerville, New Jersey 1945) and the French **Martine Dupuy** (Marseille 1952). The first has specialised in the roles of Rosina, Desdemona (Rossini's *Otello*), Cenerentola, and Elena (*Donna del Lago*). The second, instead, has specialised in the *travesti* roles, such as Malcolm (*Donna del Lago*), Arsace, Falliero, Giulio Cesare, or Romeo in Bellini's opera *I Capuleti e Montecchi*. Von Stade is famous as an intense and fascinating Mozart singer who gives a unique characterisation to the role of Cherubino and to Annio (*Clemenza di Tito*) mainly in Anglo-Saxon productions, but also at La Scala. In May, 1986, she obtained a great success in *Pélleas et Mélisande* by Debussy at La Scala. She was Tina in the first performance of Argento's opera *The Aspern Papers* in Dallas, 1988.

Dupuy does not have the beautiful pure timbre of her American colleague, but she is more creative and better technically prepared, and she always stands out in the fast vocalizing passages and in variations in the *da capo* arias. For years she has been a fixed presence at the Pesaro Rossini Festival and at the Martinafranca Festival, taking part in many important "rediscoveries" and revivals.

The first operatic steps in Rossini territory by **Luciana d'Intino** (S. Vito al Tagliamento, Pordenone 1959) and **Cecilia Bartoli** (Rome 1966) give positive indications for the future. They are two young singers who do not have large voices but who are both very musically and stylistically prepared, have a good command of the stage (especially the fun-loving Bartoli) and are both easily capable of resolving the vocal and interpretive difficulties posed by the theatrical works of Mozart and Rossini.

Recently the Swedish mezzo **Anne-Sofie von Otter** (Stockholm 1955) has won her share of the limelight as the protagonist of a noteworthy *Tancredi* at Geneva in 1990. She is a voluptuous mezzo-soprano, gifted with a warm and agile voice.

Martine Dupuy *(Romeo) in* Capuleti e Montecchi *by Bellini. (Photo: E. Bisazza. Verona).*

THE MEZZO-SOPRANO IN THE GERMAN REPERTORY

Altough chronologically she belongs more to the last century than to this, **Ernestine Schumann-Heink** (born E. Rössler; Lieben, Prague 1861 - Hollywood 1936) can be nominated as the historical beginning of the German dramatic mezzo-sopranos of the twentieth century, as her career stretched from 1876 until 1932: at seventy-one years of age she still managed to sing Erda in *Siegfried*. She had almost a hundred and fifty different roles in her repertory, thus showing an incomparable versatility. Her great voice flow, which reached up to a high b″, splendidly suited the difficult Wagnerian roles (Brangäne, Ortrud, Erda, Fricka, Waltraute), finding its ideal realisation in the part of Clytemnestra (*Elektra* by Richard Strauss), of which she was the first performer at Dresden in 1909.

She sang pop music, acted in a film (*Here's to Romance*, 1935), and made a recording of Maffio Orsini's "Brindisi" (*Lucrezia Borgia*, by Donizetti) in a belcanto version that included an excellent tight trill.

Karin Branzell (Maria Branzell; Stockholm 1891 - Altadena, California 1974) was also a wonderful *dramatischer Alt* in the Wagnerian repertory. She sang from 1912 until 1944, mostly at the New York Metropolitan, gaining notable successes in *Die Walküre*, *Lohengrin*, and *Tristan und Isolde*, and as Amneris and Azucena as well. However (according to Lauri Volpi in his book *Voci Parallele* — and he was a "live" witness) Branzell was far less at ease in the Italian *cantabile* and *legato*. Her robust voice was better suited to Wagnerian declamation; and her recordings confirm the opinion of the great tenor.

We must list **Marie Goetze** (Berlin 1865 - 1922), an historic performer of Strauss at Berlin; **Kerstin Thorborg** (Venjan, Sweden 1896 - Stockholm 1970), who had a beautiful timbrical polish which she put at the service of such roles as Ortrud, Brangäne, Fricka, and Eglantine in Weber's opera *Euryanthe*; **Maria Olszewska** (Ludwigsschwaige, Bavaria 1892 - Klagenfurt 1969), a famous Wagnerian singer in Germany, who sang at Covent Garden from 1924 until 1932, and at the Met. from 1932 until 1935.

Belonging to the next generation, **Margarete Frida Klose** (Berlin 1902 - 1968) was active between 1925 and 1961. A noble contralto with unique timbrical charm and technical mastery, she was one of the best performers of *Orfeo*, *Tristan und Isolde* (Brangäne), *Lohengrin* (Or-

Blanche Thebom *in the title role of Bizet's* Carmen. *She was at the Met from 1944 to 1967, and sang the role of Dido in London's first complete performance of Berlioz's* Les Troyens *(Covent Garden, 1957).*

trud), *Salome* (Herodias), and *Elektra* (Clytemnestra) in the post World War I period. She took part in the "live" recordings the RAI made of *The Ring* in 1953, singing Erda and Waltraute under Furwängler's magical baton.

We should also mention **Elisabeth Höngen** (Gevelsberg, Westphalia 1906); **Hildegard Rössel-Majdan** (Moosbierbaum, Austria 1921); **Hertha Töpper** (Graz 1924); **Ira Malaniuk** (Stanislav, Ukraine 1923); **Marga Höffgen** (Müllheim, Baden 1921); **Maureen Forrester** (Montreal 1930); **Birgit Finnilä** (Falkenberg, Sweden 1931).

No list would be complete without **Blanche Thebom** (Monessen, Pennsylvania 1918), who studied in New York with Matzenauer and Edyth Walker. For more than twenty years she cast a splendid figure in all the major American opera halls. Protagonist of the 1955 American premier of Stravinsky's *The Rake's Progress*, she was also famous as Dido in a magnificent Covent Garden production of Berlioz' *Les Troyens*. After retiring from the stage in the mid 60's she taught musical studies at the University of Arkansas.

The ranks of the German mezzo-sopranos gradually diminished, but it is our duty to remember the great **Christa Ludwig** (Berlin 1924) who is still in active career after forty five years of singing (she made her debut in 1946 at Frankfurt as Prince Orlofsky in J. Strauss's *Die Fledermaus*). An extremely musical singer with a vast and varied repertoire, she is able to range from the typical *komischer Alt* parts (such as the above cited Orlofsky or Clairon in *Capriccio*) to more dramatic and vocally exhausting roles such as Fricka, Ortrud, Kundry, Octavian, the Composer and Ariadne in *Ariadne auf Naxos*, Eboli, Lady Macbeth, Azucena, Quickly, Adalgisa (*Norma*), Dorabella, Cherubino, and Ifigenia (Gluck).

All this is possible because of her admirable technique and an innate scenic talent that also makes her an excellent actress; and no one can forget her splendid Lieder and concert recitals, which have always gained her the respect of the world's greatest conductors.

Brigitte Fassbänder (Börn, Berlin 1939) has become Ludwig's successor, and is the best German mezzo-soprano of the moment. Her first basic singing lessons were given to her by her father — the great baritone Willy Domgraf-Fassbänder. She completed her studies in her native city and in Nuremberg. Since 1961 she has been present in the greatest theatres in a wide repertoire that includes Mozart (Dorabella, Cherubino, Sesto), Verdi (Amneris, Azucena, the *Requiem*), Johann Strauss (*Die Fledermaus*), Wagner (*Die Walküre*), Flotow (*Martha*), Pfitzner (*Palestrina*), plus a vast Lieder and recital selection. Her best vocal characteristics are her robust and burnished timbre, her equality over all the range, her extension, and her noteworthy verve, which is best displayed in the *travesti* roles of Orlofsky and Octavian in *Der Rosenkavalier*. In 1970 she was awarded the Bavarian title of Kammersängerin. Octavian in *Der Rosenkavalier* was her debut role at Covent Garden, 1971, and the Met, 1974.

THE MEZZO-SOPRANO IN THE RUSSIAN REPERTORY

The Russian mezzo-sopranos of historic value in our century begin with **Sophia Preobrazhenskaya** (St. Petersburg 1904) who was a permanent member of the Kirov Opera from 1928 on — a grand Martha in *Khovanshchina*, Joan of Arc and Countess in Tchaikovsky's *Queen of Spades*; the contralto **Maria Ivanovna Dolina**; **Zara Doluchanova** (Moscow 1918) who was able to tackle the parts of the *contralto d'agilità* with bravura as her recordings of Arsace's *cavatina* (which she provided with interminable *cadenze*) demonstrate; and **Vera Davydova** (Nishnii, Novgorod, 1906).

They were all fore-runners of the great **Irina Arkhipova** (Moscow 1925). She began her musical career as a hobby, taking evening lessons after her day-time work as an architect. Her debut was made at Moscow in 1954, as Liubacha in *The Tsar's Bride* by Rimsky-Korsakov, making a great sensation. From then on her career was a continuous upward climb. Thanks to her superb timbre, her luminous polish, her naturally smooth emission and her excellent technique, Arkhipova was a fantastic performer in operas by Mussorgsky, Glinka, Shostakovich, and Tchaikovsky, but also a vibrant Azucena, a passionate Carmen and a singularly relevant Eboli and Amneris. She appeared in Montreal with the Bolshoï during EXPO 1967, San Francisco, 1972 and in Covent Garden, 1975.

Who best represents the Russian mezzos today? **Elena Obraztsova** (Leningrad 1939). She made her debut in 1964 as Marina in *Boris Godunov*, a part which has always suited her. Her voice is powerful, reaching up to high c''', of magnificent colour, quite agile and sweet in the *mezzevoci*, and generous in the low notes (even if she has somewhat abused the use of *poitriné* sounds, with the consequent wear and tear for the *passaggio*).

From 1975 until today she has gathered triumphs world wide, ever enlarging her repertoire: *Carmen, Samson and Delilah, Aida, Cavalleria Rusticana, Don Carlos, Boris Godunov, Kovantchina, Trovatore* and *Adriana Lecouvreur*. Sometimes, pushed by her passionate temperament, she lets herself go in some excessive exaggerations, such as at the end of Azucena's great

scene in the second act of *Trovatore* as performed at San Francisco in 1975, where she concluded with a series of sobs which were frankly out of place. Few, however, will ever be able to forget her luxuriant and voluptuous Eboli in La Scala's *Don Carlos* in 1977, or her sweet Charlotte in the *Werther* of 1976 at La Scala. Made her Met debut as Amneris (*Aida*), 1976, and her Covent Garden debut in the same role, 1985.

We conclude with the excellent **Alexandrina Milcheva-Nonova** (Shoumen, Bulgaria 1936) who has been able to include in her repertory almost all the most important mezzo-soprano roles of the Slav, Italian, French and German schools, whilst continuing a laudable concert activity.

*In a photo from 1946 we see the great **Sophia Preobrazenskaia** in* The Maid of Orléans. *Her interpretation of the farewell scene and the recognition scene in the second act of the Tchaikovsky opera long remained in the memory of her Russian audience. (Historic Archives of the Kirov Theatre of Leningrad).*

*A triple ace for the Bizet masterpiece: from left Franco Zeffirelli, director, at centre, **Obraztsova**, still with her hand on her hip, and, at right, blond and fat, **Domingo**. Carmen was performed with great success at the Vienna State Opera under the baton of Carlos Kleiber.*

José Mardones, *as Ramfis in Verdi's* Aida.

THE BASS SINGER

The Bass Voice:
Extension and Phonation

It is the lowest of the male voices. The extension usually starts from F and reaches up to f′; but in some exceptional cases it can stretch from C to g′. However the amazing basses who sing in Russian choirs often reach the octave below low F, thus obtaining that singular "organ-like" effect.

On the basis of vocal characteristics and repertory we can make the subsequent division among the basses. The *basso nobile* or *cantante* (the noble bass) of the Italian, French and Russian repertory (Verdi, Boito, Mussorgsky, Glinka) is the most commonly found category. It is an ideal fusion of a smooth, rich, powerful and extended voice with superior interpretative gifts. The *basso profondo* (the German *tiefer Bass*), because of his extension, is decidedly suited to priestly, austere and sometimes mythical characters (Fafner in *Siegfried*).

The *comic bass* (the Italian *basso buffo* and the German *komischer Bass*) is agile and fun-loving, a great actor, and a master in the art of "spoken-singing" such as that required by the parts of Dulcamara in *Elisir d'Amore*, Bartolo in *Barbiere*, or Osmino in *Die Entführung aus dem Serail*. The bass-baritone (the German *Bass-Baryton*) is the type of voice which combines characteristics typical baritone (higher extension and clearer middle register) with those of the comic and noble basses; thus he fulfills the demands of roles initially conceived for "voices" in the wider sense of the word (Mozart's *Don Giovanni*, for example, which has, in the past, been sung by tenors like Garcia and Nozzari, baritones like Gobbi, Wächter, and Milnes, and basses such as Pinza, Siepi and Ghiaurov). Lastly we would like to cite the *belcanto basso*, which has recently been reincarnated by the American star, Samuel Ramey, champion of the old style virtuoso, especially suited to the Handel and Rossini repertory so much in fashion today.

Now let's give them a closer look.

THE *BASSO NOBILE* IN THE TWENTIETH CENTURY

The music world remembers the worldwide historic appearances made by: **Leo Sibirjakov** (St. Petersburg 1869 - Antwerp 1942) a wonderful Pimen and Mefistofle; **Oreste Luppi** (Rome 1870 - Milan 1962); **Vittorio Arimondi** (Saluzzo 1861 - Chicago 1928) the first singer to perform Pistola in *Falstaff*; **Francesco Navarini** (Cittadella, Rome 1853 - Milan 1923), a great Silva in *Ernani* and Marcel in *Les Huguenots*; **Ivar Andresen** (Oslo 1896 - Stockholm 1940), an outstanding Wagner singer; **Paul Payan** (1878 - St. Juan-les-Pins, 1959); **Josef von Manowarda** (Cracow, Poland 1890 - Berlin 1942), a great Philip II, Osmin, Gurnemanz, Marke and Barak (*Die Frau ohne Schatten*) of which he was the first interpreter in 1919.

For the beauty of his timbre, his power and vocal extension, governed by a perfect technique, **Marcel Journet** (Grasse, France 1867 - Vittel,

Vosgi 1933) was practically unrivalled from 1891 right until the end of the twenties. These were the golden years of his long career, which eventually ended in 1932 at the Paris Opera. Thanks to his uncommon vocal gifts he was really able to sing everything: from the *basso profondo* roles (Baldassarre in *La Favorita*, Sparafucile in *Rigoletto*) to the most important roles of the Italian repertory (Philip II, Basilio, Mefistofele, Ramfis, Simon Mago in the inaugural performance of Boito's *Nerone* in 1924), the French repertory (Méphistophélès in Gounod's *Faust*, the Father in *Louise*) and the German repertory (the Wanderer in *The Ring*, Hans Sachs in *The Mastersingers of Nuremberg*, King Henry the Fowler in *Lohengrin*). During his last career years, he sang mostly baritone or bass-baritone roles, still possessing an enviable extension and security in the high register.

A cute photo of the great bass **Marcel Journet**, who had a voice of great power and flexibility. (Historic Archives of the Rome Opera Theatre. Photo: G. Artico).

In a photo from 1910 we see **Feodor Shaliapin** as Boris Godunov. (Historic Archives of the Kirov Theatre of Leningrad).

He sang in London, Covent Garden, 1897-1907, 1927-8; New York, Met, 1900-1908; Paris, Opéra, 1908-31, where he was the first Fafner, Klingsor, Phanuel (*Hérodiade*), Dosifey, and Sultan in *Marouf*.

Shaliapin's thousand voices

The legendary bass of our century is, without a doubt, **Feodor Shaliapin** (Kazan 1873 - Paris 1938) — one of the most sensitive and generous artists ever to have enriched the operatic world. It was already apparent in his teenage years that the phenomenal bass had the operatic stage in his blood. He actually began his career at fifteen years of age, as a bit-part player in a travelling company.

In 1892 he made his debut at Tiflis in *Rusalka*, by Dargomisky; and soon after he was offered a contract with the Leontovsky Theatre of St. Petersburg, in which he first sang in 1894 in the perilous part of Bertram in *Robert le Diable*, by Meyerbeer.

Satanic characters were perfectly suited to Shaliapin's impressive stage presence and acting. He was an insuperable master in the art of chiselling sound, and perfect in stage movement. He always found the right gesture, gaze and expression to help him touch the audience's heart.

His Mefistofele, both in Boito and in Gounod's

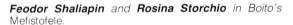

Feodor Shaliapin and **Rosina Storchio** in Boito's Mefistofele.

Nazzareno De Angelis in his favourite role as Mosè, a photo from 1926.

Faust, was truly terrifying: menacing, slimy, and calculating, with a range of vocal shadings that ranged from tenor-like *pianissimi* to amazing explosions of sound.

From 1896 until 1919 he performed in Moscow, specializing in the great Russian repertory: operas by Glinka, Mussorgsky, Rimsky-Korsakov and Tchaikovsky, each of which he studied in every dramatic detail, with a sense of analytic phrasing and an expressive power without equal. Shaliapin became famous in America, France, England and at La Scala of Milan, triumphing in his favourite operas: *Boris Godunov, Kovantchina, Mefistofele, Barbiere di Siviglia, Ivan the Terrible,* and *Prince Igor.* Often, dragged to excess by his passionate temperament, he abandonned himself to exaggerations of dubious taste: in Basilio's aria (*Barbiere*) he was in the habit of adding the words "Ma questa è la fine del mondo" (But this is the end of the world) in a squeaky little voice after the "tremuoto" and "temporale" provided by Rossini — a useless and unjustified liberty. But you only needed to watch the stage movements and expressions of this Basilio to see that he was totally immersed in the part.

In fact it was as Don Basilio that he gave his farewell to La Scala in the 1932-33 season, whilst he retired for good in 1937 after a final *Boris Godunov* at Montecarlo.

From Poland came another amazing bass: **Adam Didur** (Sanol, Galizia 1874 - Katowice 1946) who was only partially influenced by his national origins, and who was, in fact, very close to Italian taste, style and repertory.

His debut was made in Latin America (Rio de Janeiro) in 1894. Didur sang on that continent for several years before going to Italy (where he had previously studied singing). Subsequently he performed in Warsaw; then he was employed by La Scala; and lastly he settled into the New York Metropolitan, where he sang as first bass from 1909 until 1932, thus becoming Edouard De Reszké's successor.

Thanks to his more than normal extension, his equality between the registers, the beauty of his timbre, and his attractive appearance, Didur was among the greatest singers of this century to interpret parts like Marcel (*Les Huguenots*), Mefistofele (Boito and Gounod), Ramfis, Sparafucile, Kecal (*The Bartered Bride*), Wotan, Don Basilio, Boris, and even Figaro and the Count in Mozart's *Marriage of Figaro*. Listening to his records we are able to appreciate his wonderful polish and his uniquely luminescent high notes — especially in Méfistophélè's *ballata* in *Faust* ("Le veau d'or"), Basilio's *cavatina* ("La calunnia"), and in the aria from Meyerbeer's opera *Robert le Diable*.

The Devil's Trill

Nazzareno De Angelis (Rome 1881 - 1962) had an amazing voice in many respects: first of all his voice was exceptionally long-lasting, as he sang from 1903 (when he made his debut) at L'Aquila in *Linda di Chamounix*) until 1959. However the Roman bass also possessed a very powerful voice, which was flexible and very well extended, smooth in the *mezzavoce*, robust in the low notes and he controlled this voice with an excellent technique and vocal placement.

The *legato* he exhibited in the long *cantabile* passages (especially in "Celeste man placata" from Rossini's *Mosè* and in "Dormirò sol nel manto mio regal" from *Don Carlos* by Verdi) seemed more like the *cavata* of ten cellos than the sound of a human voice. As for his high notes, we had best cite Bruno Barilli's description: "He launched towards the audience ...note after note, *roulades*, as massive and incandescent as cannon balls".

He was noble but moving in the Wagnerian roles of Wotan and Guernemanz, proud and belligerent in *Vespri Siciliani*, terrifying in *Mefi-*

high notes, and finely chiselled singing) even if he could never equal his volume. His name was **Ezio Pinza** (Fortunio Pinza; Rome 1892 - Stamford, Connecticut 1957). He also had the charm of a natural scenic verve, commanding the stage with an attractive physical appearance and the intelligence and sensitivity of a great actor.

After his debut at Soncino (Italy) in 1914, he was forced to interrupt his career during the years of the First World War, when he was a soldier for six years. In 1919 he began to sing again, this time at Florence, in the small parts of Roucher in *Andrea Chénier* and Ferrando in *Il Trovatore*. His contract with the Teatro Costanzi in Rome for the 1919-20 season drew the public's attention. Pinza sang admirably in *Forza del Destino*, *La Gioconda*, *Tristan and Isolde*, *Rigoletto*, *Aida* and *Boris Godunov* (Pimen), demonstrating talent and technique.

La Scala (from 1921 until 1924), the Metropolitan (from 1926 until 1948), and Covent Garden (from 1930 until 1939) — all the world's major theatres welcomed Pinza as their absolute favourite, right up to his Broadway performances of *South Pacific* by Rogers and Ham-

*Many first-ever performances of opera were confided to the powerful vocal means of **Tancredi Pasero**, such as the* Re Hassan *by Ghedini, which we see in the photo. Other celebrated prime were Emiral (Barilli), Orseolo (Pizzetti), Gli Orazi (Porrino), Nerone (Mascagni), and Margherita da Cortona (Refice). (Historic Archives of La Fenice Theatre, Venice. Photo: Giacomelli).*

*For over twenty years **Ezio Pinza** was the principal bass at the Metropolitan of New York. He was idolised by the public and became a legend in the role of Don Giovanni. Besides the Mozart masterpiece, he interpreted more than fifty operas.*

stofele, and thundering as Oroveso in *Norma*. De Angelis made Rossini's *Mosè* his favourite role, and even managed to acquire the famous "tight trill" after assiduous study for the great scene "Eterno, immenso, incomprensibil Dio". An exploit, thankfully preserved on a disc, which will probably remain unequalled. He sang in all leading Italian theatres and with the Chicago Opera, 1910-11 and 1915-20.

Ezio Pinza: a Winning Don Giovanni

Another Roman bass inherited De Angelis' technical qualities (breath control, smooth and well-placed sounds, extended and penetrating

merstein, with which he retired from the stage in 1949.

Because of his aristocratic phrasing and his vocal quality he emerged in the typical roles of the *basso nobile*: Fiesco, Philip II, Ramfis, Boris, Mefistofele, and Oroveso; but he also managed to sing the role of Don Giovanni exceptionally well, becoming legendary in that part. Pinza had a repertory of more than 95 roles, sang *Don Giovanni* more then 200 times, and appeared more than 750 times in 50 operas during his engagement with the Met.

During an evening at the Met in the year 1942, Mozart's masterpiece was being performed by Pinza, with the famous bass Kipnis in the part of Leporello. When they came to the balcony scene in which the two characters imitate one another while disguised, the smart Kipnis began to produce funny bleating sounds (mimicking one of Pinza's personal defects), which made the public fall off their seats laughing. Pinza, however, was not able to copy the cavernous voice of the *basso profondo*, thus losing the challenge. Apparently, from then on, the two great singers did not speak to each other ever again.

Tancredi Pasero (Turin 1893 - 1985) completes the golden triangle of Italian basses (De Angelis and Pinza). His career embraced a long period of time and a wide repertory. He sang from 1918 (he began at Vicenza as Conte Rodolfo in *Sonnambula*) until 1953, and his voice remained miraculously intact until his death, according to many reliable witnesses.

Compared to many of his famous colleagues Pasero could not boast an extraordinary timbrical charm or vocal volume. However he was able to make a practically unlimited use of his voice, having complete control of his means — from his low notes to his vibrant high notes. His favourite theatres were La Scala (where he was first bass from 1926 to 1952), the Metropolitan and Covent Garden, although he often performed in other theatres the world over (South America, Spain, Portugal).

His varied and incisive accent helped distinguish him as a Verdi bass, mainly in the roles of the Padre Guardiano, Philip II, Zaccaria, Walter (*Luisa Miller*), but he did not exclude Donizetti (*Linda di Chamounix, Lucrezia Borgia*) nor Bellini (*Sonnambula, Norma, Puritani*) nor even Rossini (apart from his excellent and controlled Basilio, he was also an applauded Mosè and occasionally Assur in *Semiramide*, Florence 1933 and 1940). Pasero also performed memorably as Boris, Wotan, Gurnemanz, King Marke, Caspar in *Der Freischütz*, Mefistofele, Alvise Badoero (*Gioconda*), and in some contemporary works created especially for him.

Two important Russian basses must be noted, even if they remained in Shaliapin's shadow.

Mark Reizen as Boris *in 1930. What struck one about this artist was his colossal size and his great dramatic capacity. (Historic Archives of the Kirov Theatre, Leningrad).*

Alexander Pirogov (Novoselka, Rjazan' 1899 - Moscow 1964) was the first bass at the Bolshoi from 1924, and was much acclaimed as Boris, Ivan, Mefistofele, and Pestel in *Decabristi*, an opera by Saporin. **Mark Reizen** (Zaitsevo 1895) made his debut in 1921 at Kharkov, and was a permanent member of the greatest Moscow theatre from 1930 on; he distinguished himself in the classic role of Boris and as Dositeo (*Kovantchina*) and Gremin (*Eugene Onegin*).

His vocal longevity is to be considered legendary: he apparently still managed to sing in 1985 (on the occasion of his ninetieth birthday!) an

A close-up of the bass **Gottlob Frick**, *a celebrated Hagen and Osmin. (Historic Archives of EMI. Photo: Fayer).*

entire performance of *Eugene Onegin* at the Bolshoi (in the role of Gremin).

Moving on to the great German *bassi cantabili* we must first of all mention **Richard Mayr** (Henndorf, Austria 1877 - Vienna 1935), who was persuaded by Gustav Mahler to undertake musical studies instead of the medical studies he had already started. After his debut at Bayreuth in 1902 as Hagen, his career developed at Vienna (Staatsoper, 1902-35), Salzburg, London (Covent Garden, 1924-31) and New York (Met, 1927-30). He always favoured the principal Wagnerian roles, Leporello, Figaro (*Marriage of Figaro*), Sarastro, Barak in *Die Frau ohne Schatten* by Strauss (of which he was the first interpreter in 1919); but it was his performance of Baron Ochs in *Der Rosenkavalier* which became legendary.

Ludwig Weber (Vienna 1899 - 1974) belongs to the following generation, and was active in the theatres of Vienna, Bayreuth, London and most of Germany from 1920 to 1960. His repertoire included Mozart, Verdi, and, primarily, Wagner. He become well-known in the parts of Gurnemanz (*Parsifal*), Hagen and Daland. Thanks to his vocal flexibility and his interpretive intelligence he was able to perform in the Lieder and oratorio fields as well.

Among the best German basses between 1930 and 1970, a deserved reference to **Gottlob Frick** (Ölbron, Württemberg 1906). His voice was of a dark timbre, rich, well-extended and robust — ideal for the roles of the operatic "bad guy" in

Josef Greindl in the role of the perfidious Hagen, and, seated, Adolf Vogel in the part of Alberich during a scene from Götterdämmerung (Twilight of the Gods) given on 16th March, 1957 in Venice. The director was Wolfgang Wagner. (Historic Archives of La Fenice Theatre, Venice. Photo: Giacomelli).

the works of Wagner (Hagen, Hunding, Fafner) and Mozart (his Osmin in *Die Entführung aus dem Serail* has remained unforgettable). He was active from 1927 until the end of the seventies with all the main operatic companies the world over. Frick also was the protagonist in many contemporary compositions and included several Verdi roles in his repertoire, such as Padre Guardiano and Philip II, with excellent results.

From Valhalla, an Unforgettable Wotan: Hans Hotter

Hans Hotter (Offenbach 1909) was best suited to roles full of pathos. He was formed by the great school of Römer, a student of the mythical Jan De Reszké, in Munich (Bavaria). His timbre, rich in harmonics and governed by a superior technique and musicality, made his renderings of the Wagnerian roles like Wotan, Hans Sachs, King Marke, Hunding, Amfortas, Kurwenal and the Dutchman truely grand, and allowed him to give excellent performances in the Italian repertory (Philip II, Scarpia, Amonasro, the Grand Inquisitor) and in Lieder, especially that of Richard Strauss.

His debut was made back in 1929 as the Orator in *The Magic Flute*, put on at Opava. From then on the German bass sang in Bayreuth,

*Wagner, Die Walküre, performed in Naples in 1963. In the opera's finale, Wotan (**Hans Hotter**) is about to build a wall of fire around the sleeping Brunhild (the beautiful **Anja Silja** (Historic Archives of the San Carlo Theatre of Naples. Photo: Troncone).*

Munich, Vienna, Paris, Milan, New York, London, and, in Munich, took part in the first-ever performances of Richard Strauss's *Friedenstag* (1938) and *Capriccio* (1942). He still sings in some German theatres nowadays, after more than half a century of career, still demonstrating his gifts as a singing-actor of rare artistic sensivity.

An excellent actor and singer with a strong voice and a lovely low register: **Josef Greindl** (Munich 1912). He first sang in 1935 and became immediately popular in the Germanic countries as Sarastro, Osmin, Hunding (*Die Walküre*), Fafner, King Marke, Daland (*Flying Dutchman*), Hagen (*Götterdämmerung*), Rocco (*Fidelio*), and Sparafucile (*Rigoletto*).

We have rarely had the occasion to listen to the prayer "O Isis und Osiris" (Sarastro) sung in such an aristocratic way. Greindl filled the concert halls and opera theatres with his resonant accents and vibrant voice, of which the low notes resembled powerful "organ peddles". He was exceptional in Osmino's difficult aria "Ach! Wie will Ich triumphieren". He performed it with an extraordinary verve and ability, right down to the impossibly low D — full and sonorous. Unfortunately, after 1960, you could hear the wear in his high register. It became ever harsher and wobbly. Notwithstanding this, Griendl continued to perform as an excellent singing-actor, creating a magnificent Moses in Schönberg's opera *Moses und Aron*. He sang his last Wotan in Paris, June 1972.

The Amiable Baron of Lerchenau: Otto Edelmann

From the end of the thirties until the first half of the seventies the operatic stage boasted the presence of one of the most important singing-actors in the German repertory of this century: **Otto Edelmann** (Vienna 1916). After having completed his studies in his native city under the guidance of the famed teacher Lierhammer (his class-mates were Christoff, Welitsch and Kunz), Edelmann made his debut at Gera in *The Marriage of Figaro* in the lead role.

From 1947 on he became a permanent member of the Vienna State Opera ensemble, and after that his career was a constant upward path.

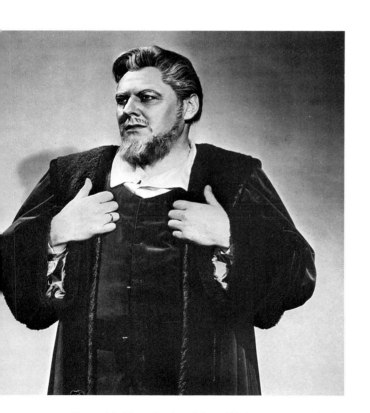

*The noble Hans Sachs of **Otto Edelmann**, a part he interpreted many times in all the world's great theatres. In particular we wish to remember the recording made at Bayreuth in 1951 with the conducting of Herbert von Karajan. The tenor Hopf, Schwarzkopf, and Erich Kunz sang in this with Edelmann. (Metropolitan Opera House. Photo: Melançon).*

*2nd February, 1979: The bass **José van Dam** has a great success as Philip II in* Don Carlos *by Verdi. Here he is during the aria "Ella giammai m'amò". (Historic Archives of the Opéra de Nice).*

189

New York, San Francisco, London, Bayreuth, Salzburg, Edinburgh and Milan were fundamental steps in a brilliant career that developed under the guidance of the most important conductors (Furtwangler, Knappertsbusch, von Karajan, Mitropoulos, Böhm). His vocal qualities (a beautiful timbre, smooth emission, perfect legato, good extension) place him half way between the *basso-nobile* and the German *Bass-Baryton*. His wide repertoire is proof. It swept from Mozart (Figaro, the Count, Osmin, Leporello, Publio in *La Clemenza di Tito*) and Verdi (Philip II and Falstaff) to his natural Wagner territory (Hans Sachs, Wotan, Amfortas, the Dutchman, and King Henry in *Lohengrin*) and his adored Richard Strauss (his Baron Ochs and his Waldner in *Arabella* are unforgettable). In addition to his purely vocal gifts Edelmann has also displayed a refined scenic art, much superior to most opera singers' possibilities.

In the roles of Hans Sach, Wotan and Ochs he governed the stage with a variety of expressions and gestures worthy of a dedicated actor. His habit of whistling nonchalantly during the letter scene when playing the part of coarse and

*A typical attitude of **Boris Christoff**, in the role of Boris Godunov. His acting talent was equal to his singing. (Historic Archives of the Rome Opera Theatre. Photo: O. Savio).*

"Le veau d'or" from Gounod's Faust, *performed energetically by the great **Boris Christoff**. (Historic Archives of the Rome Opera Theatre. Photo: Piccagliani).*

boastful Baron Ochs in *Der Rosenkavalier* has remained famous; with that simple gesture, as accurately noted by Hartmann, Edelmann expressed far more than he ever could have with words.

Another famous name: **Oskar Czerwenka** (Vöcklabruck, Linz 1924), a member of the Vienna State Opera from 1951 on, for over thirty years. He was acclaimed in seventy-five different roles as well as in many concert performances. The American **Jerome Hines** (J. Heinz; Hollywood 1921) was employed by the Met. from 1947 on and was applauded for his performances as Boris, the Grand Inquisitor, and Gurnemanz, which he even sang at Bayreuth in 1958. The English **Forbes Robinson** (Peter Robinson; Macclesfield 1926) was a permanent member of the Covent Garden Opera Company from 1954 on. He was the first Don Giovanni in that theatre after Sir Charles Stanley. He sang over seventy roles including Pizarro, Figaro, Boris, Swallow, Claggart in *Billy Budd*.

Today the true German *basso-nobile* (tending towards the *Bass-Baryton*) is epitomized by **José van Dam** (Josef van Damme; Brussels 1940), who is active in the French, Austrian and German theatres. He was much appreciated by von Karajan who often invited the bass to sing in Salzburg. His rich and velvety voice is well extended, technically well organised, and perfectly suited to melancholy, pensive characters such as Philip II, the Dutchman and Amfortas, but can also be adapted to Escamillo, Figaro (*The Marriage of Figaro*), Méphistophélès (*The Damnation of*

In our collection, we could not miss a close-up of Philip II, a character perfectly adapted to the vocal gifts and capacity of **Boris Christoff**. *(Historic Archives of the Rome Opera Theatre).*

Faust), and Jokanaan (*Salome*). He began at the Paris Opéra in 1961 and later sang in other major theatres, including Covent Garden (debut as Escamillo in *Carmen*, 1973).

Two good German basses working over the last twenty years are **Karl Ridderbusch** (Recklinghausen Westphalia 1930) and **Hans Sotin** (Dortmund 1939), both of whom possess a smooth and well extended vocality with an aristocratic vocal line, ideal for the parts of King Marke, King Henry the Fowler, Gurnemanz, Wotan, the Flying Dutchman, Sarastro, and a few roles in the Italian repertory.

King Boris

Boris Christoff (Plovdiv 1914) was a great Bulgarian bass. The name "Boris" played a fundamental role in Christoff's career: it was King Boris III of Bulgaria who awarded him the scholarship which permitted him to study singing in Italy (after the king had noticed the young singer when he was a soloist in the Gussla Choir of Sofia); and it was the role of Boris Godunov, in his superb interpretation, which made him famous the world over.

Thanks to the precious guidance of the baritone Stracciari, the Bulgarian bass was able to create a fascinating mixture between the Slav style of singing (the unmistakable *portamenti*, the slightly Byzantine-sounding accents and inflexions) with the dictates of pure Italian belcanto (perfectly placed sounds, smooth emission, use of the *mezzavoce* and of the various dynamic nuances, equality between the registers); he thus avoided the defects that often mar many Slav basses (high notes in the throat, harshness, exaggerations).

It was obvious that Christoff would excel in

An event to remember: The Don Carlos *of the 1981-82 season in Parma; the star an outstanding* **Christoff**. *"Sei un drago!" ("You are a dragon!") an enthusiastic spectator shouted. (Historic Archives of the Teatro Regio of Parma. Photo: Montacchini).*

the Russian repertory. His Boris, his Ivan the Terrible, his Prince Galitsky and Konchak in *Prince Igor*, his Kochubei in *Mazeppa*, and his Ivan Susanin in *A Life for the Tsar* by Glinka were all splendid. He perfectly amalgamated power of expression, analytic phrasing, beautiful polish and a dominant stage presence.

The characters he rendered best in Verdi were those of the proud Silva in *Ernani*, Attila, Fiesco in *Simon Boccanegra*, Procida in *Vespri Siciliani*; but, above all, Philip II in *Don Carlos*. His King of Spain was complete in all the dramatic details indicated by Schiller and Verdi. In various stages of the opera the character became proud, melancholy, a wounded father or an important king. It was a great interpretation, which he deepened with every performance, culminating in the memorable performance in 1982 at the Teatro Regio of Parma, with an "Ella giammai m'amò" whispered confidentially, which was very moving. At the end of this difficult monologue the audience burst into an interminable ovation, with the spontaneous cry of "You are a dragon!" coming from the gallery.

It was Christoff's farewell, the last performance of his wonderful career.

He was invited by the Metropolitan Opera, 1950, but was politically barred because he was from a Communist Country; he sang in San Francisco and Chicago (1956-63), but never at the Metropolitan.

"My dear Don Ottavio, fix your jacket if you want to be a Don Giovanni", **Nicola Rossi-Lemeni** *seems to be saying to tenor* **Luigi Alva***, his partner in* Don Giovanni*, performed at Venice on 14th. January, 1958. The orchestra conductor was Vittorio Gui. (Historic Archives of La Fenice Theatre of Venice. Photo: Giacomelli).*

In Shaliapin's Footsteps

Many singers followed in Shaliapin's footsteps, the best of whom were **Ivan Petrov** (Irkutsk 1920) and **Nicola Rossi Lemeni** (Constan-

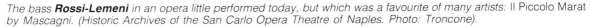

The bass **Rossi-Lemeni** *in an opera little performed today, but which was a favourite of many artists:* Il Piccolo Marat *by Mascagni. (Historic Archives of the San Carlo Opera Theatre of Naples. Photo: Troncone).*

The 1967-68 Lyric Season in Parma: **Nicola Rossi-Lemeni** had a personal success at the Regio in Assassinio nella Cattedrale by Pizzetti. The opera was written especially for him in 1958. (Historic Archives of the Teatro Regio of Parma. Photo: Montacchini).

tinople 1920 - Bloomington, U.S.A. 1991).

Petrov entered the Bolshoi Opera in 1943, where he immediately showed that he was an artist of fine vocal means and good stage presence. He preferred Russian parts like Dositeo in *Kovantchina*, Kochubei in *Mazeppa*, Boris, Konchak in *Prince Igor*, René in *Iolanta* by Tchaikovsky, but he also sang Don Basilio and Méphistophélès in Gounod's *Faust*.

Nicola Rossi Lemeni studied with Maestro Cusinati at Verona. He had learnt the first basics from his mother; but the turning point came when he began to listen carefully to the recordings of Shaliapin and De Angelis, who became his great models. With care and sensivity he succeeded in learning their interpretative skills, changing his own voice to make it resemble that of his illustrious predecessors, especially that of Shaliapin. During his golden years, between 1946 and 1960, Rossi Lemeni had a voice which was not particularly powerful, nor extended in the low register, even more or less out-of-focus (foggy) in the timbre. But it was exceptionally flexible, pliable to every expressive demand: from tenor-like *pianissimi* to the effects of *smorzando* and *rinforzando*, which were so moving. It was extended in the high register, right up to a penetrating high g', agile in the patter and fast vocalizing passages (to the extent that he was successfull in the parts of Selim in *Turco in Italia* by Rossini, Don Basilio, Mosè, Don Giovanni, Uberto in *Serva Padrona* by Pergolesi, and Handel's *Julius Caesar*).

The Italian bass was helped by a commanding

appearance, an expressive face and a natural elegance and dignity in his movements on stage. He refined his art thanks to his constant, intelligent self-control and innate musicality. Rossi Lemeni was a great Boris, Philip II Silva, Procida, Mefistofele, Don Quichotte, Giorgio in *I Puritani*, Oroveso, Basilio; he also sang in many modern compositions, the most important of these being *Assassinio nella Cattedrale* by Pizzetti, of which he was the first interpreter in 1958 at La Scala.

A Lord of the Stage

Cesare Siepi (Milan 1919) and Christoff were the last legendary exponents of the *basso-nobile* school.

Siepi's unusually long career is worth notice (it is a clear example of class and superior, correct vocal technique): Siepi made his debut at Schio, near Venice, in the distant year of 1941, singing Sparafucile in *Rigoletto*. In recent years audiences have been amazed to hear his still magnificent portrayals of Philip II, Fiesco, Don Basilio, Baldassarre (*Favorita*), Don Giovanni, and Roger in Verdi's opera *Jerusalem* (in a memorable performance at Parma in January 1986).

The vocal characteristics of the Italian bass begin with the smooth, rich consistency of his timbre, and a naturally dark colour which resembles that of a *basso profondo*; it is a voice sustained by a faultless emission, flexible and light, based on the right breathing technique. His low notes are wide and resonant, of equal quality, reaching down to low C (a note which Siepi produces easily in the brief aria "Splendon più belle in ciel le stelle" from *La Favorita* and in

Cesare Siepi: a gentleman of the stage. The photo was taken in April, 1986, when Siepi performed Fiesco magnificently at the San Carlo. The low F sharp of the aria "Il lacerato spirito" resounded full and round, in a way that no one today can do. (Historic Archives of La Fenice Theatre, Venice. Photo: L. Romano).

Seneca's death scene from the *Incoronation of Poppea*).

Until the end of the sixties, his high notes sounded well-placed and powerful, reaching up to g'. With the inexorable passing of time, however, this register became a little worn and wobbly; but this did not significantly damage the splendor of such a vocal organ.

During the course of his extraordinary artistic history Siepi has sung at La Scala, Covent Garden (1950-62), the Metropolitan (succeeding Pinza from 1950 on), Vienna, Salzburg, and in all the major Italian theatres. Amongst his favourite roles we must also include Mefistofele, Padre Guardiano, Zaccaria in *Nabucco*, Ramfis, Silva, and Sparafucile.

Nicolai Ghiaurov (Velimgrad 1929) came from Bulgaria with a magnificent voice, to give new life and honour to the long line of Slavic basses. He began by studying violin and piano; then he took his diploma in singing at Sofia, and did a post-graduate course at Moscow. He made his debut in 1956 at Sofia, singing Don Basilio in *Barbiere*. It was immediately apparent to everybody just how unique Ghiaurov's talent was: his quality and polish, his notable extension and the equality of his sound, his ability to colour each one of his beautiful notes with a special expressive meaning, made his singing always varied and interesting. He accompanied these gifts with an impressive physical appearance and good acting skills; and so Ghiaurov was soon enrolled by the world's major opera theatres as Boris, Mefistofele (both Boito and Gounod), Mosè, Philip II, Ramfis, Fiesco, Zaccaria, the Grand Inquisitor, and Don Giovanni.

Halfway through the seventies, Ghiaurov began to have some difficulty in governing his high notes — they became harsh and opaque. Nowadays, despite the fact that time has been merciless, we can still wonder at the vocal splendor of this singer in his central register. He also remains an expressive actor. He often performs with Cappuccilli in *Attila*, *Simon Boccanegra*, *Don Carlos*, *Macbeth*, and *Aida*, thus forming an ideal and insuperable pair (on record as well as live).

An important Italian bass has emerged over the years as one of the best prepared and gifted singers, notwithstanding the fact that the Italian companies discovered him rather late. His name is **Bonaldo Giaiotti** (Ziracco, Udine 1933). His debut took place at Milan in 1958; but it was the Metropolitan that soon took the initiative of assuring his fixed presence in the roles of Zaccaria, Fiesco, Basilio, Silva, Mefistofele, Ramfis, Philip II, Oroveso, and Alvise Badoero. His voice is rich, equal, thick, and sustained by a professionality and musicality that cannot be criticized. Perhaps it is actually his excessive professionalism and introversion that kept him out of the big-time

In the first years of his career **Ghiaurov** frequently sang Don Giovanni, *succeeding in creating an excellent portrayal, both vocally and scenically. Here he is in a photo from 1964 together with the bass* **Ganzarolli** *(Leporello). (Historic Archives of the San Carlo Theatre of Naples. Photo: Troncone).*

Another famous characterisation of **Siepi**: *the High Priest Ramfis in* Aida. *Parma, 1988. (Photo: Montacchini).*

194

"La calunnia è un venticello": **Ghiaurov** often played the role of Don Basilio. (Photo Archive Stinchelli).

Principal singer of Attila at the Staatsoper of Vienna, 1980 - a new triumph for **Nicolai Ghiaurov**. (Photo: V. Claser. Vienna).

agencies and recording companies. But Giaiotti appears in all major international theatres, and always with excellent results.

We do not want to leave out some basses who, without being superstars, have passed on the great tradition with artistic honesty: **Nicola Moscona** (Athens 1907 - Philadelphia 1975); **Agostino Ferrin** (Padua 1928 - Rome 1989); **Norman Treigle** (New Orleans 1927 - 1975); **Carlo Cava** (Ascoli Piceno 1928); **Raphael Ariè** (Sofia 1920 - Milan 1988); **Paolo Washington** (Florence 1932); **Ivo Vinco** (Verona 1927); **Nicola Zaccaria** (Athens 1923); **Ezio Flagello** (New York 1933); **Giorgio Tozzi** (Chicago 1923) at the Met from 1955; **Robert Lloyd** (Andrew Lloyd, Southend-on-Sea 1940); **Gwynne Howell** (Richard Howell; Gorseinon, Wales 1938); and **Paul Plishka** (Old Forge, Pennsylva-

nia 1941) who were one and all essential in thousands of performances.

In the latest generation of Russian basses the best is without a doubt **Yevgeny Nesterenko** (Moscow 1938), who made his debut in 1962 as Gremin in Tchaikovsky's *Eugene Onegin*. It is more than twenty years now that he has been walking the boards, even if his fame has only recently spread to the West. His repertory includes, obviously, all the main Russian operas, plus a vast selection of characters from the Italian repertory, such as Mefistofele, Philip II, the Grand Inquisitor, Massamiliano Moor (*Masnadieri*), Zaccaria, Colline, Mosè, and Attila. His voice is of good grain, smooth and extended, even if, in his high notes, he tends to sing in the throat (but this is a defect common to most Slavic basses).

195

THE BASSO PROFONDO

Representing the voice of baroque opera in our century there is a restricted platoon of singers who are all more or less worthy of the title of *basso profondo*. Let us see who they are.

The flag bearer for this prestigious category is, without a doubt, **José Mardones** (Fontecha, Alava 1869 - Madrid 1932) who had a voice which was unique for its volume and timbrical beauty. Between the end of the nineteenth century and 1926 he was much acclaimed, especially by the American public (he sang at the Met from 1917 to 1926), in roles such as Ramfis, Mefistofele, Oroveso, Marcel in *Les Huguenots*, Pimen in *Boris Godunov*, and Zaccaria. In his formidable executions, these characters became fantastic thunderbolts of sound.

Alexander Kipnis came from Russia (Zitomir, Ukraine 1891 - Westport 1978) to collect and better Mardones' inheritance. He had made his debut in 1915 at Hamburg, and was very active in German and American theatres. What was amazing about Kipnis' vocal performances was his flexibility and his interpretative intelligence: his voice spread easily over all the range from the bottom of the stave (full, sonorous notes) to the high notes, with an extraordinary homogenity. The bass could also obtain all the shadings he wished from his compliant vocal instrument — from the most delicate *pianissimi* to *rinforzando* effects. So he was able to excel in a vast repertoire. Kipnis often sang Don Giovanni, but also Leporello, Sarastro, Osmin, Gurnemanz (*Parsifal*), an extraordinary Pogner in *The Mastersingers*, Fiesco, Philip II, Sparafucile, Boris, Gremin in *Eugene Onegin*, Rocco in *Fidelio*, Hagen, King Marke; and he was also a worthy Lieder singer, excelling in the Brahms repertory. He was a sensitive actor, moving well on stage, and he became irresistible in comic parts, where he showed a verve and musicality without comparison. Forced by Hitler to leave Germany, he settled in America, and eventually became an American citizen.

There is always time to list **Juste Nivette** (1865), an unequalled Sarastro, Alvise in *La Gioconda*, and Hagen at La Scala in 1907; the powerful **Mansueto Gaudio** (Vignale Borbera, Alessandria 1873 - Santiago, Chile 1941); **Giovanni Gravina** (1872 - Havana, Cuba 1912), successful as Ramfis and Sparafucile; **Wilhelm**

A cruel Mefistofele, that of **Giulio Neri**. The audience were thunderstruck by the terrible glares cast by his enormous blue eyes. (Historic Archives of the Rome Opera Theatre. Photo: A. Villani).

"Aô! Ammazza che voce!" *("oh What a voice!") says Alberto Sordi to* **Giulio Neri**, *exhibiting his own undoubted quality as a basso-profondo! The two were acting in the amusing film* Mì permette babbo? *(Will you let me, Daddy?) in which they performed a formidable duet. (Historic Archives of the Rome Opera Theatre).*

Strienz (Stuttgard 1900 - Frankfurt 1987), famous above all as Sarastro; **Umberto Di Lelio** (1890 - Milan 1946); and **Emanuel List** (Vienna 1890-1967).

The Neri Phenomenon

The last true *basso profondo* was **Giulio Neri** (Torrita di Siena 1909 - Rome 1958). Everybody agrees upon the virtual impossibility of describing his monumental voice in words: whole theatres, even open-air ones, would tremble under the sea of sound produced by Neri.

By 1938 he had established himself as leading-bass at Rome, Teatro dell'Opera, and appeared there regularly until shortly before his death. His last performance was in *Norma* in 1958.

His timbre was naturally cavernous. Neri could sink down to C, without losing any of the power and richness of his central notes, with an entirely unique "organ" effect. Between 1935 and the year of his premature death in 1958 he was unsurpassed as Sparafucile, Ramfis, the Grand Inquisitor, Mefistofele, and in Wagner's operas, which he sang in the Italian version.

Martti Talvela *as Fafner (left) in* Das Rheingold, *with* **Karl Ridderbusch**, *as Fasolt.*

*Because of the strength and power of his voice **Neri** was able to affront even the Wagner repertory without difficulty. Here he is in the role of Hagen in* Twlight of the Gods. *(Historic Archives of the Rome Opera Theatre. Photo: A. Villani).*

Together with the Italian comic actor Alberto Sordi (who, having studied singing before beginning to act, would have been able to have had a successful career as a bass if he had continued) Neri made a fun-filled movie film entitled *Mi Permette, Babbo?* (Will you let me, Daddy?) where he sang a duet with the Roman actor, who was playing the part of a young hopeful *basso profondo* who, despite his ardent desire to emerge on the stage, was destined (as so often happens in real life) to remain an eternal student.

Martti Talvela (Hütola 1935 - 1989) and **Kurt Moll** (Buir 1938) have all the characteristics of the typical *basso profondo*, and they are the only two singers in recent years who have been able to perform the roles of Sarastro and Osmin live, with due stylistic fidelity.

Talvela, from Finland, a real giant in stature, first sang at Stockholm in 1961, and from then on his wide, resonant voice was mostly heard in Wagner (Fasolt, Hunding, King Marke, Daland), Mozart (Sarastro, Osmin), and in Verdi's *Don Carlos*, where he played the part of the Grand Inquisitor with a good vocal rendering. Sadly, due to a sudden heart attack, he died whilst still in the full of his career.

197

Kurt Moll is very active in German and Austrian opera houses, with a repertoire which includes: *Tristan und Isolde; The Mastersingers of Nuremberg* (Pogner); *Die Entführung aus dem Serail* (Osmin) — an opera in which he is able to perform the aria "Ach! Wie will Ich triumphieren" like a real virtuoso, singing the complicated *cadenza* in one breath and finishing with a well-emitted trill; *The Magic Flute, Parsifal* (Gurnemanz); *Der Freischütz* (Caspar); *The Flying Dutchman* (Daland); and *La Forza del Destino* (the Padre Guardiano).

THE COMIC BASS: FUNNY BUT NOT FARCICAL

Many basses perform in the comic repertory; but few are truly great in it. Those few, however, are the rare singers who do not indulge in jokes and exaggerations to win the public's favour. A real buffo — that is, a comic but not a clown — should not be a failed *basso nobile*, a flop of a Philip II to be more explicit. Quite the opposite. He must unite the vocal elegance of the *basso nobile* with a refined phrasing and acting skill. Fun-loving or grumpy, chasing after servant girls, youngsters, or whoever else happens to pass by, he must never surpass the limits of correct, respectful acting, never becoming vulgar.

Therefore not many qualify for this title. In our century there are few worthy of being called *buffi*. We would like, first of all, to talk about **Antonio Pini-Corsi** (Zara 1858 - Milan 1918), the first Ford in *Falstaff*, chosen personally by Verdi for the historical *prima* at La Scala in 1893.

Such a choice makes us understand just how special this singing-actor was. He could don the costume of Dandini in *Cenerentola* by Rossini (his debut opera in 1878 at Cremona) and that of Rigoletto, King Alfonso in *La Favorita*, Germont in *Traviata*. His favourite roles were those of Dulcamara (*Elisir d'Amore*), Don Pasquale, Don Bartolo, and Taddeo (*Italiana in Algeri*), - characters which he virtually transformed in his interpretations. To counterbalance this long praise session, we must repeat what the publisher Ricordi said about him after the opening night of *Falstaff*. He declared that Pini-Corsi was a third rate singer, who hammed the part and was also anti-musical. His recording of the aria "Udite, udite o rustici" actually confirms what Ricordi said.

Virgilio Lazzari (Assisi 1887 - Castel Gandolfo 1953) was one of the most acclaimed Leporellos, both in American theatres and at Salzburg. He had a clear voice, which was governed by a controlled and aristocratic taste. A fine singing actor with a repertory of some 55 operas. He studied in Rome with the famous Antonio Cotogni.

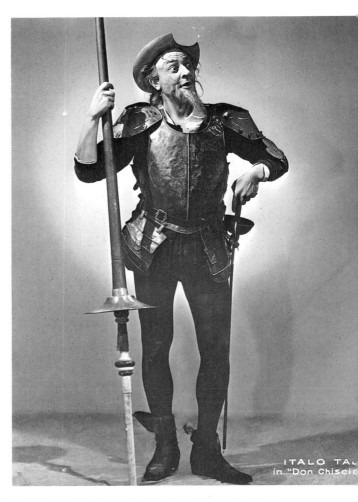

Italo Tajo in Don Quichotte *by Massenet. Today the bass from Piedmont, Italy still performs with success, especially at the Metropolitan Opera of New York, where he is assured of the public's affection. (Historic Archives of the Rome Opera Theatre. Photo: A. Villani).*

Vincenzo Bettoni (Melegnano 1881 - Milan 1954) alternated serious and comic repertories: in fact he made his debut as Silva in *Ernani* in Pinerolo in 1902. He often sang at La Scala (1926-40) and in England, covering a sizeable repertory (*Tristan und Isolde, Faust, Gioconda,*

Mignon, Comte d'Ory, Fra Diavolo, Barbiere di Siviglia, L'Italiana in Algeri, Cenerentola), thanks to his flexible and well-extended vocal means.

Between 1922 and 1962 **Salvatore Baccaloni** (Rome 1900 - New York 1969) dominated the stage with his amiability, his sense of humour, and his refined singing. It could not have been otherwise, considering the formation of this singer from Rome. He was a boy singer in the Sistine Chapel and afterwards studied with Talli and Kaschmann. He was a perfect Don Pasquale, Bartolo, Don Magnifico, Taddeo, Mustafà, and even Osmin. After 1940 he performed almost exclusively at the New York Metropolitan Opera, where he was proclaimed the "new Lablache".

Andres Perello de Segurola (Valencia 1874 - Barcelona 1953) obtained a memorable success as Leporello at Salzburg in 1910. **Wilhelm Hesch** (Elbeteinitz, Czechoslovakia 1860 - Vienna 1908) was a remarkable *buffo*. **Vanni Marcoux** (Turin 1877 - Paris 1962) made an exceptional Don Quichotte in Massenet's opera and Gianni Schicchi, but also performed in the most important parts for *basso nobile* over forty years of career. He had a repertory of 240 roles.

Nowadays we must list among the important comic basses the following singers: **Fernando Corena** (Geneva 1916 - Lugano 1984) and **Paolo Montarsolo** (Naples 1923), who both often overdo things a little but have an irresistible sense of humour. Lastly a word for **Renato Capecchi** (Cairo 1923), whose limitless repertory begins with the seventeenth century and ends with contemporary composition (including Ghedini's *Billy Budd* and *Lord Inferno* and Napoli's *Un curioso accidente*; his versatility is said to have embraced 300 roles).

The Never-Ending Tajo

Italo Tajo (Pinerolo 1915) is one of those miraculous cases of artistic longevity that can only be explained by his rigid self-control, a correct and constant study, intelligence and sensitivity. Of course we cannot limit his successes to the category of comic basses (the *buffi*): in fact Tajo made his debut in 1935 at the Teatro Regio of Turin in the role of Fafner in *Das Rheingold* (a *basso profondo* part). During the first part of his fifty year long career (Tajo has continued singing in small parts such as that of the Sacristan in *Tosca*, Alcindoro and Benoît in *La Bohème*, and Simone in *Gianni Schicchi* throughout all the eighties and into the nineties), the Italian singer showed a marked inclination towards the classic repertory of the *basso nobile*: Ramfis, Banquo, Don Giovanni, Méphistophélès in Gounod's *Faust*, Attila and Sparafucile. He did not give these parts mere vocal splendour, but

Salvatore Baccaloni as Don Pasquale. From 1926-1940 he sang at La Scala, where Toscanini worked with him and suggested that he specialise in the comic roles of Italian opera, in which he had great success. He was one of the most famous and celebrated Met stars from 1940 to 1962.

added a psychological depth achieved by a variety of accents and a lively, vivid phrasing, always perfectly suited to the character.

Tajo's voice was never particularly attractive as far as timbre is concerned, nor was it powerful enough to stun. What was amazing was his ability in producing any shading he wished, starting from an almost inaudible trill in *pianissimo*; he also offered an elegant and incomparable acting style. So, side by side with his serious repertory, he gained a huge success in the comic repertory: from his legendary Dulcamara to Don Basilio, from Figaro (*Marriage of Figaro*) to Don Pasquale, and his wide selection of characters from the Neapolitan repertory of the seventeen hundreds, many of which have been preserved by RAI recordings. He gave his farewell performance in 1991, at the Met, as the sacristan in *Tosca*.

"A Doctor of My Standing...,": (*Barbiere di Siviglia*)

Enzo Dara (Mantua 1938) is the *basso buffo* of the moment. Few people can ever imagine him as Ramfis or Monterone, Angelotti (*Tosca*) or Timur (*Turandot*), or even less as Klingsor in

Parsifal; yet his first performances, from 1960 until 1966, were actually in these parts.

After having sung Bartolo and Dulcamara in 1967, Dara discovered that his real vocation lay in the comic field, and he dedicated himself entirely to it from then on. His best quality is that of vocal agility — in the fast vocalising passages and especially in the patter pieces where he enunciates so perfectly, and at such supersonic speed, that every word can be understood. (His "Signorina, un'altra volta..." by Don Bartolo, or his execution of Don Magnifico's demanding aria "Sia qualunque delle figlie" are unsurpassed).

To his gifts as a virtuoso, Dara adds a great natural sense of humour, never going over the top, never trying for easy laughs. Dandini, Don Pasquale, Geronimo in *Matrimonio Segreto*, Taddeo, Dulcamara, Don Magnifico, and the already mentioned Don Bartolo are all roles in which the Italian bass has eliminated many bad performance habits which had accumulated in the bass tradition.

Wladimiro Ganzarolli (Venice 1932) was a good Leporello and Mozart singer during the sixties and the seventies; **Domenico Trimarchi** (Naples 1940) was often engaged by many theatres to sing Don Bartolo, Dandini, Taddeo, and Frà Melitone, with excellent results.

FAMOUS BASS BARITONES

We decided to take the voices of **Mario Petri** (Perugia 1920 - Rome 1985), **George London** (George Burnstein; Montreal 1920-1985), and **Ruggero Raimondi** (Bologna 1941) out of the section given to the *basso nobile* because we believe them to be ideal exponents of the ambiguous category of the bass baritone. They are voices which are well extended, with an indefinable vocal colour, always changing repertory because of their peculiar characteristics, varying over a wide number of roles.

Petri (who was really called Mario Pezzetta), sang from 1948 until 1960, and then he interrupted his operatic career to act in sword-fighting, swashbuckling films and to sing pop music, until the beginning of the seventies, when he returned to opera — this time as a baritone, but without great success. He had been acclaimed in many performances of *Don Giovanni* and *The Marriage of Figaro* (the Count), often under the guidance of Herbert von Karajan, who numbered him amongst his favourite singers. His voice was never very beautiful; but it was extraordinarily expressive, well modulated, put to the service of a dynamic acting ability and an attractive physical appearance. Without exaggerating, singing with taste and style, Petri was also a good Don Magnifico and Mustafà in *L'Italiana in Algeri*.

Canadian born, but Austrian by adoption, George London was one of the most acclaimed bass-baritones between 1940 and 1960. He gave intense and vigorous performances of *Don Giovanni*, *The Flying Dutchman*, *Boris Godunov*, *Parsifal* (Amfortas), *Carmen* (Escamillo), *The Marriage of Figaro* (Figaro), *Aida* (Amonasro), and *Tosca* (Scarpia). His career was interrupted at the height of success after an operation on his vocal chords failed. The operatic stage thus prematurely lost one of its most interesting and sensitive personalities. He began producing Opera in 1971, with *The Magic Flute* at the Juilliard School, New York, and the *Ring* in Seattle and San Diego, 1973-5.

Ruggero Raimondi began at Spoleto as Colline in 1964. He immediately exhibited a smooth emission, an ease over the whole range, and a power that placed him amongst the most gifted young *bassi nobili*. In the decade which went from 1965 to '75 he sang in a vast repertory: *Vespri Siciliani*, *I Lombardi*, *Faust*, *Boris*, *The Marriage of Figaro*, *Simon Boccanegra*, *Ernani*, *Carmen* and *Don Carlos*. But he identified himself almost totally with the role of Don Giovanni, and in Losey's 1979 film of that opera he gained great popularity. However when he performed parts more strictly limited to a bass voice, his low register showed more clearly what it was — artificial and unnatural. He was saved exclusively by his technique.

He has no difficulty, however, in his high register (his a' is easy and penetrating) to the extent that over recent years he has been able to make frequent excursions (sometimes only discographically) into the baritone repertory: Escamillo, Scarpia, Iago and Falstaff. His appearance as Don Profondo in *Il Viaggio a Reims* by Rossini, at Pesaro in 1984, was surprising. His agility was noteworthy and his rapid vocalization was that of a true belcanto bass. However these gifts were only partially confirmed by his following Rossini performances (*Turco in Italia*, and *L'Italiana in Algeri*).

Raimondi moves with elegance on the stage, and he takes part in the drama with the credibility of a great film actor: this is why he is so much

Mario Petri, at right, with two illustrious colleagues, **Ferruccio Mazzoli**, at left, and in the centre, **Boris Christoff**, in Handel's Julius Caesar; presented in Rome on 26th December, 1956. The reading of the score was certainly not philological; but-as to the voice — the audience was very well satisfied. (Historic Archives of the Rome Opera Theatre).

During the performance of Aïda conducted by von Karajan at Salzburg in 1980, Ghiaurov was substituted in the role of Ramfis by **Ruggero Raimondi**. Here he is, involved in this difficult and not very satisfying role for a bass. (Historic Archives of the Salzburg Festival. Photo: Rabanus).

Mario Petri, an exuberant Don Giovanni. In this role he was the favourite of von Karajan, who called him to his side in many performances. Petri was also active as a film actor. One remembers an amusing film made with Totò (Totò against the Black Pirate). (Historic Archives of the Rome Opera Theatre. Photo: Villani).

in demand by the greatest directors and opera conductors, without forgetting the film industry, which has captured his interpretations of Don Giovanni, Boris, and Escamillo (in Rosi's *Carmen*).

To list a few other famous bass baritones: **Jean-François Delmas** (Lyons 1861 - Saint Alban de Monthel 1933), very active in the Wagnerian and French repertories (he was the first Athanael in *Thaïs* by Massenet); **Nikolai Schewelev** (1868 - Tiflis 1929), able to sing Escamillo, Rigoletto, Hans Sach and the principal roles of the Russian repertory with success; **Arthur Endrèze** (Chicago 1893-1975) famous as Hamlet; **Jaro Prohaska** (Vienna 1891 - Munich 1965), a Wotan and Baron Ochs of extraordinary means.

In the following generations, some of the most famous names were **Alfred Jerger** (Brünn 1889 - Vienna 1976) the first Mandryka in *Arabella* in 1933 at Dresden and an acclaimed Mozart singer; **Gustav Neidlinger** (Mainz 1910-1991) a specialist in the role of Alberich in *The Ring*; **Ferdinand Frantz** (Kassel 1906 - Munich 1959) a noteworthy Wotan; **Herman Uhde** (Bremen 1914 - Copenhagen 1965) who worked in all the most important German theatres, Covent Garden, and at the Metropolitan, giving unforgetable performances of *Lohengrin*, *The Flying Dutchman*, *Tales of Hoffmann*, *Wozzek*, until his death in Copenhagen while he was singing *Faust III* by Bentzon; **Franz Crass** (Wippenfürth 1928) specialised in the roles of Sarastro and the Flying Dutchman; **Theo Adam** (Dresden 1926) who performed in a vast repertory, with a particular predilection for the parts of Jochanaan in *Salome*, Wozzek, and Pizzaro in *Fidelio*; **Tom Krause** (Helsinki 1934) active in the Mozart repertory and as a concert artist; **Roger Soyer** (Thiais, France 1939) a famous Don Giovanni; **Nicolai Ghiuselev** (Pawlilceni, Bulgaria 1936) who is really more of a bass than a baritone, despite his frequent excursions into an ambiguous repertory (Escamillo, Scarpia, Alfonso in *Lucrezia Borgia*); **Jules Bastin** (Brussels 1933); **Simon Estes** (Centerville, Iowa 1938). As for **Justino Diaz** (San Juan, Puerto Rico 1939), despite the fact that the Kutsch-Riemens dictionary dares compare him to Ezio Pinza, we have always found him a singer of poor taste and mediocre technique.

Don Carlos: *"Nel posare sul mio capo la corona"* sings **Raimondi** *(Philip II) and so opens, very solemnly, the scene of the autodafé. (Historic Archives of the Teatro Comunale of Bologna. Photo: P. Ferrari).*

THE BELCANTO BASS: SAMUEL RAMEY

and his ability to vary with taste and imagination, can be traced back to the eighteenth and nineteenth century basses mentioned previously. He is the only bass in this century to restore the force and incisiveness of an unsurpassed belcanto class composed of head-spinning *roulades* and incredible *passaggi di sbalzo* (which show that he can jump easily from low D to high a') , trills and interminable vocalizing. His roles are Assur (*Semiramide*), Maometto (*Maometto II*), Mosè (in the double version of the opera *Moïse* and *Mosè in Egitto*) and Argante (in Handel's opera *Rinaldo*). Thanks to these particular vocal qualities, Ramey is practically the singer-symbol of the Rossini Opera Festival of Pesaro. There he is often the protagonist and star of the summer opera season (*L'Italiana in Algeri, La Donna del Lago, Edipo a Colono, Maometto II, Turco in Italia, Viaggio a Reims, La Gazza Ladra* (The Thieving Magpie), and the *Stabat Mater*).

An amiable extrovert, Ramey moves with great ease on the stage, and is capable of playing comic roles very well, such as Don Giovanni, Mustafà (*Italiana in Algeri*), Selim (*Turco in Italia*), Figaro (*The Marriage of Figaro*) and Don Basilio.

As a personal experience of Ramey's incredible voice we describe the following episode: in

Samuel Ramey *wouldn't even be recognised by his own mother decked out like this! Looking at him he seems almost a painting, an ugly sketch - but instead it is Mefistofele, ready to enter on stage and terrorise the audience. (Giandonato Crico Collection).*

Samuel Ramey, *magnificent principal of Maometto II. As a Rossini interpreter the American bass has no equal in our century. (Photographic Archive of the Rossini Opera Festival. Pesaro).*

The Handel and Rossini renaissance could not help but have stimulating effects among the basses, as we have already mentioned in respect to Dara and Raimondi.

Samuel Ramey (Colby, Kansas 1942) is the best product of this belcanto revival. He is a bass who traces an ideal *fil rouge* from the legendary Boschi, Montagnana, and Galli (historic basses of the 1700's and 1800's) through to the teachings of Pasero. From this last singer Ramey has taken the smooth singing line, his impeccable legato, his varied phrasing, which is always expressive, and his ability in vocal shadings. Ramey has displayed these qualities from 1973 on, in many operas which had also been dear to Pasero, such as *Don Carlos, Mefistofele, Barbiere, Puritani, Rigoletto,* and *Faust*.

Ramey's spectacular agility, his rare extension

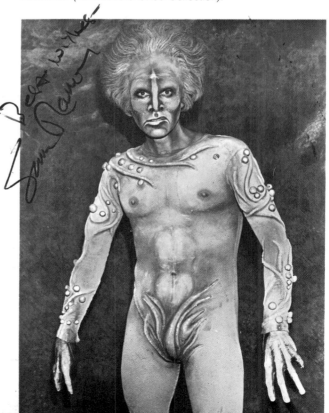

A moment from Turco in Italia *by Rossini. At left Donna Fiorilla (the soprano **Lella Cuberli**) kneeling, entreating; Don Geronio (**Luigi De Corato**); and at right, **Ramey**. (Photographic Archive of the Rossini Opera Festival. Pesaro).*

L'Italiana in Algeri the two *buffi*, Mustafà and Taddeo, compete with each other, by the use of their high notes, in the "Pappataci" duet. The first to pronounce the perilous "Pappataci Mustafà" is Taddeo, who then invites the gullible Pasha to repeat the vow: at that point Ramey launches his thunderous "Pappataci Mustafà" — two powerful high g''s, perfectly placed and as penetrating as any tenor's; of course, at this point, the public never fails to break into a murmer of amazement and admiration.

*With majestic and imposing carriage, **Samuel Ramey** makes his entrance in* Rinaldo *by Handel, in the role of Argante. The tremendous entrance aria "Sibilar gli angui d'Aletto" provides passages of very long and elaborate vocalizing, resolved with incredible ease and power by the American bass. (Giandonato Crico Collection).*

APPENDIX

GLOSSARY

Agility: An ease, lightness and flexibility of vocal execution - a special gift of the virtuoso singer.

Appoggiatura: An appoggiatura is a vocal ornament mainly used by composers and singers in the seventeen hundreds. It is an unharmonised auxiliary note which falls on the strong beat of a measure, a half tone above or below the essential note to which it is smoothly connected.

Aria: An air, song, melody or tune: often for solo voice, with accompaniment by an instrument or orchestra. Opera composers use the aria to enable singers to display their ability.

Belcanto: An Italian term for beautiful singing, now frequently used to imply a style of voice production especially suited to the operas of Rossini, Bellini, Donizetti, early Verdi, etc.

Bis: The Italian term for "Encore".

Bravura: A striking display of ability and technique in a difficult passage.

Break: When a singer passes from one register to another there can be an abrupt change of vocal quality.

Breath: Air used in respiration. A singer inhales normally and exhales either with the glottis wide open and without producing vocal vibrations, that is, silently, or with the glottis closed, thus activating the vibratory action of the vocal chords.

Breath control: The mastery and correct use of the three breathing techniques used in opera singing. These tecniques are breath renewal, breath retention and breath support; and their mastery enables the singer to conserve breath during phonation and to keep a well-regulated, continuous pressure for the production and projection of his voice.

Breathing: The act or process of drawing air into the lungs for oxygenating and purifying the blood, and its subsequent exhalation (Webster). Let us quote from *Human Physiology*, by Starling: "The constant renewal of air in the lungs is brought about by rhythmical movements of the thorax or chest cavity which cause an alternate increase and diminution in their size. As the lungs swell up with each enlargement of the thorax, air (breath) is sucked in through the Trachea or windpipe. This is the process called *inspiration*. As the thorax relaxes it contracts and its capacity is diminished causing an explosion of air and deflation of the lungs. This is *expiration*. The completed cycle of inspiration and expiration is called *respiration*. The frequency of respiratory movement varies with age, muscular effort, fatigue, and emotional excitement.
During full inspiration the thorax is enlarged in all dimensions, from above downwards by the contraction of the diaphragm (diaphragmatic breathing) and in its transverse diameters by the movements of the ribs (costal breathing)." Breathing is important to the singer because normal voice production or phonation depends upon the presence of a steadily expiring stream of breath.

Buffo: The Italian word for comic or funny. It is used in opera, and particularly Italian opera: eg. *basso buffo*, *tenore buffo*, but also *buffo* by itself - meaning a comic bass. We also find *opera buffa*, meaning comic opera.

Cabaletta: The word originates from the latin *copula*, coming from the Provençal *cobla*. A *cabaletta* is a verse, a brief opera aria with a simple rhythm and lively time, sometimes varied, placed at the end of a scene or a concertato. The term entered into common usage during the nineteenth century in Italian opera, especially in Verdi operas (The famous *cabaletta* "Di quella pira" from *Trovatore*, "Sempre libera" in *Traviata*, "Sí, vendetta" in *Rigoletto*).

Cadenza: Here we are referring to the vocal *cadenza*, that is to a series of ornaments performed, without instrumental accompaniment, before the end of the virtuoso aria. Initially, in the eighteenth century, the singer inserted *cadenze* (even three in 'da capo' arias) of his own invention, even improvised. From Mozart on, the composer himself placed them in his work (celebrated ones: the *cadenze* of Gilda, "Caro nome" in *Rigoletto*, and that of Lucia, the "Pazzia", Mad Scene, in *Lucia di Lammermoor*, not written by Donizetti however). The singers, however, continued (and continue) to insert their own *cadenze*: the famous cadenza del "Brindisi" from *Hamlet*, the opera by Thomas, added by Titta Ruffo; and that, with a final trill, insisted on by Roberto Stagno for the "Brindisi" of Turiddu; or the *roulade* with a high c″ sharp which Lauri-Volpi executed at the end of "La donna è mobile", sending Toscanini into a fury. Today, baritones such as Sherrill Milnes and Leo Nucci are in the habit of adding brief *cadenze* in the arias of *Trovatore, Barbiere di Siviglia, Ballo in Maschera* — not to show-off their agility (as did Galvany or Battistini) but to display their power and extension in the high register. The restoration of the amazing, at times even excessive, nineteenth century *cadenze* is due to singers such as Sutherland, Sills, Horne, the bass Ramey and the tenors Merritt and Blake, specialists in vocal arabesques in the operas of Rossini recently revived in philological style.

Cavatina: Diminutive of *cavata*. A short aria in one or two sections (not like the classical 'da capo' aria in three sections), often preceded by a recitative, which has the purpose of presenting the character. Some famous cavatinas are those by Figaro in *Barbiere di Siviglia*, "Largo al factotum"; by Dulcamara "Udite, udite, o rustici" from *Elisir d'Amore*; the "Casta diva" by Norma.

Claque: A French term used to signify a group of people paid by a singer or theatre (or even sometimes without any financial reward) to be present at a performance to applaud this or that interpreter (irrespective of the quality of his performance) and, viceversa, the "anti-claque" to whistle and boo a performer. The claques have always operated in favour of one artist or against another, so much so as to feed famous rivalries (Banti and Morichello, or Cuzzoni and Durasanti in the eighteenth century; Callas and Tebaldi, or Caballé and Gencer, Domingo and Pavarotti in this century). Berlioz has left an unforgettable essay on the claque, describing its members, their ways of applauding or disapproving, penetrating the psychology of this particular category of music-maniac. To a special category belong the so-called *Vedovi* (Widows), nostalgic supporters of Maria Callas, ready to whistle any artist who dares to sing "her" operas.

Coloratura: Brilliant vocalizations, such as florid ornaments, arabesques, runs, trills, rapid scale passages. Thus we get the *coloratura soprano*, a specialist in music that requires a virtuoso rendition.

Colour: The quality or timbre of the voice; the various shades of vowel quality. Colour refers to the features of a particular voice which give it a character or individuality of its own, and give life and imaginative intensity to the expression. It is a composite of gradations in tonal quality and dynamics which vividly renders the text of the song or aria.

Colpo di glottide, Coup de glotte, Glottal Stroke: A little trick used by some singers to assist in attacking a note. The vocal chords are put into rapid vibration by a tiny, almost imperceptible movement resembling a cough, which, closing the larynx orifice, provokes the attack of the sound. It is a very useful technique, in fact even fundamental for producing staccato sounds, the famous *picchettati*, even if it is important not to abuse its use. The *colpi di glottide*, hiccup-style, of Leyla Gencer are famous, almost proverbial.

Concertato: A musical moment placed at the end of a scene or act of an opera, with the participation of the solo voices, the orchestra and often the choir. Celebrated *concertati* are: those which close the first act of *Barbiere*, "Mi par d'esser con la testa" (Rossini); the final acts of *Don Giovanni* (Mozart) and Bellini's *Norma*.

Corona or Punto Coronato: A graphic sign placed above a note or a pause prolongs *ad libitum* its length. In use since the fourteen hundreds, in the eighteenth century it served to indicate the start of a *cadenza* or, in case the corona was placed at the start of an aria *di portamento*, to indicate the possibility of performing a *messa di voce* closed by a trill. The interpretive tradition of the last century and this has inserted *corone* where the composer never dreamed of putting them; thus we have the high a′ of "Sacerdote, io resto a te" in the version by the tenor De Muro or by Del Monaco, which seem unending; and also the phrase of Don José in *Carmen* "Dragon d'Alcalà", sung back-stage; or the "Amami Alfredo" of Violetta Valéry.

Critical edition: A musical edition prepared on the basis of strictly philological criteria, in absolute respect of the original text and the relative documents. They can be about a composer in his global production (*opera omnia*), or various composers of similar period and background (*monumenti musicali*).

In recent times the principal critical editions relate to the *opera omnia* of Rossini (care of the Rossini Foundation of Pesaro, since 1969) and of Verdi (care of Ricordi and the Chicago University Press), an operation initiated with valid criteria and praiseworthy intentions. The musicologists entrusted (and our comments essentially regard Verdi) with this work often forget, in the impetus of their philological enthusiasm, to be concerned with the philology of tradition, to integrate the primary source of the text with an accurate choice of the principal ornamentations, of the *cadenze* and of the *puntature* added, right from the first performances, by the great singers. As a result we have, as an example, the philological *Rigoletto* presented at Vienna by Riccardo Muti: away with the high notes, modified time in some pages, away with the soprano ornaments; the original score was absolutely respected, but the end result was lacking. Even Verdi himself, perhaps not even too unhappily, accepted the virtuosity of his singers, fully aware that, thanks to them, the opera would be a success: he even asked his friend Donizetti to write the *puntature* for the singers in his opera *Ernani*.

Da capo: Repeat from the beginning. "A da capo" aria, often used by Handel, is one in which the first section is repeated after a contrasting section.

Diapason: In the music of ancient Greece it was the name which indicated an octave; a basic sound, usually the A, used for establishing the pitch of all the other notes and for tuning the instruments. The placement of the sound is fixed at 440Hz, or double vibrations, a second; but for centuries the diapason varied from region to region.

Only in 1700 was there an effort to resolve the problem, studying a method to uniform the tuning and pitch of the instruments; however the congresses and conferences organized by acoustic physicists during the Romantic period did not succeed in establishing an identical diapason for everyone; also because there was, in fact, a tendency (especially in string instruments) to increase the pitch, little by little, as the lute-makers strove to give their instruments an ever more brilliant and incisive sound. The present measure was established in 1939 at a congress in London, with a later decision in 1971 by the Council of Europe to confirm the frequency of 440Hz. Despite all this, from Bach to our time, the A has passed from 563 Hz to 377Hz a second, that is to say that it has grown by more than a semi-tone: the mythical high c″ in chest voice of Duprez would correspond today to a b′, or even a b′ flat. This does not authorize certain singers, however, to lower the pitch of the most difficult arias: the tenor Penno sang the "Pira" in B flat major; Pavarotti today performs "La gelida manina" and the duet "O soave fanciulla" (*Bohème*) a half tone under; Frederica von Stade adjusted to her own pleasure the arias of *Sonnambula* in San Francisco. These habits have always existed in the theatrical world: the same things were done by Malibran, Garcia, Pasta and Alboni.

Diaphragm: A partition consisting of muscles and tendons which separates the chest from the abdominal cavity. The diaphragm is convex upwards and flattens on contraction, thus increasing the capacity of the chest or thorax. The diaphragm is a most important factor in the breathing process, especially for opera singers.

Diction: The manner of enunciation in speaking or singing. Good diction requires clear and accurate formation, production, and projection of the elementary sounds of a language, subsequently combining them into fluent patterns which are suited to the expression of the words and music of a song or aria.

Diva: The term originates from the latin and meant goddess. It is used to denote a great or especially gifted female singer.

Dynamics: The variation and control of the force or power with which vocal tone is released and radiated into space. The term can be broken down into loudness and intensity.

Encore: A French word used in English (but not in French) to mean "Perform it once more". An encore is a repetition or extra piece performed in response to such a demand. The word "Bis" has the same meaning and is used in Europe.

Enunciation: A projective, energising or dynamic process whereby vocal sound, audibility, and distinctiveness are applied to the vowels and consonants being articulated.

Falsetto/Falsettone: A singing technique which uses the resonance cavities of the head. The voice which results is penetrating, high, sweet if well emitted, otherwise querulous and chirping. With the use of the chest resonance cavities you can obtain a mixed sound, the reinforced *falsettone* with which the tenors of the early eighteen hundreds pushed their voices up to high e″ flat, f″ and g″ (David, Rubini, Nourrit).

Fila di voce/Filatura: Literally to draw the voice out into a mere thread of sound.

Flautato: The so-called *attacco flautato* (fluted attack) of a note is, in imitation of the flute, the abrupt passing from one note to another, without intermediate passages or *portamenti*. Some singers prefer to reach their notes using this type of effect; whilst others (Corelli, for example) adopt a technique of *portamento*.

The Gods: Term used in Anglo-Saxon countries to indicate gallery seats high up in the theatre.

Habanera: A Cuban rhythm (the word derives from the name of the city Havana), originating from Spain, in moderate 2/4 time, similar to the tango. *Habaneras* were composed by Ravel, Debussy, Albèniz; but the nost famous of all is that of Bizet "L'amour est un oiseau rebelle", which marks Carmen's entrance in his opera. The motive did not originate with Bizet, but with the Spanish musician Sebastian Yradier (1809-1865) who wrote the celebrated melody for his opera *El arreglito*. The entrance of Carmen was very difficult: the first interpreter, Célestine Galli-Marié, obliged the poor Bizet to write thirteen different versions, and she was only satisfied with the present *habanera*. As a recompense for so much trouble, after the early death of Bizet, the singer collected the funds necessary for a fine monument dedicated to the composer.

Heldentenor: A German term signifying, literally, a hero-tenor. A Heldentenor uses his big voice for singing the heavy tenor parts in Wagner operas or others of this type.

Inflexion: Variations of the voice in pitch.

Intonation: Singing in tune.

Legato Singing: A passage marked *legato* should be sung smoothly, without noticeable breaks between the notes.

Lied/Lieder: A German word meaning aria, song or melody. It comes from medieval times, when it emerged in the soloist verse form of the troubadours and *Minnesänger*.
   In the thirteenth and fourteenth century the Lieder underwent a polyphonic elaboration, transforming into *conductus, rondeaux, Diskantlied, Tenorlied*, always acquiring more poetic and expressive value.
   With the sevententh century production of the accompanied solo, the Lied rapidly spread, often using more than one voice with an accompaniment of *basso continuo*. In the eighteenth century many odes and Lieder verses were published and used in *Singspiele*.
   The pre-Romantic Lied has its base in *Volkslied*, simple and inspired, reaching its time of greatest brilliance in the last years of the eighteenth century. The *Kunstlied* developed with the support of the classic composers (Haydn, Mozart, Beethoven) and reached its peak with Schubert, Schumann, Brahms, and Wolf. Words and music intergrated perfectly, as did the solo voice and piano accompaniment. Lieder are often grouped together in song cycles: *Die Schöne Müllerin, Winterreise* (Schubert), *Dichterliebe* (Schumann); or are presented with sumptuous orchestral accompaniment, *Lied von der Erde* (Mahler). In this century the *Kunstlied* has not been given much attention by composers, with the exception of those coming from the New School of Vienna: Schönberg, Berg, Webern.
   Singers from Germanic countries specialize in Lieder, be they tenors, sopranos, basses, mezzosopranos, or baritones; whereas singers from the Italian school literally vanish when confronted with Lied, with the exception of some little lullabies, *Ave Maria*, or a few other melodies frequently given as encores by Gigli, Schipa, and their like, at the end of their recitals. Latin singers have stubbornly ignored the formidable patrimony of German **Lieder** — musically fundamental and an excellent form of voice training.

Loggionismo: (derives from Italian "loggione"=The Gods). This Italian word relates principally to a favourable or critical attitude towards the singers performing the opera. The term comes down from that epoch in which the first real divas of the opera stage appeared and is paragonable to the fanaticism of some football supporters, or political or religious bigots.
   Loggionismo comes from the word *loggione*, the last row of seats (not divided into boxes) generally destined to those opera lovers who cannot afford the exorbitant prices of other places in the theatre. However, apart from the limited vision of the stage (both in height and depth) the *loggione* is the best

place to follow an opera and every music critic should be seated there! *"Le son monte"*, say the French, and in fact, the best acoustics are found right there - up in the "gods", where the voices are perfectly amalgamated with orchestra sonority; and, in addition, the critic who sits in the *loggione* flees from the perilous proximity of parents and close friends of the singer who are decidedly more annoying than the most exuberant loggionists; in the third place, perched up in the "gods" the critic escapes from venomous gossiping with theatre managers, artistic directors and theatrical agents.

Loggionismo has a good side (friendly and folkloristic) and a bad side. For decades the world capital of *loggionismo* has been Parma. In the small bars scattered around the Teatro Regio the fanatical Parma opera lovers gather - mostly from the *loggioni*, but some also from the box seats. In the box seats in particular they practise the dreadful habit of consuming red wine and ham, whilst waiting for the tenor or primadonna to sing a famous aria. The loggionist from Parma was unmerciful. The tenor who didn't please was insulted, even under his hotel windows; and even the railway porter might refuse to load his luggage onto the train. Carlo Bergonzi, born at Vidalenzo (near Parma), and therefore a local glory, was severely contested for having sung in *pianissimo* the b′ flat of "Celeste Aida"; and from that time he has never again sung at the Regio. Cornell MacNeil, exasperated, threw an inkwell whilst crying out to the audience "Enough - Fools!". Elena Mauti Nunziata could not continue her performance of *Traviata* (with Maestro Previtali conducting) because of the protesting whistles and jeers.

Today times have profoundly changed and opera lovers from Parma are content with the good and the less good; as has happened in almost all Italian opera theatres. The anger and the enthusiasm of the loggionist has dissipated, even if every now and again you still hear an "old-style" objection. We remember, among the latest, most clamorous incidents; the *Traviata* interrupted during "Parigi o cara" at Genoa (the innocent victim being Joan Sutherland - forced to withdraw from the performance because of the inadequacies of the tenor); the *Lucia di Lammermoor* at La Scala when they booed Pavarotti; the much worse *Lucia* at the opening of the 1988-89 season of the San Carlo of Naples; the ugly *Luisa Miller* at La Scala with Katia Ricciarelli in 1989, culminating with the diva cursing the audience; and the *Vespri Siciliani* which opened the 1989-90 season at Milan, severely criticized by the public on opening night.

To end, we want to note the different forms of protest which change from country to country. In Italy the "Boo" and a protest whistle are the norm, and, in cases of more extreme confrontation, explicit insults are hurled (and sometimes even programmes or bunches of vegetables). The "shushing" is reserved for the less grave cases of a failed aria. In Austria the "Boo" is used but not the protest whistle; and in serious cáses the loggionists (who occupy the *Stehplätze* - standing places) hurl insults, sneeze, or laugh during an aria. In American theatres the whistle is a sign of approval and vast enthusiasm, as is the stamping of feet; dissension is rare and is limited to shouts and a few isolated "Boos". In France you manifest, disapproval with "Uh! Uh!". In the Soviet Union you just don't applaud; and the same is true in England. In China you always applaud.

Mask: The hollow bone cavities of the skull found behind the eyes and the back of the nose. In singing the words "placing the voice in the mask" or "in the facial mask" are technical terms which refer to the obvious: that is, using these cavities in the emission and projection of sound.

Melisma/Melismatic: The word originates from the Greek and meant "song". It is used to signify the extension and prolongation of a single vowel or syllabe into an expressive but non-florid vocalisation.

Messa di voce: In vocal technique this consists in gradually swelling the sound from a *pianissimo* to a very loud (*fortissimo*) sound and then dimishing the volume until *pianissimo* is again reached, all on the one breath; a technique also known as *filare il suono*, that is 'to thread the sound'. In Belcanto the *messa di voce* had great importance because it allowed a singer to exhibit the length of his breath, the fullness of his sound, and his technical ability. On the score a composer would mark the opportunity to execute a *messa di voce* with a *punto coronato* at the beginning of an aria of *portamento*. (In some Handel arias, and in the Malcolm aria in *La Donna del Lago* (Rossini) Marilyn Horne gives an example, and a singing lesson, of the perfect *messa di voce*, with a final trill as well!).

Mezzavoce: The sound is emitted very, very softly or with a muffled tone. The true *mezzavoce* requires a quantity of breath equal to, if not more than that used for a high note, as well as a perfect positioning of the sound in the facial mask. Only the greatest singers know how to correctly use the *mezzavoce* (Pertile, Schipa, Kipnis, Pinza, Callas, Kraus); others willingly substitute the *falsettone rinforzato* (Gigli, Lauri Volpi, Tagliavini) if not the *falsetto* (Carreras, Di Stefano, Domingo), which is the easiest way of getting over it without too much trouble.

A good use of *mezzavoce* assures a varied interpretation and participation in the text's expressive demands. Verdi wanted the entire prologue of *Simon Boccanegra* to be performed with *mezzevoci*, and the entrance of Nabucco "Tremin gli insani" (often declaimed by baritones at full voice), and the attack for "Sì, vendetta", far more effective and logical if murmured by the baritone — not to even mention the "Sogno" of Iago or the difficult "Parmi vedere le lagrime" by the Duke of Mantua.

Rossini agility, on the other hand, should be performed with strength, on the precise instructions of the composer; a rule always respected by Horne and Valentini-Terrani, but ignored by Caballé and Gasdia, who resolve the most complex Rossini melismatic passages with an out-of-place use of *mezzavoce*.

Mezzofiato: A virtuoso effect obtained with a sort of interruption and immediate release of the flow of air on a held note without resorting to any intake of breath. Today this technique has almost completely fallen into disuse; but it was often adapted in the Liberty period by Mattia Battistini, the tenors Anselmi, Schipa, Gigli, and Pertile, who placed it, often excessively, in the middle of an aria or in the *cadenza* of the aria.

Oratorio: A composition, usually for solo voices, choir and orchestra, based on a sacred text, and usually performed in concert form, often in a church, without acting, scenery or costumes.

Ornament: A term used to describe the vocal, melodic decorations which were not written into the score by the composer but were improvised by the performer according to his or her personal taste. Many of these ornaments have become traditional and frequently are believed to be an integral part of the score; and their performance is expected and demanded by the public.

We must distinguish between the *improvised or Italian ornaments*, not indicated in the score and entrusted to the taste and fantasy of the interpreter, and the *fundamental or French ornaments*, marked in the score by specific symbols and placed in precise points of the melodic line, respecting both pitch and rhythm. Among the principal fundamental ornaments are the *acciaccatura*, the *appoggiatura*, the *arpeggio*, the double *cadenza* or *gruppetto*, the *mordente*, the *tremolo*, the trill, and the *vibrato*.

Opera Critic: He is an expert in "antique" voices, an avid collector of dusty old recordings, of vintage static and crackle, of dates, quotes, relics of every kind, lists of names, addresses, certificates of birth and death; ready to describe the voices of David or of Malibran with a precision and sureness which he would be incapable of using to comment a performance of Pavarotti heard the evening before.

Passaggio: As a techical term used in voice production, it refers to the break between the various vocal registers. e.g. from low to middle register, from the middle register to the high register.

Phonation: When vocal sound is produced in the larynx or glottis this process is called phonation, that is, the vibratory activity of the vocal chords producing pulsations sufficiently rapid to create the sensation of tone. When these tones are sustained they form the singing voice.

Phrasing: The use of vocal patterns and expressive technique that are appropriate to the musical thought in a song. Phrasing needs to be the result of genuine feeling and not be a cold analysis of the musical structure. Unobtrusive phrasing, clearly and correctly applied to the piece, constitutes one of the greatest refinements in performing.

Picchettato: In vocal technique, the term refers to the quick emission of *staccato* notes, often in the high register. It is a type of virtuosity especially used by coloratura sopranos; and the absolute champion of this skill was Maria Galvany, who sang at the beginning of the century.

Pitch: The degree of acuteness or graveness of a tone. The greater the number of vibrations per second the higher the pitch that is heard.

Portamento (French, *port de voix*): The *portamento* is usually indicated by a slur mark connecting two notes of different pitch; the *portamento* is characterised by passing from one note to another by sliding rapidly above all the intermediate notes. Some singers make excessive use of this vocal technique, with the intention of facilitating their rise to the high notes, or more simply, from bad habit (Gigli, Corelli, Bergonzi, Tebaldi).

Prima Donna: These Italian words meaning "first lady" refer to the leading lady in an opera company. The term comes from the beginning of opera in the seventeenth century, when the term *primo uomo* was also used; but then it was applied to the *castrati*. In our time the title *Prima donna* is often given to a female vocalist of high reputation and vast earning ability; as a result the term *prima donna assoluta* (the absolute first lady) has arisen to satisfy the vanity of certain eminent singers.

Projection: The act of transmitting the voice through the atmosphere from singer to listener.

Puntatura: The substitution of a note with another (usually higher) by a singer, for the purpose of better putting on show his or her ability. The *puntature acute* (high points) by now have become part of the tradition of certain operas (the c″ of the "Pira" in *Trovatore*, the e‴ flat of *Traviata*, the a′ flat in the Prologue of *I Pagliacci*) and should not be considered whims or caprices by the lead singer. The composers were conscious that the success of a super-high note could determine the success of the entire opera, and were more than willing to meet the requests of their singers. During a concert recital at Rome, the soprano Editha Gruberova used a score of the aria "Ebben ne andrò lontana" (*La Wally* by Catalani) which finished with a high e‴, that is, a traditional *puntatura*.

Range: The pitch range of the singing voice. See "Tessitura".

Recitative: A type of singing in which the words are delivered in a declamatory way with the intention of emphasizing the natural inflections of speech. Another name is *musica parlante*, speaking music. In opera and oratorio recitative commonly serves for dialogue or narrative. Recitative is divided into various types, the principal ones being *recitativo secco* (dry) which is a quick patter, with a simple accompaniment of chords, and *recitativo strumentato* (instrumented) which has an orchestral accompaniment and was brought to its apex by Wagner.

Roulade: A French term meaning a fast vocalised passage, as found especially in Rossini and Belcanto composers.

Smorzatura: A gradual dying away of the sound.

Sprechgesang: German, meaning "spoken song". The term was used for the first time by Schönberg in *Pierrot Lunaire* (1912) and then by other composers of the New School of Vienna, to indicate a form of declamation which synthesises the values of singing and acting, in full respect of the rhythm. The intonation oscillates in a continuous *crescendo, glissando, diminuendo* (Italian terms commonly used in music and meaning "growing", "sliding", and "diminishing") without ever remaining fixed (or if so only for a fraction) on any one note. The word is particularly suitable to describe the recitative used by Wagner and especially the type used by Richard Strauss in his operas.

Staccato: The word means detached, and in singing the *staccato* sign requires a disconnected attack for each note or tone, each of which is cut short or separated from the next note by infinitesimal gaps of silence. There are two ways, in singing, of attacking and releasing a staccato note. These are: diaphragmatic action, such as we use when we laugh; or glottal attack, similar to the mechanism used when coughing.

Stecca: A familiar term amongst opera singers, especially those of the Italian school, to indicate a vocal accident - that is, a singer's mistake. It may be an off-key note, hoarseness, a break, a sob, a yell, a scream or a flop; but also a note simply not sung, that is: "eaten". The *stecca* of the tenor Gayarre in *The Pearl Fishers* is famous; it happened during the performance on 8th December, 1899 at Madrid: after having failed the first high note in the aria "Mi par d'udir ancor" (worth translating as it says "I seem to hear again"!) he repeated the aria at the end of the opera; but, alas, he failed again. He then turned to the audience and said *"Esto ce acabò"* (It is finished!). Shortly afterwards he died of consumption.

Style/Stylistic: In opera these words refer to the particular way in which a singer performs - his own special characteristics.

Tessitura: A term used to indicate the approximate extension of a musical piece in relation to the voice for which it has been written. The *tessitura* is, therefore, the ambit of sounds, from the low to the high, in which a singer finds himself most at ease. It is not to be confused with "extension" (or range), which regards the complete orbit of sounds possible for a certain voice. In the following table we have listed the tessitura and extension of the various categories of voices.

	Tessitura	Extension
Tenor	g—g′	c—d″
Soprano	g′—g″	b flat—g‴
Baritone	d—d′	G—a′
Mezzosoprano	e′—e″	g—b″
Contralto	b—b′	e—g″
Basso	B—b	C—f′ sharp

Timbre: Timbre is the tone quality or tone colour which distinguishes, for example, the note sung by a boy soprano from that same note sung by a tenor or by a mezzo-soprano. It is the special resonance quality of a tone which makes it distinguishable from other notes of the same intensity and pitch. Timbre is determined by the form of the sound wave being emitted by the singer and the relative frequencies and intensities of its harmonic parts and overtones. It is the identifying quality of a vocal tone which has been mainly determined by the resonant properties of the singer's facial mask.

Transposition: The changing of the pitch of a composition, without making other changes, in order to make it more suited to a particular singer's vocal range.

Travesti Roles "Trouser" or "Pants" Roles: As can be guessed by looking carefully at both words, these terms refer to roles which are written for a female mezzo-soprano when the character being portrayed is male (Octavian in *Der Rosenkavalier*). There are a few, but rare, *travesti* roles for men - in Wolf-Ferrari's *Il Campiello* two old women are played by two tenors.

Tremolo: In singing, the *tremolo* is an uncontrollable unsteadiness or faulty trembling of the pitch. It is caused by an inability to maintain stability in the laryngeal mechanism during phonation, which frequently results from muscular weakness, or nerves and tension. The *tremolo* must not be confused with vocal *vibrato*. The *vibrato* varies within a semitone interval whereas the *tremolo* varies more than a semitone.

Trill: Not to be confused with *vibrato* or *tremolo*. In singing, the trill is the controlled rapid alternation of two distinct pitches in the musical interval of a semitone, a third or a whole tone. Joan Sutherland and Selma Kurz are two singers famous for their trill.

Verismo/Verist School: The term describes a style of Italian opera composed mainly in the late 19th and early 20th centuries which presented "real-life" situations instead of the rather idealized subjects and characters of operas written before this date. Some composers of the Verist school are Leoncavallo, Puccini, and Mascagni. Some singers have specialized in Verist roles (Magda Olivero).

Vibrato: The vocal *vibrato* is a regular periodic oscillation of vocal tone above and below its normal pitch level and always within a semitone interval. In *vibrato* the concept of interval is completely missing; *vibrato* is not to be confused with *tremolo* or trill. The *vibrato* adds life to and enriches a tone, but it is never exaggerated.

Voice: To reproduce the sound of the human voice (phonation) the following is needed: a. the respiratory muscles of the thorax closed in the rib cage with the lungs functioning as bellows (capacity of approx. 3500-6700 cm^3 of air); b. the vocal chords (four) functioning as source of the vibrations; and c. the cavities of the forehead, nose, mouth, trachea and lungs in use as resonators. The highness of a sound depends on the tension and length of the vocal chords. The shorter the larynx, the higher the voice, and vice versa. This is why basses are, generally, men of tall stature.

The timbre of the voice is conditioned by the resonance cavities (the trachea and lung cavities below the larynx, and above the larynx the oral cavity, the nasal fossae, the forehead cavities and the vibrations of the facial bones).

The quality of the voice depends on the number of harmonic frequencies (below 9 frequencies it is opaque, and above 14 it is shrill). These frequencies can be aumented with a good breathing technique. The sound can be very powerful and penetrating using only, and exclusively, the right pressure of air flow on the vocal chords, thus exploiting the principle of resonance without using any other energy form.

Volume: Fullness or quantity of tone.

Zarzuela: An idiomatic Spanish opera with spoken dialogue.

214

A LESSON IN SINGING:
A. KRAUS

High Class Master Class

The following transcription includes the major points discussed by tenor Alfredo Kraus in a two hour Master Class held in Rome at the Brancaccio Theatre, on May 22, 1990. This Master Lesson offers a full discussion of singing technique, a fount of valuable information and insight for professionals and non-professionals alike.

The audience, formed by young singing students and various singing teachers, listens and comments. Many have their eyes (and ears) opened for the first time; others are undecided what to think. Numerous questions arise. "But what about the roundness of the sound?" "Don't you risk singing in the nose?" "My teachers always told me to cover during the break, to darken the sound!" "I have always breathed sending my stomach in during the expulsion of breath!" etc., etc. Kraus never loses one bit of his proverbial calm. It is the outlook of a person who is sure of what he is affirming. He knows that any misunderstanding or unresolved doubt could be fatal for many immature talents, so he repeats for the fourth time his explanation of how to breathe, indicating his abdomen, making the students touch it when on the stage, singing with them the most difficult phrases and sailing up to any high note with no effort at all.

Initial explanation and the concept of voice placement

Thank you for your warm welcome. I am pleased to see that so many of you have joined us for our friendly chat this afternoon.

I must first say that the voice is a mystery. It is not tangible. It is a sound and not at all material. We cannot even hear how it really sounds, because our ears perceive at the same time both an external and internal sound; this is its mystery. It is the most fascinating musical instrument that exists, because we are ourselves the instrument, and we control it by means of internal sensations.

Why do we always hear people talking about voice placement without ever giving an explanation? We say "Putting the voice in the mask" and the reason for this term is that placing the voice correctly we use the internal cavities behind our facial bones (the so called "mask") as a natural amplifier, because in the throat we have none. On the contrary, the area that surrounds the vocal chords tends to absorb sound as it is made of soft mucous tissue and flesh. It is up to us to project our voice as close to the listener as possible, as "forward" as possible, using a column of air that passes through the vocal chords. The further forward the sound is placed, the closer it is to the listener's ear. The further forward the sound is, the more it is sustained in the mask. The more it is sustained in the mask, the better we use the facial amplifiers (ie. the cavities we were speaking of before: the frontal sinuses, the nasal sinuses, etc.).

Why do we say "voice in the mask"? We say so because a very intelligent person discovered that there is one sound that is naturally placed in the facial amplifiers: it is the Latin sounding vowel "i" (as in "igloo"). It is also the least tiring vowel to sing on. When we say "i" the sound is already there, forward, and correctly placed in the mask; when we say "e" (as in "excellent") we notice that in respect to the "i" it is further back; as for the "a" (as in "arrive") we may as well wave good-bye, for the sound sinks completely into the throat. However when we talk we can mostly get away with this, even if many people end up having to go to specialist voice doctors (phoniatritians) because they speak badly. If we could manage to put all the sounds in the position of the "i" simply while talking, there would be no work for these doctors.

The "I" vowel opens the throat

There is a real obsession in most schools of singing: that of darkening the voice. But why should I darken my voice if it is naturally clear? It is nature who decides if a voice is clear and bright or dark and rich; we cannot make it become so by artificial colouring. Many of my collegues, (even famous ones), when they come to a Latin "i" tend to sing a French "ü"; or when they come to a Latin "e" they pronounce it "ö" (as in "earth"); instead of "a" they say "o". This is all mistaken. It is wrong to think that this darkening of the sound helps technique and rests the voice: this method sends the voice backwards into the throat, making it lose colour and sonority. Up until a short time ago all that I am saying was mere theory (put to practical use by those singers who have a correct techique; unfortunately they are hard to come by).

Now thanks to new studies, and to a video made by professor Tapia of the Santandér University in Spain, we are able to actually see the movements of the vocal chords and the surrounding area during the emission of the voice. The revelations are amazing. It can be clearly seen that the vowel that most widens the cavities (the famous "open throat") is the "i", the "weakest" vowel. They have also measured the sound frequencies, and the results show that the "i" has the largest number of frequencies. How can we explain this? Simple: the "i" may seem small but it has the right resonance; it is sustained in the natural amplifiers and therefore has a larger number of frequencies; you can hear it better. Volume doesn't count. The sound must vibrate correctly and carry well, arriving to every listener in an auditorium.

As you can see studying singing simply becomes a matter of placing the voice in the natural position of the "i". That is all. Seems easy, doesn't it?

I am no genius; neither am I a freak: if I am able to do it so is anyone else. The problem is that very few people have talked about this until now.

It has become a technique in disuse. When I debuted at the Rome Opera a Spanish friend of mine presented me to Giacomo Lauri Volpi. Lauri Volpi himself accompanied me at the piano as I sang "Questa o quella" and "La donna è mobile". He exclaimed straight away: "This is the right technique. These days nobody sings like this anymore". He also told me to be careful in my choice of repertory, because if I kept to my correct repertory I would be able to continue singing for a long time. Lauri Volpi knew what he was talking about!

Everybody has their virtues and their defects. I think that Lauri Volpi, apart from the style and taste of his time, had an excellent technique. He sang a bit of everything, this is true... even if he told *me* to be careful of my repertory. On the other hand, it was customary to do so then. He was, in my opinion, a "heroic" tenor, but he also sang light lyric roles with the aid of a reinforced falsetto. Today this may be questionable, but then it was perfectly acceptable. I think that both Lauri Volpi and Gigli denaturalized their voices by the use of this reinforced falsetto. They were also somewhat lacking in taste, as this is a very dated and strange way of lightening the voice. Aside from this, Lauri Volpi had a good technique, based on the principles I have just explained to you, and what's more, he breathed excellently.

Intercostal-diaphragmatic breathing

Lauri Volpi confirmed that the right breathing method is "intercostal-diaphragmatic". When we open our ribs as widely as possible the elastic membrane we call the diaphragm is completely flattened. In this way it is able to sustain the column of air that is needed to sing. This is very important: while expiring all the ribs widen; then you must sustain by increasing the outward pressure of the diaphragm, so that it remains as flat as possible during the whole process. It is wrong to pull in your stomach while exhaling; I'm sorry if someone disagrees. By pulling in your stomach the membrane loses tension and can no longer sustain the sound. Therefore, to sustain the sound the diaphragm must remain tense and as flat as possible, and during the emission of breath you must push outwards. This is essential. Of course there are many small tricks and techniques to think about as you study. They may seem stupid, but are often very useful. To understand singing we need a special language, and also a lot of imagination. It cannot be explained in any other way. It is not like the piano that we can touch, and that has visible keys which we touch. A person with little imagination will always have difficulty in studying singing. Great difficulty.

The mobility of the facial muscles

An example: let's imagine that there is a small hole in our forehead, between our eyes, and that it is from this opening that the sound passes. This hole is always the same size; it will never change. If this opening is the right size for the "i" ("igloo"), and it passes through it perfectly (and it would seem so) how can the "e" ("excellent") which is larger, and the "a" ("arrive") larger still ever pass through it? Of course if I had a magic power that automatically reduced the larger vowels making them lighter and placed higher they would be able to pass easily. But instead it seems almost impossible to put the "e" and "a" sounds into the same opening as that of the "i". To do this we must be assisted by our facial muscles. The heavier and the larger the vowel is, the more we must lift it by raising our cheek muscles, lightening the sound as we ascend towards the high notes. Many singers pronounce "ü" (as in "soon") and "eu" (as in "earth") with their mouths tightly pursed, or open in a O-shape, without moving their facial muscles at all. It would be best to remember that in singing neither "u" (as in "book") or "o" (as in "octopus") exist, even if we are sometimes obliged to sing them. The "u" is the most difficult of all, as the "o" we may pronounce like a French "a". For example the word "amore" correctly becames "am-a-re" as if you were saying the Italian verb "amare" and not the noun "amore". The "u", however, has hardly any frequencies so we have to make do by putting it as near as possible to the "i", in the cavities surrounding the nose. Be careful, do not put it *in* the nose; many people tend to confuse the two things.

People, used to hearing voices placed in the throat, hear a correctly placed voice and exclaim: "He is singing in his nose". It is true that we are close to the nose, but we are not in the nose. I can easily block my nose and continue to sing or speak when my voice is sustained in the "mask". There are people who have difficulty in understanding this difference because they are used to hearing a guttural or backward placed voice. It is a problem for that listener to resolve. We must go ahead and forget about the people who don't want to understand. Another useful example is to consider the length of piano strings: the low notes have long strings, the high ones have short strings. Let us imagine that our vocal chords are not in our throat, where we cannot control them, but between the eyes where we can manipulate them thanks to the air pressure exerted by the diaphragm. Now let us make believe that we are singing normally and climbing towards the high notes. As we increase the outward pressure of the diaphragm, therefore the air pressure, the vocal chords are shortened, and the sound becomes higher and more resonant. It is like a river that is at first wide and calm, but when the banks tighten it begins to flow faster and with more force.

Avoid an "O"-shaped mouth

Another thing to avoid is the "O"-shaped mouth that so many singing teachers recommend: a round mouth and the chin lowered. One must articulate logically, using the upper jaw, and not the lower one. If you lower the chin the sound becomes closed, but using the upper jaw and keeping the lower one still, gives much more space and sonority to the voice. A few days ago I was watching the Callas Competition on television, and I was particularly struck by the *mezzosoprani* who were amongst the finalists. It was easy to understand that their

teachers had always told them: "Cover, darken the sound, for you are a mezzosoprano" (it would be interesting to see if they actually were mezzosopranos). The poor girls kept darkening, losing both colour and sonority, and sending the voice backwards. When, suddenly, on the high notes, they were physiologically forced to open their mouths wide and lift their cheeks, the sound became far more brilliant.

This is the basis of singing. Everyone has their own individual instrument; each one of us is unique, but there is only one technique. The fact that many people manage to sing with other techniques does not mean anything; there are voices that are as strong as iron, that can survive any sort of treatment. However they all have their defects, and serious ones at that. Try listening to how many tenors fail the "To-o-sca, sei tu" passage from Mario Cavaradossi's first aria! This is because they almost all say "Tu-u-scou" strangling the high b′ flat and sending the voice backwards. Instead you must forget the "o" and think of a dark "a". The audience will hear a clear, easy "To-o-sca", but you have really said "Ta-a-sca". These seem like silly little tricks; perhaps they are, but there is no escaping from them.

Q: Can you explain how to approach a note?
You must forget about the throat and you must drop the sound from a height downwards, as if it came from above your head. In this way the note will be perfectly clean from the beginning, and stylistically correct, without those awful *portamenti* from below, that touch the throat, or hiccups. Think about those small balls that balance on top of water shoots in village fairs: the pressure must be always maintained or else the ball falls off. It is the same sort of mechanism that works for the breath in sound production. You must maintain a constant air pressure, and sustain every note, including the descending ones, always keeping the position high. The notes preceeding a high note are particularly important; they function like the steps of a ladder.

The *passaggio*? You must be joking!

I never think about the *passaggio* (or the so called "break" between the registers). The further I climb the more I increase the pressure, raise higher the position, and widen the sound. It almost feels as if your very head is widening to give more space to the voice. Like when I want to call to a friend standing on the other side of the street: I don't shout "üüüü!", which is a tight and closed sound; I shout "aeeee!", which is open and wide. Almost every teacher makes his student close the sound, cover it, or turn it. Some even say you must vomit it. This is not the right way to do things.

Q: *I would like to ask you to explain breathing again, because singing teachers are very often so confusing on the subject. Did you say that during expiration we must push downwards?.*

No, not at all. Not downwards: outwards! When I widen my ribs as much as possible and begin to emit the sound I feel as if there are external forces that pull my diaphragm, extending it always further. These forces are, of course, not external but inside my own body. It is I who push outwards.

Q: *But doesn't the stomach have to be pulled in during the process of exhalation?*

No, never.

Singing is the simplest thing in the world, but many people seem to want to complicate it. I never talk about the "passaggio": there are various changes of registers (a low register, a middle register and a high register), but there is no change in position. We do not have various throats in different parts of our body, but only one, and one position in which we can control it. Why create such problems over the *passaggio*? Many people make a sort of vomiting sound when they "pass", a sort of "augh!" that instead of opening the throat closes it. The point of resonance is the same for every sound, chest voice and head voice. Women have great facility in their chest voice, however it must also have a high placement. We use technique to render similar all the notes in our range, without the need of so called "breaks" or *passaggi*. If someone had a problem on their high or low notes what should they do? What *passaggio* should they look for? Should they pass over a bridge, or in a tunnel perhaps?

Q: *You criticized the reinforced falsetto used by Lauri Volpi and Gigli, but I find the* mezzavoce *used by Gigli sublime. Is the* mezzavoce *out of fashion as well?*

The *mezzavoce* is out of fashion because nobody knows how to produce it. However I never spoke about *mezzavoce*. I spoke about reinforced falsetto. They abused this falsetto, while *mezzavoce* is quite another thing.

Once we have asserted that the "i" vowel is the most open and free of all, we can do nothing else than attempt to put all the other vowels in the same position.

It is obvious that there are other parts of our phoniatrical apparatus that participate in forming the sound. They are the mouth, the larynx, the pharyngeal cavities, etc., but we cannot control them consciously. We can only manipulate the voice once it is in the facial amplifiers; so you must start from the "i", which has the

highest position and, therefore, is the most distant from the throat.

Q: *In 1964 I remained very impressed by Luciano Pavarotti who sang* La Traviata *at the Rome Opera, even after having heared Franco Tagliavini who at the time had the more robust voice of the two. Pavarotti was amazing for the homogeneity of his voice, even if it was quite small. Today his voice has become more robust and he has changed repertory. Do you think this is a correct evolution?*

Let's forget about Pavarotti. I think that a correct technique allows a voice to maintain its best features intact throughout the years...

Q: *Excuse me, but I have always heard that a voice becomes more robust as time goes by.*

Look: Gigli started his career singing the repertory of a light lyric without being one; this doesen't mean anything. Juan Oncina, one of my colleagues, always sang parts for a light tenor. Once upon a time, thanks to a frequent use of falsetto or *mezzavoce*, you could sing the light lyric repertory and at the same time many works of the verismo school. Caruso did so at the beginning of his career, but he did not really have a light voice. Why should a voice change? Then should all our configuration change? It is clear that with time we grow older, but our height remains the same. I may put on three kilos of weight, or loose five kilos, but I won't change that much. Technique must help preserve the voice as best as possible during the years. Of course there will always be some slight change as time goes by; the voice might darken slightly, or might gain sonority in the low notes, but mainly the vocal features must remain the same. Certain tenors begin their career singing the "gelida manina" in the original key, and only five years later they have to lower it by half a tone. Does this seem right to you? What has happened? It is simple: they have made their voice heavy, pushing on the middle register and losing the high notes. It is not natural. Any respectable tenor must have a high c".

Q: *Could you please explain, once again, the correct method of breathing?*

You haven't understood it yet?

I have heard different theories on this subject, but I only have one. The breathing method is intercostal-diaphragmatic. You don't push your stomach out, or pull it in. You must widen your ribs, thus flattening the diaphragm: once the diaphragm is completely flat all the way around, you emit the voice while pushing outwards. We must continue to make the note "travel" until the end. For example when I emit an "a" it is not only one "a" but millions of "a's", like machine gun fire.

Q: Maestro, I would like to ask you about vocal agility. There are many singers with light voices that should have no problems with it, but instead they have many difficulties. What would you advise them to do?

It is a question of practice. You must make sure that every note is part of a single flow and are all sung legato without that awful "ha-ha-ha" sound. We Latins have the habit of adding a sort of "h" before each note. It is quite dangerous as with this system we risk losing the sustainment of the sound. The secret for singing well is that of singing legato. This will also give you the agility needed.

Q: Without discussing the specific virtues of your colleagues, I would like to ask you what the difference is between the open method of singing (like Di Stefano) and the rounded method (like Bergonzi)?

I cannot talk about singing methods. For me there exists only one method for singing, only one technique. You must pardon my presumption, but I insist that the correct technique is the one I use myself. The fact that anyone manages to sing well because of their gifts does not mean anything. As I said before there are the so called "iron voices", that can survive any sort of treatment. You must know how to listen accurately, to hear if a "round" voice can really resolve the high notes, or if a voice placed in the throat can resolve them at all. Most listeners know nothing of these terms: they only want to listen to a beautiful voice, especially one that screams a lot.

Q: You mean as in the case of some much publicized voices?
Exactly.

Q: Can you explain how to perform the mezzavoce?

This is one of the many contradictions of singing. To diminish the sound we must increase the pressure and decrease the volume (that is: we must compress the diaphragm further while reducing the weight of the sound, lifting it ever higher and lightening it). This is not easy. We cannot resolve this problem in five minutes. However it is the only way to reduce the sound, keeping the same position, without having to use any falsetto. The facial muscles are very helpful in this as well. We must train them to be elastic and mobile.

Q: When you talk about the sustainment of the voice, you make a vertical gesture. How can the widening of the ribs horizontally have anything to do with this vertical pressure?

Of course singing is full of these contradictions. If I breath pulling my stomach in, the diaphragm would lose tension. How could I sustain the voice then?

Q: So we must keep a constant pressure, pushing outwards along the whole circumference of our abdomen?

That's right. On all sides. Thus the diaphragm remains as tense as possible.

Q: When you talk about tension of the diaphragm I don't understand what you mean. Can you explain yourself better please?

The diaphragm is an elastic membrane. When it is relaxed, in its normal position, it is not completely horizontal. If I keep it horizontal during expiration, by pushing outwards, I can support the column of air needed to sing. Otherwise where could I sustain it to be able to project it forwards? Take a trampoline artist, for example. From whence does be project himself when he jumps? He is sustained by something that resists his pressure; then he jumps. Have you ever watched a small baby crying naked on a bed? What does he move? The ribs. And where does he sustain the sound? In his facial mask. You can be sure that the baby will never lose his voice. The parents will jump out of the window from desperation, but the baby will cry for days on end without losing his voice. This happens because he is using a physiologically perfect technique. He breaths naturally, widening the ribs to extend the diaphragm and projects the column of air into the facial amplifiers. I am afraid that I cannot be any clearer.

Conclusion

I believe above all that there is no lack of voices, but a great lack of voice teachers. Plenty of voices arrive, even if periodically. There are probably no more dramatic sopranos or tenors or mezzosopranos only because they are ruined by the conservatoriums, the singing teachers, and schools. Then there is another phenomenon: that of the voices that manage to survive even the worst training and the worst teachers. These singers have such gifts that they can keep on singing and, if they know how to manage themselves, they can go ahead with a career despite their defects. The teacher is important only to a certain extent. He can give advice, some clues, some indications of technique; but if the student is as hard-headed as a donkey it is all useless. The student must already be talented when he decides to become a singer. The teacher is important especially if he can recognize the student that has no problems, or defects, or the student that starts off straight away with many doubts and mistakes.

Yes, today we have a crisis situation; but it's not all the fault of the singers.

(Translation by: HELLÈ THEOPHILATOS)

219

INDEX OF NAMES

This is an index of the singers cited in the book, and excludes those mentioned in the glossary of terms. The page numbers in italics refer to singers' picture captions.

Abbreviations:

s soprano
t tenor
ms mezzo-soprano
bt baritone
bs bass
c contralto